Together in Love

Also by Roberta Showalter Kreider

From Wounded Hearts:
Faith Stories of Gay, Lesbian, Bisexual, and Transgender People and Those Who Love Them

TOGETHER IN LOVE: Faith Stories of Gay, Lesbian, Bisexual, and Transgender Couples.

Copyright © 2002 by Roberta Showalter Kreider

Cover design by Steven Olofson.
Photograph by David Brenneman.

For orders, information, or reprint permissions:

kreiders@netcarrier.com
Roberta@EmpoweringDiversity.com
P.O. Box 101, Sellersville, PA 18960   (215) 257-7322

Also visit our website at:

www.empoweringdiversity.com/robertakreider

ISBN 0-9664822-1-2

First Printing: August 2002

Library of Congress Cataloging-In-Publication Data

Kreider, Roberta Showalter
    Together in love: Faith stories of gay, lesbian, bisexual, and transgender couples / Roberta Showalter Kreider
        p. cm.
    Includes bibliographical references and resource materials.
    ISBN 0-9664822-1-2

    1. Gay and Lesbian — Christianity   2. Christian Faith   3. Relationships
    I. Title   II. Kreider, Roberta Showalter

Published in association with:
Strategic Press. P.O. Box 277, Kulpsville, PA 19443   (215) 723-8422

Printed in the United States by Morris Publishing
3212 East Highway 30
Kearney, NE 68847
1-800-650-7888

Together in Love

Faith Stories of Gay, Lesbian, Bisexual, and Transgender Couples

Compiled and Edited by
Roberta Showalter Kreider

Have you not known?
Have you not heard?

The Lord is the everlasting
God, the Creator of the ends
of the earth.

He does not faint or grow weary;
his understanding is
unsearchable.

He gives power to the faint,
and strengthens the
powerless.

Isaiah 40:28-29

To the gay, lesbian, bisexual, and transgender friends

God has given to me,

and

to all the GLBT friends who are yet to be.

~ ~ ~

I thank God for the diversity of God's creation

and for the joy I have

in being part of the lives of

such beautiful, sensitive, and loving individuals.

…mercy draws us to recognize
our solidarity with any part of
creation that is suffering,
oppressed, handicapped,
or victimized.

It moves us, as it moved Jesus,
to act with love and integrity,
at whatever cost, to do whatever
the situation requires of us to
resist, expose, advocate, remedy.

Jesus is God's firm promise to
be present in all of our reality,
always intent upon bringing
life out of death.

In Jesus, we know that God's
love is, relentlessly, mercy.

Elaine M. Prevallet, "Living in the Mercy,"
Weavings **(Sept/Oct 2000) p. 12**

Together in Love

Table of Contents

God's grief is simultaneously a cry for justice. It enters creation like a mighty storm, rousing God's people from their sleep. While we wait in the darkness and ask God, "Why did you let this happen?" God hurls the question back to us: "Wake up, people, to what is happening. Why do *you* let this happen in the world that I gave you?"

Whenever people are being exploited, violated, injured, killed, deprived, or degraded, God wants the oppression to stop immediately – not by divine intervention, but by ours, with God's help.

Elaine V. Emeth, "Lessons from the Holocaust: Living Faithfully in the Midst of Chaos," *Weavings* **(March/April 1998) p. 24.**

Foreword

Nothing is quite so important in understanding the human story as the stories of humans.

We read the story of Ruth and puzzle over the reason she chose Naomi's people over her own. We read the story of David and see how closely his sons followed in his footsteps. We read of Peter's dream upon being invited to meet Cornelius, and we realize that the dream arises from his struggle with his religious culture. We find it exciting that the remembered words of Jesus are able to change and strengthen him.

So the stories continue through the ages, and the biographies that appeal to us the most answer the questions of what it means to be human.

My own story of interest in and concern for gay and lesbian individuals began more than twenty years ago when I was beginning a residency in psychiatry (my second career). I remember to this day two gay men and an elderly lesbian who told me their stories that first year. Then just before the Triennial Conference of the General Conference Mennonite Church at Estes Park in 1980, a consultation of the Mennonite Medical Association concluded that we knew too little about human sexuality and less about homosexuality and that we needed more study.

At that same conference, a young man in our small group shared his story of coming to terms, as a young boy, with the fact that he was different from other boys. That story prompted me to accept the invitation in 1980 to serve on the Commission on Human Sexuality, a joint study of the General Conference Mennonite Church and the Mennonite Church. My assignment was to particularly address the issue of homosexuality.

So I began to study, and my life was changed. As I heard more stories of gay and lesbian individuals and later those of bisexual and transgender individuals, I was distressed by how culture, society, and the church treated them. I have heard many stories over the years. These stories and the accumulation of medical information – including the general conclusion that sexual orientation is not chosen – have driven me to go to bat for these individuals that they may be loved, affirmed, accepted, and treated equally and fairly. The church should do no less.

There are many stories and such a wide variety of experiences. We all have stories, and we need to listen and learn like Peter.

This book gives us another opportunity to do so. Roberta Showalter Kreider (who briefly lived in the same small Kansas town where I grew up) has made these stories available – first in her book, *From Wounded Hearts* – and now in this book. Read them with open hearts. May they help us understand the human story, and, like the remembered words of Jesus, may they change us.

Elsie Enns Steelberg, M.D.

Dr. Steelberg is a psychiatrist with Prairie View Hospital, Wichita, Kansas.

A Personal Message to Our Readers

As I pedaled away on my exercise bike, the words on the cards in front of me were impressed upon my consciousness with new meaning and importance:

Jesus said, "Neither this man nor his parents sinned, he was born blind so that God's works might be revealed in him."

~ ~ ~

Some of the Pharisees said, "This man is not from God, for he does not observe the sabbath." But others said, "How can a man who is a sinner perform such signs?" And they were divided.

~ ~ ~

His parents said this because they were afraid of the [Jewish authorities] for the [authorities] had already agreed that anyone who confessed Jesus to be the Messiah would be put out of the synagogue.

~ ~ ~

Then they reviled him, saying, "You are his disciple, but we are disciples of Moses. We know God has spoken to Moses, but as for this man, we do not know where he comes from."

~ ~ ~

They answered him, "You were born entirely in sins, and are you trying to teach us?" And they drove him out.

~ ~ ~

Jesus said, "I came into this world for judgment so that those who do not see may see, and those who do see may become blind."

~ ~ ~

Jesus said to them, "If you were blind, you would not have sin. But now that you say, 'We see,' your sin remains."

xiii

I was endeavoring to memorize the Gospel of John and was working with John 9, the chapter from which the above verses were excerpted. It was significant to me that these words were being drilled into my consciousness a few weeks prior to the spring session of our Mennonite church's district conference. That session in 1995 was the time designated for the first vote about the fate of Germantown Mennonite Church in Philadelphia, Pennsylvania.

Following the mandate of Jesus to "love your neighbor as yourself,"[1] the Germantown church was providing a haven for GLBT[2] individuals, as well as all other people God brought to the congregation. Because this church had members living in same-gender, covenanted relationships, its conference membership was in jeopardy.

Several months earlier, my husband Harold and I embarked on a journey of listening to voices from the other side of the debate about homosexuality. We pledged to each other and to God that we would listen without judging and be open to any truth God's Spirit would lead us to.

As a retired minister, Harold was one of the delegates who needed to vote on this matter when conference convened. Even though some of our conference leaders were recommending that people do intensive study of the subject and learn to know people from Germantown Mennonite Church, very few people were willing to devote any time or effort to consider that God's Spirit might lead us to a different understanding of truth. A new interpretation of Scripture was too threatening to the status quo.

Because of our personal experience with homosexuality through the tragedy of my youngest brother's death with AIDS

---

[1] Matthew 22:39

[2] Here and in all the following chapters, GLBT or LGBT refers to gay, lesbian, bisexual, or transgender individuals.

ten years earlier,[3] we had already been exposed to the reality of homosexuality. Even though we were sporadically exploring what we could find about the subject, we had never diligently determined to look at resources that presented the other side of the debate. Everything we read enforced the judgment that homosexuality is a learned experience – a chosen one.

Now with the vote looming on the horizon, we felt there was no way that it would be honest or fair to vote about other people's lives if we had never met them or listened to their stories. Consequently, we began to search diligently for resources that presented the other side of the debate, and we went to Germantown Mennonite Church to learn to know the people there.

When we set our minds to the task, it was amazing to see how God brought people and experiences into our lives that affirmed to us that we needed to stand in the gap for GLBT people and their families.

We felt it was very unfair that in over two years of debate in our conference sessions about what to do with Germantown, never once was a gay or lesbian individual or any of their family members asked to share their faith stories. It was always a discussion about them – *them!*

In my own experience, learning to know these people and listening to their stories brought a completely different perspective to the dialogue. Telling the stories became very important to me, and I began to feel that God was asking me to provide a forum where our friends could tell their stories.

Now God has brought a second book of stories to birth. It is my prayer that as you read the stories in this book, your life will be transformed by God's love and grace, so that you may see GLBT individuals with new eyes.

---

[3] In *From Wounded Hearts* (Chi Rho Press, 1998), I wrote about the experience of learning to know that my brother had AIDS only two weeks before he died. The story is also available in booklet form, along with "Fifteen Reasons Why I Have Changed my Mind." This booklet can be ordered from Ray L. Moyer, 6 Eagan Street, Pottsville, PA 17901-1002. For more information, contact Mr. Moyer at rlm@infi.net.

The purpose of *Together in Love* is not to elevate couples above single individuals in the GLBT community. Couples and singles are all equally valued by the one who created us all.

Together in Love is a tribute to the many faithful GLBT couples in our world who are loving and caring for each other "for better or for worse, for richer or poorer, in sickness or in health" and intend to do so until death parts them. The couples who have shared their stories in this book have been together from three to over forty years.

I had hoped that in this volume no one would need to be anonymous. The fact that there are a few who did not dare to use their own names attests to the sad reality that there is still risk involved to be openly GLBT. These stories are just as authentic and real as the rest, but in order to protect themselves or their family members, the authors needed to use fictitious names. It is my hope that all who read these stories will accept the responsibility to help make the way smoother for the GLBT community.

To truly embrace all of God's creation as good and worthy of respect and love is the most freeing experience I know. Never again do I want to judge another person by skin color, status in life, gender, sexual orientation, religion, or by what those in authority determine for me. I am experiencing in a much deeper way than ever before God's unfathomable heart of love for me. May this also be true in your experience.

Roberta Showalter Kreider

Editor's note: When *and* is used on the byline, both partners have written the story together. *With* denotes that one partner has written the story with the approval of the other.

Acknowledgments

Before I begin to thank the people involved in the birthing of *Together in Love*, I want to acknowledge the guidance of God's Spirit throughout all this endeavor. In my own strength, I could never have accomplished this task.

I thank my faithful husband Harold for all his patience, love, and encouragement throughout the strenuous months of work on this project.

Many people need to be involved in a book where there are multiple authors. I am grateful for all the authors who labored to put the right words together to faithfully portray their spiritual journeys to an unknown audience. I thank them for their courage to be vulnerable in this way. Without their stories, the book could never have happened. I value each of these individuals as my brother or sister on life's journey, and I thank them for sharing their lives with me.

One of the authors, Rick Alderfer, deserves special recognition and appreciation for the many hours he worked to prepare galley sheets and help me with the intricate details of self-publishing a book. He also was a great encourager through all of the difficult obstacles that were thrown into my path.

Thank you, too, to Steven Olofson, another author who designed the attractive cover and was always ready to help with other details.

Ed Meyers, from my church community, gave many hours of his time and resources to keep my computer working.

Hilda Landis, also from my church family, did a great job keeping me challenged with her excellent proofreading. I learned a lot from her.

Peggy Campolo and John Davis put me in touch with several prospective authors. Their suggestions led to three couples who were willing to share their stories.

How wonderfully God has blessed and guided this birthing process from beginning to end! As we were finishing the final details, Libby Smith and Ruth Hinkle graciously gave their time to help with the final proofreading. I want to include both Libby and Ruth in my gratitude for their friendship and their willing participation in this challenging endeavor.

I am grateful for all the friends who cheered me on with their words of encouragement. Thank you to every one who prayed and gave time or resources so that these valuable stories could be shared.

The greatest thing that can happen in the life of any person is to discover that God's love is not conditional. In reality, that is what new life in Christ is all about. We enter new life when we hear God saying: "You've gotten it backwards. You don't need to win my love. I have already given you my love."

~ Robert Stanley

Together in Love

~ Part One ~

Faith Stories of Gay, Lesbian, Bisexual, and Transgender Couples

God's grace comes to the last, the lost, and the least. Divine mercy overlooks conventional social structures and lifts up the marginalized; it even reaches beyond the borders of the people to embrace the excluded and outsiders (Samaritans and Gentiles). Sinners are saved while the place of the "righteous" becomes increasingly precarious. It is the powerless, the sick, and the sinful who rush into God's realm, while many who are powerful, healthy, and respected lodge their protest and turn away.

Within Protestant Christianity in North America today, many churches are preoccupied with their own survival. In such a context, concern with purity, with boundaries and exclusion of those who do not belong, is understandable. It would be a pity, however, if pursuit of such an agenda led churches to forget Jesus' own radical challenge to the prevailing purity rules. When we are yearning for clear structures and boundaries, how will we serve a Lord who subverts them and extends compassionate care to the most unlikely of persons?

John T. Carroll, "Luke 17:11-19,"
Interpretation 53 (October 1999) 407, 408.

~ *one* ~

The Church at the Top of the Hill

Steven Olofson and Robert Roush

Robert:

Steve and I have been together since 1989, when I moved to Jamestown, New York, to take a job as the director of the local American Heart Association office. As I looked for a place to live, I saw a block of townhouse flats. They were some of the most picturesque apartments in the city of Jamestown, but there was no indication that any of them were available and no phone number to call. I went into the optician's office on the first floor to ask if there were any apartments available. The optician answered, "Why, yes, the one upstairs is for rent." He gave me Steve's phone number.

When I dialed, I heard a recorded male voice with a slight Jamestown Swedish accent. I thought nothing of it and explained my desire for an apartment. Later when he showed me the apartment, I knew it was the one for me. Steve said to me, "I have a really *good* feeling about this."

I knew what he meant without knowing what he meant. I was preoccupied with moving from my home city to take a job raising money and running health programs. This was a major change for me. The tall, smiling local boy (he was thirty-two at the time) was a curiosity that I wasn't ready to think about, not to mention that his teeth were less than perfect.

Afterwards, we discovered that the rental sign with Steve's phone number had fallen from the window, but the townhouse apartments had caught my eye. Coincidence? We have cohabited for twelve years and currently share a hundred-year-old house that we bought together in Pennsylvania in 1995.

I grew up in a German-American family with close ties to the Lutheran church. My mother chose the Lutheran church in her East Buffalo, New York, neighborhood to be her church home. After her divorce from her first husband, my maternal grandmother married a man whose brother was a Lutheran minister. The church is, without question, a presence in individual communities, and the love and openness of its members are the magnets of faith – regardless of the denomination. I was raised and confirmed in the Lutheran church, but now I am no longer a member.

My maternal grandmother firmly maintained that her father, who came from England as a merchant marine and fought in the Spanish American war, was a Jew who kept faith with both Jewish and Christian traditions. This family story has influenced me more than any other in forming my faith. I can feel the blood of my Jewish mothers inside of me.

My faith has run from childish blind acceptance to adolescent rebellion to finding a collegial relationship with God as a loving friend. By searching for the Christ that dwells within, I have found that God wants to relate to us on an intensely intimate and personal level, which speaks only of one thing – equality in existence together, between the Creator and humankind and humankind with each other. While I believe God is incomprehensibly grand, divine, and powerful, I also believe that God is my partner, and I feel this is reflected in my relationship with Steven.

Like many children, I established my sexual identity at an early age. My interests ranged from the stereotypically feminine for a young gay male to average boy interests, including mechanical science and comic books. These things defined me as a person, encompassing both the masculine and feminine, even before the question of sexual attraction or identity.

I know from memories of at least as early as seven or eight years old that my sexual fantasies were focused on men and other boys. It was only later that I discovered what this meant in relation to cultural and religious acceptance. I kept my heart subdued throughout my high school years, not daring to mention what Oscar Wilde termed "the love that dare not speak its name."

Steven:

I honestly can not remember a time when I did not know that God was around and with me. Likewise, for as long as I can remember, I knew that I was gay. I did not always have a word for it, but I knew it. I grew up in a family that at times resembled *All in the Family* more than it did *Father Knows Best*. Our family of three sons (with me in the middle) was a typical upstate New York family, except that I was the only one who attended church. Church was not a priority in our house, but I felt very much at home there and dreamed of being a pastor.

As a teen, I found all the Scripture passages that I believed were relative to homosexuals in the Bible (all seven of them versus more than 360 references for heterosexual persons). I was very forceful in pushing those views – trying to convince myself and others that all gays were going to hell. I did not understand the background of those and other scriptures, as I do now. Because of my frustration, suicide was a consideration on more than one occasion, but God always seemed to have the right person in my life when I needed someone.

I can not count – nor would I attempt to add up – the hours of tears, fist pounding, fasting, Bible reading, begging, pleading, and bargaining with God. I was trying to rid myself of this affliction. I ran from my feelings, pounding them into the deepest marrow of my being. And, yes, I even got married! My rationale was that if I got married, God would see how earnest I was to change and that the attractions I felt would fade.

For nine years of faithful and faith-full marriage nothing changed! I was lying to God, my church, my wife, and myself. During that time I was very active in my church and served in many capacities, including preaching when pastors were on vacation.

It was after a counseling session that my wife asked me point-blank if I were gay. Here I was, driving down the road, tears running down my face, fearing to speak a word. She asked me again and then asked why I would not admit it if I were. I told her, "Because I would be afraid of losing my friends." She said it was nobody else's business. She also said that if I were gay, she did not want to remain married to me because that would be unfair to both of us. The fact was, it was safer to remain married – easier to hide and not face the truth.

After much prayer, my wife and I decided to divorce. At this same time the United Methodist district superintendent asked me if I would be available and interested in taking over a small country church that could not afford a pastor of its own. I was excited, but I explained to him what was going on. He said that he would give me some time to settle things and we would talk again. That talk never came, and I was not surprised.

During our divorce proceedings I pulled myself out of the church – thinking that neither the church nor God would want me. I also feared that no one else would want me either. I was preparing myself for a very lonely life as a single gay man condemned by all. People around me told me that gay people are unhappy, hopping from bed to bed, from backroom to backroom, and condemned to hell. It was a long time before I realized that God loves me as I was created. This has been confirmed in many ways.

In 1998, I shared my story in a mailing to all the ministers of the United Methodist churches of the Western New York

Conference (where I was active) and UMC bishops throughout the USA. I was amazed at the positive responses. Of course, there were a couple of negative responses also. To open my life up completely as I told my life story was a very difficult thing for me to do. It was scary, but Robert's encouragement helped me to follow through with it.

The same year we met, Robert invited me to join his family for Christmas. I was very nervous about meeting the in-laws. On Christmas Eve, Robert and I babysat for Meghan and Brendon (Robert's niece and nephew) while the others went to Mass. (Robert's sister converted to Catholicism for her second husband.) After they came home, we went to a Methodist church midnight service. When we returned, everyone was in bed, the sofa bed had been pulled out, and the sheets turned down for us. Included on each pillow was a mint – Robert's father's sense of humor. To me this was amazing, as I had only heard the horror stories of how families rejected a gay child. I was made to feel like a member of the family.

As for my own family, a few years ago my father and stepmom came to visit. They had not met Robert previous to this meeting and quite frankly I wasn't sure how this would go. At the close of their visit, Dad walked up to Robert and gave him a hug. This meant so much to me. However, there are other family members who will not speak to me anymore, and while I'm sorry they feel this way, I can not and will not hide behind a mask of heterosexuality anymore. GLBT persons are often blamed for the breakdown of the family, yet we crave and value birth- and extended-family togetherness. Faith is a major part of the cement for any family relationship – whether it be with our Creator, between spouses, or child and parent.

Perhaps the most significant thing that we have accomplished together was the establishment (and co-directorship) of the Lehigh Valley Gay Men's Chorus in 1994. We both felt strongly that there should be a musical group in the area that would not only provide good music and entertainment, but would also help break down the stereotypes and be a conduit for discussion and understanding of gay and lesbian issues. LVGMC has created a safe space for the singers and also a non-bar situation where GLBT people and their friends could get together. There were times when we were harassed by phone and mail, but we both knew the chorus was important to the life of the gay community.

In 1999, we were nominated for the Pennsylvania governor's *Excellence in Arts Award* for launching the chorus. We could not have accomplished this if we did not have the kind of faith and relationship with each other that we do.

After moving to Allentown, Pennsylvania, I felt the pull to get back into a church, and Robert supported me in this. I missed the Christian fellowship terribly. While dusting the house, Robert found a love poem on my desk – lyrics to a song I was composing. He read the words describing an exceptional love and realized the words were talking about my personal love for God. Like the words of St. Chrysostom centuries before, they spoke about a committed love to Christ.

A newspaper article about Wesley United Methodist Church in Bethlehem, Pennsylvania, constructing a new building aroused my interest. I decided to check it out and fell in love with the music program there. However, I was not going to get involved in a church that would not welcome us as a couple, so I met with Pastor Bill. The pastor spoke of his love and acceptance of all people, including gays and lesbians, and confirmed that both Robert and I would be welcome at Wesley. Robert is not an official member of the church because of the strong United Methodist policy, as listed in the *United Methodist Book of Discipline*, that "homosexuality is incompatible with Christian teaching."

This congregation allows the Gay Men's Chorus to rehearse and perform in their building. Even though Robert is not an official member, his family is made to feel at home at Wesley when they visit us. On one of the many Christmases that we have played host to Robert's family, his Aunt Sharon from Phoenix, Arizona, sang with our church choir on Christmas Eve.

I was instrumental in studies being done at Wesley regarding the church and homosexuality and continue to challenge the church's official stand as I work to facilitate change from within. While Robert and I agree in many matters of faith, we also disagree. "It's part of the vibrancy of our relationship," Robert says. "We don't want to give the impression that we think only believing one way is the basis of faith. Faith in God can be expressed in vast and different ways."

Robert:

Steve has a job with a contracting company, and we feel very blessed that I am as welcome at company events as the husbands and wives of other employees. Our partnership also gave us the opportunity to fight employment discrimination in my workplace.

When I was employed at a comparatively large organization that served youth in the Lehigh Valley of Pennsylvania, I felt clearly called to address a situation involving a gay youth program that was established by a gay male student intern. He was subsequently ill-treated in the uphill battle of beginning such a program. My employer moved the program from the influence and jurisdiction of the gay community members, who had created it, and hid it from both them and the public.

When faced with whether or not to mention my concerns to my employer, I was met with the resounding realization that fate had employed me there in order to address this issue. Even though I feared losing income and my job once again in my life, Steve helped me. He assured me we would make it through together even if I did lose my job. He listened to me while I was on the phone with the people involved with the situation and was a good sounding board for me, sharing his concern, support, and his own views of how to handle the situation.

Steve says: "We sometimes approach problems from opposite directions. This may appear as though we disagree; yet to us, we are making sure we are seeing the issue from all sides before we act. We both utilize and recognize the power of prayer and meditation."

On several occasions, my employer told me that the organization was concerned that gay men were potential predators on youth. It was clear that they felt they were somehow protecting the youth by keeping members of the gay community away.

For those who grow up gay and know in their hearts the fear of violence and retaliation that might be directed at them if their difference is discovered, the idea of being a predator is simply absurd. Men who are such aggressors rarely identify themselves as homosexual, nor have they developed a gay identity.

In the end, the gay community members joined me to meet with the organization's executive director and were able to make it clear that gays and lesbians know when they are being mistreated and are organized to address issues of discrimination when they arise. Without Steve's support, I would not have felt able to address the subject at all. We share a very strong concern over the gay teen suicide rate and are concerned about programs like this one.

Together:

As we work toward our individual goals, Steve in his job in construction and Robert working toward his doctorate in complementary and alternative health, it has been very important to have the support we know each other gives.

For many years, the idea of being "gay and okay" has been out of the closet. The American Psychological Association removed homosexuality from the list of disorders in 1974 and, more recently, has become more aggressive in denouncing the therapists who say that they can change a person's sexual orientation. Oddly enough, homophobia, especially the type that led to the beating death of Matthew Shepard[1] and the execution-style murders of gays and lesbians across the country, *is* now classified as a psychological disorder.

In spite of that opposition, GLBT persons are now more accepted in the workplace and at a growing number of churches across the country. The issues we face are not really the issues of fundamentalist resistance to our acceptance; they are the issues of where to fit into a world of acceptance and visibility. The days of lurking in the shadows and sneaking around in a world of hidden sexuality are over for many of us.

The behaviors of self-loathing and self-hatred that seem to justify dangerous and promiscuous lifestyles, filled with alcohol, drugs, and sex, can no longer be accepted by the gay community. Indeed, we can no longer say, "I am going to hell anyway because of my lifestyle, so what does it matter what else I do?" Those days can be happily over because there is a *church at the top of the hill.*

However, something is wrong when we can have services of blessing for buildings sanctioned by our churches, but not for a committed same-sex couple. This kind of message stabs at the hearts of those couples who want nothing more than to live faithful lives together, supported by those around them, including their church.

When we win the battle of acceptance as couples, what then? This image of a church at the top of a hill is a symbol for the

---

[1] Matthew Shepard was a twenty-year-old student at the University of Wyoming in Laramie, Wyoming. During the night of October 6, 1998, he was taken from a gay bar by two other young men to a place about a mile from Laramie. They mercilessly beat him with a pistol, tortured him, then tied him up to a split-rail fence, and left him for dead. Two bikers found him some eighteen hours after the brutal attack. When the bikers first saw Matthew tied to the fence, they thought that they saw a scarecrow. Matthew was taken to a hospital where he remained in a coma until October 12, when he left this world in the early morning hours with his family by his bedside. The Matthew Shepard Foundation has been set up to help fund programs to educate youth and the public about hate crimes and what they can do to prevent tragedies such as Matthew's brutal murder. (Information from http://mattshepardresource.freeservers.com/)

long and perilous climb that gays and lesbians have endured, toward the ultimate goal of every human being – spiritual growth and understanding. These truths are not separate from our sexual identities, but intertwined with them. We both have come to this realization, and we both agree that we would not be here without the love and commitment of our relationship. We do not mean to imply that *not* having a relationship means one *can not* climb a path toward greater spiritual light and understanding. It is Christ, that internal sense of spirituality, that guides our journey, not a picture of gay romantic love. In our own experience we have discovered that when we can depend on each other for economic and emotional support, we can also begin to explore spiritual longings with one another, even though those longings may be expressed in different ways for the two people in a relationship. After all, there is a lot of ground to cover in the vastness of God's love.

We believe that to be closed out of the political structure of churches and religious organizations presents a challenge to the gay community, but it also presents the opportunity to develop a God-centered spirituality. Christ's blessings are not just for those on membership lists at certain denominations of churches. There is so much opportunity going on across denominations for gay and lesbian people! There is a vibrant life and a vibrant call to gather together.

The Metropolitan Community Church of the Lehigh Valley held a blessing service for gay and lesbian couples in February of 2001 with nine ministers of different denominations participating. After eleven years together, we were one of the thirty-three couples who were blessed. During the service we had the opportunity to perform the vocal duet composed by Eric Helmuth, "Finally Here," – a song about gay relationships. It was a wonderfully moving experience and probably the largest religious gathering ever of GLBT people in the Lehigh Valley.

Having faith and being gay are not mutually exclusive as some would have us believe. It is our spiritual faith and our faith in each other that has helped us make it this far, and it will continue to be the foundation of the road to *the church at the top of the hill.*

In 1978, **Robert Roush, Ph.D.**, co-founded the Western New York Alzheimer's Disease Association and began his career in healthcare. He has held executive director positions with the American Heart Association in southwestern New York and the AIDS Services Center in Bethlehem, Pennsylvania. Robert is currently an adjunct professor of Yoga and Meditation at Northampton Community College. He holds a Ph.D. in Complementary and Alternative Health from Westbrook University in Aztec, New Mexico. He also holds a bachelor's degree in Music Composition and a master's degree in Non-profit Administration.

Also originally from western New York State, **Steven Olofson** is a project manager for a contracting/manufacturing company in New Jersey and is a freelance graphic artist. He was a certified lay-speaker in the United Methodist Church for many years and held many conference and local church positions. Steven is a member of Wesley U.M. Church in Bethlehem, Pennsylvania, where he sings in the chancel choir. He studied voice at the University of Denver, Colorado.

The couple lives in Allentown, Pennsylvania, with their bird, Baby. They will celebrate thirteen years together in August of 2002.

~ *two* ~

Dancing with God

Ken White with John Linscheid

"Those who hear not the music think the dancers mad."[1]

I put on the "Fame" album and waited for "The Body Electric." Then I took John's hand and pulled him from his seat. We were at a party in Lawrence, Kansas, where John was a Mennonite pastor. I was assistant pastor at nearby Topeka's Metropolitan Community Church. From the party we went to Perkins Pancake House and discovered we shared common friends, life dreams to serve the church and God, and visions of creating safe spiritual space for queer people to explore their spirituality. That was in 1983. So far, the Dance has lasted eighteen years.

John and I have danced together through many trials over the last eighteen years: John's being thrown out of pastoral ministry, our local congregation being thrown out of the Mennonite Church, a liver transplant, and the loss of both of our fathers – to mention a few. We have also danced the joy, wonder, and awe of finding a soul mate, companion, and lover with whom to journey through life. This Dance has allowed me to reunite my body, mind, and soul. Our Dance together has been inspired by our love of God and each other.

I realized over the years that I was not just learning to dance with John; I was also learning to dance with God. This wonderful metaphor reminds me how many different ways I can physically express my spirit. As humans we dance individually,

---

[1] From a greeting card received from a participant of a workshop led by Ken White and John Linscheid.

with partners, and collectively. Sometimes we dance slow and close, holding our partner tightly. Sometimes we dance fast and separately, oblivious to the other person's presence on the dance floor. We sometimes dance collectively with multiple partners, and we sometimes dance alone. We find ways to express our individual spirits and identities and our unique cultural backgrounds. We are always creating new dances and dance steps that grow out of our experiences of others and of the spirit in our lives. It is truly powerful to watch people weave together their individual movements into a unique and mutual expression of their spirits, physically acting out their innermost thoughts and feelings.

I love this idea of God and John and me co-creating the Dance, sensing each other's spirit, responding through movement or action. John McNeill, a friend and mentor, once quipped about dancing with God, "When I was young, sometimes God even let me lead."

John and I have learned this about God as well. We do not control the Dance. We may be dancers – we are not the choreographer. Often we struggle to follow God's lead. It reminds me of the comment about Ginger Rogers made by former Texas governor, Ann Richards. "Remember, Ginger did everything that Fred did – only backwards and in high heels." Sometimes I feel this way about our journey together toward God – like I'm doing it backwards, unsure of my footing.

Both John and I started our dance toward and with God in traditional ways. We each attended seminary to learn the basic steps (rituals), music and language of the holy that were considered critical and foundational by our teachers. We each embraced the "Lord of the Dance" as teacher, mentor, and friend.

I came out as an openly gay man in 1977. John came out to his family in 1979 and publicly in 1983. We came out because our bodies and spirits demanded it. We both craved the loving touch of another man, to be held by men. No matter how much we tried to think, talk, or pray away this desire, our bodies had a mind and a wisdom of their own. We have learned over the years to trust this wisdom of our arms and hearts and thighs.

We desired to dance unfettered in the sight of God and with God. But the institutional church told us that two men couldn't dance with God or with each other. So after my graduation from seminary and John's short four-year pastorate, we found ourselves barred from entering the traditional dance halls of God. John had lost his pastoral credentials. The United Methodists had made it clear that they would never give credentials to me as an openly gay man.

The church engenders hatred toward those who trust the wisdom of their bodies' responses to unsanctioned music, because it fears that the Dance's physicality must lead to sex. We have discovered the opposite. Sex – when loving, selfless, consensual, and mutual – leads to Dance. It expresses Love. Word must become Flesh.

I believe that sex is God's gift of grace and love. God experiences joy in creation when people have sex. And our being loved by another is our way of experiencing God's love for us. God's love manifests itself in and through our beloved. In a way, all sex is sex with God. A quick way to evaluate how well you have integrated your spirituality and sexuality is to imagine having sex with your beloved in the palm of God's hand with God looking down at you. What is the expression on God's face?

The institutional church's sex-negative attitudes have labeled our most sacred moments of contact with each other and God as sinful, perverted, and incompatible with Christian teaching. Yet our desire to dance with each other, our communities, and God persists. We have had to find new places to dance, new friends to dance with, and new steps or rituals to more fully express God's profound gift of gay spirit. We have had to seek – in ourselves, each other, and these communities – a wisdom beyond seminary teaching in order to respond to God's call in our lives.

John and I began to discover new ways to minister to the churched, to the unchurched (too often the overly and badly churched), and to those who walk with us. We assisted friends in blessing their homes, celebrated with them the sacred act of coming out, "officiated" at holy union ceremonies, participated in rites of separation, and grieved with folks in times of loss. We led gay men in ritually considering the passages in our lives, the Source of Holy Spirit in our lives, and the divine expression in each of us.

When we reached our tenth anniversary of life together, we considered how to mark the event. A holy union ceremony seemed redundant after ten years of union. A traditional anniversary party didn't seem quite right. Reflecting on our life to that point, John and I realized that friendship was the soul of our relationship. From our earliest days together, our commitment was not "till death do us part," but rather to a lifelong process. We pledged to love each other and seek each other's spiritual growth – whether or not that resulted in living together "forever." If spiritual growth required separation, we agreed we would seek a year of couple's counseling to learn how to separate in a way that enabled us to continue to love and support one another in the process.

So we decided to observe our tenth anniversary with a Rite of Spiritual Friendship. We gathered our friends and family at the historic Germantown Mennonite Meetinghouse to celebrate friendship with each other, with our friends, with our communities, and their friendships with each other.

The morning of the ceremony, a small round table stood at the front of the meetinghouse. Two metal-sculptured figures raised their arms in celebration, surrounded by a white candle burning with divine light, two green pillar candles, and many tea lights waiting to be lit. A wind chime hung nearby, symbolizing the presence of the Spirit.

John's mom surprised us with a quilted wall hanging. The center block read "John and Ken, Ten Years"! As guests entered, they signed the surrounding quilt blocks and lit the tea lights to commemorate friends no longer present or those unable to attend. The tea lights symbolized the "great cloud of witnesses" (Hebrews 12:1) who accompany us on our journey. John's family lit one for his father who had died a year before. My parents and I lit one for my brothers who were unable to attend.

After reflections on friendship from one of our pastors and singing about "new light streaming" and "gathering us in," we shared vignettes from our lives. I recalled how we had danced around our different expectations in making a new home. In our first home together, John and I were always disagreeing about how high to hang our pictures. We agreed they should hang at eye level. But my eye level was about six inches above John's. So when I came home one day and found something hanging in the bathroom three feet from the floor next to the toilet, I thought John had stooped to a new low in this conflict. When I looked closer, I found a table of New Testament Greek conjugations. I realized John was conjugating verbs so he could read the Bible in its original text. I learned two things about John that day: he truly loves the Bible, and he doesn't believe in wasting time.

John, in turn, said that he appreciated my role in our relationship as a visionary, seeing things and people as they could be. He has said on many occasions that if I had not come into his life he would probably still be living in Kansas. He shared with everyone that from that first time when I pulled him on the dance floor, I've always been dragging him along to discover new possibilities. Once it was a caboose – that I envisioned moving to our Topeka farm and remodeling into a small hermitage. John, of course, was stricken with panic at the thought of trying to remodel heavy gauge steel. But he shared how this ability to see possibilities has helped him grow and taken us places he had not dreamed of. We never got the caboose, but I have learned to cut and melt metal in my jewelry-making endeavors.

After we spoke, our friends reflected on their friendships, our friendships with them, and theirs with each other. We concluded with a litany to the Divine Friend who ignites us with the fire of love.

As the years have passed, I have tired of fighting with the institutional church. It has robbed me of spiritual energy which I could have used ministering to the spiritual needs in our queer community. I have watched too many friends struggle to come out, succumb to HIV/AIDS, be unable to publicly grieve lovers, and have to hide from family shame.

I watched as our local Mennonite congregation was repeatedly called to task by the larger Mennonite Church. John was often in the thick of it, on committees attempting to negotiate our relationship to the larger denomination. But, rather than seeing beloved children of God with whom God is well pleased, the larger institution pursued a course to rid itself of self-affirming gay and lesbian individuals and our supporters. Eventually our local congregation, Germantown Mennonite Church, was excommunicated from the larger Mennonite denomination.

When the denomination's representatives came to announce the expulsion to our congregation, I felt its power in my life and spiritual journey. I knew the chilling effect it would have on other queer Mennonites and supportive churches. So I requested that the officials embody their words, escort me to the door, and throw me out of the body of Christ in the Mennonite Church. It was important to me, after years and years of struggle, that the larger church realize that they were leaving me, casting me and others like me out of the church.

But the church is not the only force constraining the Dance and making the steps more agonizing. The larger culture assumes that pleasure and vigor require youth. As queer communities rediscover the gifts of sensuality, too often we adopt this view and make gay culture a culture of youth.

As John and I reached middle age, we felt the challenge of that culture. In response to our own aging, we sought the wisdom of our gay brothers to reinvigorate the Dance. In 1994, we were attending a "Gay, Lesbian, and Christian" retreat led by John McNeill, who was advancing in years. We had been asked to lead a Friday evening session that annually gathered the male participants separately to deal with gay men's issues. But the session had a history of deteriorating into unfocused debates.

We decided to put debate aside and make ritual the center of the evening. We hoped to enable the participants to begin to listen to the music of gay wisdom that had been hushed so long among us. We asked the men to consider the gifts of aging by honoring John McNeill as a sage among us and by recognizing all participants over sixty as elders.

In order to do that, we first had to acknowledge the great number of gay men who, because of bashings and the plague of HIV/AIDS, had never been given a chance to age. So we began our ritual by again calling to our presence a "great cloud of witnesses." The men cast faggots – small pieces of wood – into a central fire to remember the men who had gone before us.

Then we assembled the men into age cohorts. Men in their twenties. Men in their thirties. Men in their forties, fifties, and sixties. Together each generation considered the music they had to dance to and how they had fashioned their steps in response. As each generation reported to the larger circle, the wisdom flowed in two directions, from age to youth and from youth to age.

At the climax of the ritual we presented John McNeill with a phallic staff as a symbol of his office as a sage. We put a purple cord around his shoulders and invited him to place a similar cord on the shoulders of each elder.

The ceremony ended with a circle of light as the flame of gay wisdom passed from man to man, candle by candle. Then in the perfect stillness of the Pocono Mountain night, the Spirit suddenly waltzed through the circle with an unexpected breath, making the candles flicker. When it was all over, many men headed off to the local disco, looking forward to old age for the first time. A fifty-seven-year-old participant recalled:

As a man who had lived in the deep closet for fifty-five...years. As a man who did not choose to gently open the closet door and test the air but was blown out by forces which gave no freedom of choice, the men's ritual at the 1994 Gay, Lesbian and Christian retreat was emotionally and spiritually a moment when doors and windows began to open on a new and positive outlook.... It was a time to affirm the goodness, care and concern for one another that was evident in the community of assembled Gay men – and, it was about hope that we can live lives rich with meaning, relationships and wisdom.[2]

Four years after leading the Saging Ceremony, we found ourselves again leading a workshop. This time we were responsible for the entire event. We had titled it "Simply Divine." In one session of that workshop, we asked a gay dancer to show us ways to feel the divine energy in our bodies. We learned to move our bodies with new freedom, shuffle off our stiffness, and begin to dance again alone and with each other, to touch and be touched. At a climactic bonfire, as men shared the wisdom they had learned from being gay, we began to dance around the fire in joy. We were embracing our bodies and each other's bodies, shuffling off the shame that had so often silenced our sensuality and our sexuality.

Often the music that has been silenced by one community can only be given new voice in another. Many participants had ceased to feel the Spirit because the shame of their churches and the larger society had repressed it thoroughly. They had been

---

[2] The Saging of John McNeill, self-published booklet, copyright 1995 by Ken M. White and John Linscheid, p. 4.

frozen by their communities. Now a new community had warmed them up from shivering to dancing.

As we left that mountain retreat, however, I was painfully aware that John and I would have to leave the dance floor to rest for a time. John's liver was failing. He was on a transplant list. By the end of the summer of 2000, John, other friends, and I began to wonder if his dance would end entirely. Each step in John's life was now truly agonizing because of edema in his legs. It became harder to hear the music, and sometimes all I could do was hold him in stillness. But in September 2000, John received a new liver. The Dance continues. God has given it new life.

So we are turning our attention back to this ministry we seem called to: to do our part to reinvigorate this gay spiritual Dance. We are still learning new steps, both individual steps and common ones. We dance closer than ever. Then, suddenly we find ourselves far apart. Sometimes I can't tell if I'm dancing with God, with Jesus, with John, or with the queer community – or with all four of them together. As we look around us, John and I are increasingly convinced that it is really one Dance.

We have come a long way since I put that "Fame" album on the turntable in Lawrence, Kansas. In hindsight I should have put on Ann Murray's "May I have this Dance for the rest of my life?"

One way **Ken White** and **John Linscheid** continue to dance is by queering spiritual space (making room for difference). In addition to providing supportive space for spiritual healing and exploration to a close family of friends, they share additional articles, resources and ideas on John's webpage at www.seas.upenn.edu/~linsch/JLpage.htm. Ken is Director of Undergraduate Advising and Admissions for Temple University's School of Social Administration. John is Assistant to the Chair in the University of Pennsylvania Chemical Engineering Department.

~ *three* ~

Shared Seasons:
A Lifetime of Faith and Love Concealed

Jim and John

Spring.............................into the '60s

Our story of togetherness spans four decades which, analogically, parallel the seasons that quarter each calendar year. We have grown our relationship over time, only because of God's guidance and constant blessings. Through God's wisdom we learned how to preserve and sustain our alternative lifestyle while coexisting within an unaccepting society during its most intolerant period.

It was spring and the year was 1959. Jim had moved to New York City from out of state in pursuit of a career in the field of advertising. Short of resources, he began work with a Madison Avenue firm in an entry level position. At precisely the same time, John was separating from active duty with the U.S. Army, preparing to return to his former job at the same ad agency from which he had been drafted into military service.

Soon we would meet as coworkers, little realizing that a life connection was about to develop. Performing duties side by side at work afforded the perfect opportunity for discovering areas of mutual interest and background. Discussions of personal issues established that, among other things, we had both been baptized, confirmed, and raised Roman Catholic. As such, we understood that any expression of feelings toward members of the same sex was considered intrinsically evil and must be resisted. We believed that if we limited our social contact to dining, theatre, and sporting events, God would find our behavior less offensive. However, as with most dating, we ultimately advanced to the next level.

The attitude of the general public towards homosexuality at that time seemed to reinforce church teachings. For our part, we knew we were being forced to live a double life in order to continue our ties with family and friends. Protecting our privacy and concealing true feelings quickly became second nature. We prayed that, though God might not approve, God would understand.

We decided if we were going to live together, the most comfortable area of the city for us would be the Upper West Side that acknowledged its large gay population. We still have fond memories of that first apartment and the beginning of our new life. The inconveniences of living in a meagerly furnished, fifth floor walk-up studio did not matter as long as we were sharing the experience.

We did visit neighborhood bars in our quest of new friendships. However, we much preferred spending free time outdoors taking in the sights and sounds of Manhattan and Central Park, which was only a block away. Life seemed to be a romance novel in progress! We discovered a Catholic church nearby that we attended on a semi-regular basis, even though we felt no strong attachment.

The pleasures of being a Manhattanite proved to be short-lived, as *gay-bashers* transformed the streets and park into a hunting ground – seemingly sanctioned by the police, who had also increased their harassment against homosexuals. Without provocation, the NYPD was conducting nightly raids on the bars and making mock arrests. Although we were not part of the bar scene, we concluded that it was time for us to move to the suburbs.

For a surprisingly small difference in rent, available apartments in the borough of Queens were larger and more luxurious. We had come a long way from the former walk-up to our new high-rise abode. Our routine had become as traditional as any *married couple's*, but choosing not to engage in role-playing, we agreed to share household responsibilities, such as shopping, cooking, and cleaning.

The only thing missing in our *family* was a formal religious connection. Even though we were still occasionally attending mass at the local chapel, we no longer went to confession or took communion. In light of the church's constant condemnation of homosexuality, it seemed hypocritical to receive the sacrament. We had always attempted to live and conduct ourselves daily as Christians; therefore, we felt unfairly denounced by this doctrine.

We became great friends with two young lesbian neighbors. They, in turn, introduced us to another lesbian couple who had already been together for twenty-five years. We had never heard of any such arrangement lasting so long and wondered how it could have been so successful. Perhaps that encounter served as the inspiration for our future endurance.

The World's Fair, showcasing the traditions and technology of countries and cultures worldwide, was the major event of the mid-'60s. Located in Queens within walking distance of our apartment, it attracted millions from all over, including countless relatives and friends who opted to visit and frequently stayed with us. Our guests, for the first time, had an opportunity to observe that ours was other than a typical roommate relationship. No doubt each faced some reckoning with the issue, but none of them ever confronted us concerning the closeness of our contact.

Prior to the fair's opening, John had established a travel service that evolved into a housing bureau for the throng of Mormons who traveled from Utah and other places in the West to worship in their tabernacle at the exposition. Since we did not share their religious beliefs, we initially questioned our own capability and qualifications to handle these family groups.

However, the experience proved most enlightening, and when the fair ended its two-year run, we felt truly enriched by the gentleness and depth of their lives.

Many other religious organizations, including the Vatican, whose pavilion showcased the original sculpture of Michaelangelo's *Pieta*, enjoyed a significant presence. This masterpiece, depicting Mary clutching the body of Christ after his crucifixion, was displayed in the solemn sanctuary, and we were blessed with many opportunities to gaze upon it. How ironic that the church has for centuries proudly presented the works of this gifted homosexual artist in the Sistine Chapel!

Gay churches had not yet formed in the United States, and our community was conspicuously absent at the event. However, it would not be many years before we would emerge to claim our equality! During a nightly raid four years after the close of the fair, courageous patrons of a Greenwich Village gathering place known as *Stonewall* risked life and limb to successfully counterattack constant police harassment. Two close friends, who were in the bar at the time, phoned us the following morning with a firsthand account of what had transpired. None of us could have realized then that the incident was about to send shock waves throughout pro- and anti-gay forces worldwide.

Summer............................the '70s

As a result of *Stonewall*, gays and lesbians everywhere began to feel a sense of freedom and pride. The condemnation of gays by homophobic extremists was finally being challenged and debated openly in all forms of the media. The general population, already dealing with racial civil rights issues, suddenly became aware of an additional form of discrimination. Fearful of backlash, homosexual men and women throughout the world seized the moment to secure their fundamental God-given right to live in peace and love. This would, indeed, become the decade of advancement for our cause, despite the ongoing outrage of the opposition, who still oppose our entitlement to equality. As gay citizens, we are eternally indebted to those activists who became founding fathers in their own right two hundred years after this nation was born.

There was much to celebrate in terms of liberty and justice as the bicentennial approached! Because of his impassioned love of American history and all things early American, John was especially enthusiastic about the upcoming birthday bash. When an opportunity arose to work as a hands-on craftsman at a historical site near our newly acquired country home in Pennsylvania, there were many things to consider because that would require relocation and our living separately. The driving distance between our country place and New York City was only sixty-five miles, but was apt to take the better part of three hours during the rush hour commute.

By this time, Jim had become president of a large travel firm in lower Manhattan, a long-sought position that he was reluctant to relinquish. Was the job offered to John worth the consequences that being apart for the first time since our original meeting might have on our relationship? We prayed that God would guide us to a prudent decision and eventually concluded that our bond was strong enough to withstand one remaining alone in the big city while the other moved to the *boonies*!

British by birth, but American by choice, John loved stepping back in time in his new role. Clad in colonial garb, he would daily instruct and demonstrate crafts of the early settlers such as tinsmithing, glassblowing, decorative painting, and many other essential talents required for survival in those days. Visitors to the village included students, seniors, and religious groups. Everyone in the United States seemed to be gearing up for the celebration. July 4, 1976, will forever be remembered as the day when Americans united in their love for God and country to party across the nation as never before.

Taking advantage of the fact that his offices overlooked the New York harbor, Jim invited four hundred clients and associates to enjoy a bird's-eye view of the *OP SAIL* activities and parade of tall ships from all over the world. However, as quickly as it had begun, the hoopla began to fade, and average citizens returned to their previous lifestyles.

As attendance began to drop dramatically at the colonial village, we anticipated that John might also move back to New York, to Jim, and to the travel business. We had successfully, through faith and trust, managed to sustain our long-distance love affair, but it would be oh so much better to be together again! That plan proved to be short-lived when John received an offer to catalog the tool collection of a local historical society for display and publication. Consequently, we decided at that point that Jim would also move to the country. Even the long daily commute to the city appeared to be a better alternative than continuing to live apart.

Fall.....................................the '80s

The '80s arrived with an unexpected jolt. HIV and AIDS began to surface, primarily among gay and bisexual males. The promise and advances of *Stonewall* began to disintegrate as quickly as the leaves of autumn. The community was stunned by this so-called *gay disease* that seemingly appeared from nowhere to strike homosexuals down without warning in the prime of their lives. Each of us wondered, as we pondered our own risk, could this be some form of retribution by God?

Preachers of fundamentalism seized their chance to espouse that theory! As a result of widespread negative media, the general population initially expressed little compassion for the victims of the monster virus. Most were not impacted by the ravages of this indiscriminate killer until *seemingly straight* loved ones began to fall ill. The time finally came when the Centers for Disease Control acknowledged that all active members of society are equally exposed through either sexual transmission, blood transfusion, or both, and warned that AIDS does not discriminate. However, some understandably still believe to this day that our community is particularly vulnerable due to the promiscuity of many in our ranks.

We hope continued education on precautionary measures will result in decreasing the number of fatalities among us. As many of our longtime friends lost their battle with this vicious disease, we prayed for a cure that would remove the threat from our midst. In Jim's firm alone, three of our dearest acquaintances were stricken. In helplessness, we witnessed their suffering as each became totally emaciated and disappeared from our circle. We could not help but wonder how a loving God let this happen!

Our place of worship in the country was a tiny chapel in the woods to which a priest would travel on horseback to offer one early morning Mass each Sunday. The main parish church was several miles away, but we felt less conspicuous in the smaller sanctuary than in the family-oriented larger body. Whether imagined or not, we felt we would be viewed suspiciously in light of all the press coverage on our people and the plague.

It was around this time that many churches and synagogues were being founded within the gay and lesbian community for those seeking spiritual direction and fulfillment of life's reward. Lesbians and gay men of every denomination, including Roman Catholic, were affirming by their faith and worship that all of God's children are equally favored with God's love. Despite the faithfulness in their beliefs, the church held fast to its position, denying any affiliation with the gay Catholics. Therefore, we saw no purpose in attending their Mass or meetings.

While some Christian sects and Reform Jews were more accepting on the subject of membership and ordination, many Protestant faiths also refused to address the issue. The Bible-bangers continued their relentless condemnation and preaching their perception of the Scriptures. AIDS activists reacted with massive demonstrations and civil disobedience. Desperation provoked desperate measures, which sometimes proved counterproductive in the eyes of the general public. We prayed that the liberating power of the Holy Spirit would provide those committed individuals with the strength to carry the battle on to a worthy victory.

Our more pleasant memories of the '80s resulted from the fact that Jim was able to avail himself of countless travel opportunities in the course of his business. Because most departures were from New York, and due to the increasing stress from the five-hour commute daily, he returned to Manhattan and the Upper West Side where it all began. We had learned to equally value and respect separateness as well as togetherness. Jim's recounting of his safari, sea voyages, and world-wide travel experiences aroused John's own sense of journey, so he reentered the travel industry, joining an agency in Pennsylvania on completion of his museum project. Under God's protection, we safely traveled thousands of miles, and we are thankful for those opportunities and experiences.

Winter.......................the '90s

The last decade of the century began with the somber bleakness of a dark winter's night. The ever increasing AIDS numbers sent a chilling message that there was still no cure in sight. As we observed many in our community struggling to establish partnerships, we were even more grateful to God for the security of our own monogamous relationship. Many celebrities, particularly in the theatrical industry, had succumbed to the disease. This prompted many television and movie stars to rally in support of AIDS activists. Jarring productions about AIDS, presented in prime time, raised the consciousness of the public to the seriousness of this health crisis. Many weekly series and sitcoms introduced characters and scripts dealing with the disease. Suddenly, HIV, AIDS, and homosexuality were being discussed openly and in more sympathetic tones.

Pride took on a special significance as leading figures in the field of arts and sports began to emerge from their closets. As gays and lesbians everywhere chose to reveal their sexuality, we felt obliged to reexamine our own approach to openness. We agreed that no useful purpose would be served in raising the issue with family and friends, who had been so inclusive and respectful of our closeness for over thirty years.

Perhaps, unknowingly, we had come out to them decades before. After all, Jim's parents had always offered the bedroom with the double bed versus vacant rooms with single beds during our frequent visits. Jim's sister had always been supportive, considering John to be her other brother. Although we had never denied our relationship, we vowed that we would be less guarded as future friendships developed.

Pride festivals and parades were taking place all over the world and in most U.S. cities. We were astonished to learn that the extended lesbian relationship of those acquaintances made in early years was now beyond fifty years. For their volunteerism and efforts in the AIDS fight and the longevity of their golden status they were selected for the honor of being Grand Marshalls of the huge New York City celebration. Politicians and the corporate world were finally acknowledging that our diversity did not justify the discriminating practices of the past. It was now appropriate to commemorate, with the blessings of the Holy Spirit, the changing attitudes and events taking place. As the Gay '90s wound down and Y2K approached, we were reminded that God has indeed given us reason for renewed hope!

The New Millennium

We had made it to the year 2000 – a milestone that would have been impossible to fathom some forty years ago! It was an appropriate time to reflect on our shared life experience and the many blessings that God had bestowed upon us.

Although both of our dads had been called into eternal rest, we could rejoice in still having our mothers in reasonably good health and, also, our siblings and many long-cherished friends. Individually, we had enjoyed good health throughout our years and were grateful that up until this time we had not spent a single night separated by a hospital stay.

We still identified religiously as Catholics, although it had been decades since we had fulfilled our Easter Duty, the church's minimum requirement for receiving holy communion at least once a year. We had continued to attend Mass with family members on holidays and at regular intervals every few months. In all probability, that would likely have been the extent of our future church attendance had we not, by sheer chance, discovered the existence of a Metropolitan Community Church, less than an hour's drive from home.

On entering the church for the first time, we were warmly welcomed by the pastor and congregants. The service was most impressive, and we were especially grateful to be invited to partake of the body and blood of Christ along with the members of the church. Receiving communion again, after so many years, provided the instant inner comfort and spiritual nourishment we were seeking.

Praise God! We had finally found this place of worship that offered an affirming outreach to *all* people, including gay, lesbian, bisexual, and transgender Christians. Our only regret is that we were unaware of the establishment of this church some sixteen years before. We attended the very next membership class so that we could expedite our entry into this special fellowship. Our lives have been forever enriched as a consequence of that action.

With the arrival of 2001 came another memorable occasion. There had never been any sanctioning of our partnership in a religious form, so we were delighted and privileged to participate in a special Ecumenical Blessing of Relationships service organized by our church. The ceremony took place in the candlelit sanctuary. Despite the lack of legal significance, it attracted widespread media coverage. In the presence of God and friends, we had the opportunity to reaffirm our shared love. Together with thirty-two other participating couples, our relationship was blessed by nine clergy members from different denominations. The significance of that event will remain with us always.

Jesus has shown us how to enjoy life's great gifts and how to bear the pain of seasons less bright. We pray and trust that he will one day deliver us to the Almighty and that together we may dwell in God's house forever. Amen.

Truth is my authority,
not some authority my truth.

~ Mary Dyer

(A Quaker woman hanged by Puritans in 1660 for daring to believe and live the truth shown to her by God.)

~ four ~

A Journey of Surprises, Pain, and Love: One Mixed Orientation Marriage

Jay W. and Ruth E. H. Martin

We have been together in love in a mixed-orientation marriage, since 1968. These years have not always been easy, but they have been years of much joy and fulfillment for us. We are looking forward to more years together. They have also been years of learning about aspects of human sexuality and companionship that we knew little or nothing about at the time of our marriage. We do not take our love relationship for granted. Our commitment to stay married and enjoy our life together is based on our strong emotional bond and is intentional.

Jay:

When Ruth and I were talking recently about our life together, I made the comment: "When I got married, I would have denied being gay." This surprised me, and Ruth, too, but it is true! How did I get where I am today?

I am the youngest of five children, three girls and two boys. My brother, who is the second child, could not have been more different from me. He is bigger than I and was always athletic and interested in boy things. I was not interested in athletic things, and while I liked cars, I was not interested in trucks. When I was a child, my brother and I had a difficult time getting along with each other, but I was comfortable with my two oldest sisters. I did not relate well to the sister just older than I until we were in college. I am pleased that we all get along well together now. They all know of my bisexuality and continue to love and support us! Basically, I had a happy childhood and felt loved and supported by my parents.

Before I went to school, my closest friend was a neighbor boy. After beginning first grade, my closest friends were primarily girls. I did not like the athletic activities which other boys seemed to enjoy, but preferred being with girls. I was frequently called a sissy on the playground. This was very painful and difficult for me, because I did not know how to respond and did not feel I could talk about it with anyone. As I reflect on this, I think I knew it was true, but had no idea what I could do about it. The strong social message was that I was different and it was not acceptable. One elementary school year I was the only boy in my class. The principal phoned my mother to ask if this would be a problem. Mother assured him it would not be a problem for me. Fortunately, I was a good student in the classroom and that was acceptable, but it did not carry over onto the playground or into gym class.

My interests were in the arts. My parents did not discourage this, but one of my earliest interests in becoming an interior decorator was not encouraged. In seventh grade, I became the manager of the basketball team and continued through high school. This helped me to have a relatively good relationship with my male athletic peers. Though I felt good about that position, I was becoming more aware of being *different*. I wonder now what the gym teacher might have known or suspected, because he facilitated my being the basketball team manager and was always very nice to me.

The awareness of my sexual attraction to my own gender made me uncomfortable. I did not understand this, but was aware that I should not talk about it. I also felt other boys were uncomfortable with me. (Now, with hindsight, I think it probably was projection on my part.) I also enjoyed dating during high school and assumed that I would eventually marry, have a family, and live happily ever after. There were no gay role models and no discussions about homosexuality. I was very aware of the negative feelings about *homos*, and I knew that sex between two males was not acceptable.

My childhood church was a place where I felt loved and cared for. Most of my family's closest friends were from the church. Now that I am involved in other Mennonite churches, I realize how cohesive that church community was and how important it was to me. My father was a well-known and highly respected public school teacher in my hometown. He was an intellectual, but did not deal as well with emotional issues. In contrast, my mother, while an intelligent woman, was not so intellectual but much more emotional. I recognize some of both in myself. Even though I can get very emotional, my faith has always been more intellectual.

My road to faith has not included personal earth-shattering events. Following a catechism class, I was baptized into church membership when I was almost fourteen. I have never been a very *pious* person; consequently, I felt that I was not very religious. I was not comfortable in the few tent meetings I attended. The god of fear and retribution preached there did not fit my concept of a loving, caring God.

I am a Christian today because I have experienced Jesus as the best teacher and example of a life of love and concern for others. Christ's message of redemption for my (our) brokenness draws me to faith in God. This belief has enabled me to come to self-acceptance and an awareness of God's love for me. It has also influenced how I read and understand the Scriptures.

I enjoyed my years at Bluffton College, a Mennonite liberal arts school in Ohio. There were occasional academic discussions about homosexuality. I recall a bull session in my dorm room with about eight other fellows when the topic of conversation turned to homosexuality. At one point, someone commented that about ten percent of the male population is homosexual. I vividly remember wishing that I was not there when someone wondered aloud who that one was in this group! Fortunately, that point was not pursued.

During my senior year of college, I was accepted into a master's program in international relations; however, later that spring (1964), I received my *Greetings* from Uncle Sam and had to change my plans. Instead of graduate school, I went to Kings View Hospital, one of the Mennonite mental health facilities, in Reedley, California, to do my 1-W service as a conscientious objector. This work was in lieu of military service. On my first day, June 22, 1964, I met Ruth Hartzler, a staff nurse there. The milieu at KVH focused on being a therapeutic community. I learned a lot about myself and mental health, became more aware of my feelings, and was able to be more honest with myself. Ruth and I soon became good friends.

Ruth:

The path to our marriage commitment had a very traditional start. I was born in the mid 1930s on a small farm in northern Indiana into a rather conservative Mennonite family. My parents took their faith seriously and were active in our local Mennonite congregation. My father was definitely the authority person in our family on most matters. In addition to farming our few acres, my father worked as a machinist in a factory.

My mother, a full-time homemaker, had lived in Ontario until she married my father. She was a gentle, caring person. As an adult, I am aware that my parents loved us and took good physical care of us. They were usually not explicit in affirming our gifts and achievements or helping us deal with our emotional concerns. Responsible behavior and good grades in school were expected. As the oldest child in a family of seven – four girls and three boys – I learned early the expectations of obedience and compliance. Questioning the views and decisions of parents and elders was not even considered. Overall, my childhood was a comfortable balance of play and work, although we took life seriously.

At the age of twelve, I responded to the invitation to accept Christ during annual revival meetings at my church and was baptized and became a member of our local congregation. I tried to follow the teachings of the Bible as they were interpreted by my congregation. Although my faith in God was sincere, my perceptions of the emphasis on obedience crowded out a meaningful sense of God's love and redemptive work for me.

In my baccalaureate nursing education at Goshen College, a Mennonite liberal arts school in Indiana, I became vaguely aware of homosexuality via lectures, textbooks, and conversations with other students, but it did not seem relevant to me or to my peers. I occasionally heard certain students described as homosexual, and the implication was that such a condition was not consistent with the values of the college. An instructor at the state hospital where we received our clinical psychiatric nursing experience was rumored to be a lesbian. This did not seem to be an issue for any of us. We liked her as an instructor. Later, while working at Kings View Hospital, I learned to know some gay and lesbian patients, but their sexual orientation was not addressed as something to be changed. There was little, if any, education for staff about sexual orientation or sexuality.

When I met Jay at Kings View Hospital, where we were employed, we were both dating other people from out of the area fairly seriously. Jay and I soon found that we had many common interests and enjoyed doing many things together. We became good friends. Several years after we met, the serious dating relationships we each had with others ended. I began to seriously evaluate what I wanted in a marriage partner. My work in psychiatric nursing and observations of couples that I admired for a good relationship helped me see that much of what I hoped for was available in my relationship with Jay.

I was surprised and amazed to receive a letter from him which clearly indicated that he was also realizing that our relationship could be more than just friendship. He was attending graduate school in Pennsylvania at that time. We had corresponded occasionally after he left California. After an intensive exchange of letters for several months and a visit together, we decided to marry a few months later. I had been concerned about some of his feminine characteristics, but gradually these became less objectionable. Our mutual friends were very affirming of our decision to marry. Some even shared that they wondered what took us so long to recognize that we belonged together!

Jay:

Early in the first year of our marriage, I knew that my sexual attractions to men had not gone away and were not going to. I gradually told Ruth about my homosexual feelings, and she tried to be understanding. During this time, I began to be very concerned about being a good father; consequently, we decided not to have children, even though we both are very fond of children. Instead, we have chosen to enjoy the many nieces and nephews our siblings share with us. Ruth is seven and one-half years older than I, and she was then getting close to being thirty-five years old, at that time considered to be the deadline for having children.

Ironically, it was during our first year of marriage that my *gaydar* began kicking in. I began picking up signals from other gay men. Why this did not happen before marriage I do not know. Subsequently, I occasionally acted on the signals. This eventually led Ruth to ask questions which I answered truthfully, and I agreed to see a psychiatrist. He helped me to become more comfortable with myself. I soon realized that I was not going to change my orientation.

After that period of counseling, I occasionally acted on my feelings, and I again sought counseling. This time I made an appointment with a psychologist from our church. We met only a few times, but he, too, worked with me to become accepting of who I am. In addition, he talked with Ruth and helped her view these events less painfully. After this counseling, Ruth and I talked about whether or not to stay together in our marriage.

This psychologist was the person who first told me about BMC (Brethren/Mennonite Council for Gay and Lesbian Concerns). He had recently learned about this organization. I promptly phoned Martin Rock, the founder of BMC, took a day off work, and drove to Lancaster County, a few hours away, to meet and talk with him. This was in January of 1977. I have been involved with BMC ever since.

Shortly before this, some friends gave us a house gift subscription to the magazine, *Faith at Work*. One issue had a small ad from Kirkridge, a Christian retreat and study center in the Pocono Mountains of eastern Pennsylvania, for their first "Gay and Christian" conference. We decided to go. We were scared, not knowing what to expect. This was in May of 1977. We were the only married couple there, but I was *not* the only married man. The group composition was about one-third clergy, primarily from the main line Protestant denominations and the Catholic Church. There were only six women, including the mother of a lesbian and Ruth. Father John McNeill, a Jesuit priest at the time, was one of the resource persons. His book, *The Church and the Homosexual*, had just been published. We found his book very helpful in understanding the *clobber* passages in the Bible, and we still highly recommend it. The retreat was extremely helpful to us.

Although we can talk about this time rather calmly now, it was a very painful and difficult time for both of us. I think the Kirkridge conference was one of the major turning points to help us be more understanding and accepting of the impact that my orientation was having on our relationship.

It was also about this time that I came out to a gay graduate student I learned to know in the sociology department where I worked at Penn State University. He organized a men's lunch group on campus to provide an opportunity to learn to know other gay and bisexual men, some of whom were also married. It was a great thing for me. I was not alone. He also organized a group for wives that Ruth participated in.

Ruth learned from a friend about "Lifespring," a human potential education program, and decided to attend it. This program helped her to live more comfortably and confidently in her interpersonal relationships. With her encouragement, I also took the "Lifespring" courses, and they had a major influence in my life. I faced myself as I never had before, both the positive and the negative, and was able to accept both in my life. I became a changed person.

Prior to that, I was an angry and very cynical person. After the "Lifespring" experience, the anger was gone, and I was not the cynic I had been. I was able to accept others where they were more easily, and I became more concerned about and aware of what was going on in other people's lives. I was able to accept my sexuality. It was such a freeing experience!

The "Lifespring" community was the safest place I had ever experienced. While we had told a few close friends about me, after "Lifespring" it was easier for me to do so. We have continued to tell close friends when we are fairly sure there will be acceptance.

I have been involved in the music program of the church since college days as a substitute organist and occasional pianist. I enjoy most being a song leader and frequently serve in that capacity. Since 1988, I have become more involved in planning and leading worship in my congregation. Leading worship was a big stretch for me initially, but I have found it very satisfying. I have become aware that I am a more spiritual person than I previously recognized, though I never felt that God had abandoned me. The traditional interpretations of Scripture just never felt accurate. This is why John McNeill's book was so helpful. Although I was very aware of society's difficulty with homosexuality, I felt it was not a problem for God, but only for human beings.

Ruth:

When we married, I had not heard the word *bisexual* – much less, *mixed orientation marriage* – so I did not know such marriages existed. Both of us were serious about our commitment to live as faithful Christians and to marry for life. I assumed that our love could handle any concerns! I soon learned that my assumption would have some big unexpected challenges. We were not long into our marriage when Jay shared with me that he still had fantasies about having homosexual sex. I did not know how to respond except to continue to be loving, try to understand, and hope the fantasies would not interfere too much with our life. I certainly had no understanding of the implications of this for our relationship. We had no idea what to do.

About the time we were making the decision not to have children, I was offered an opportunity to begin a career change to nursing administration as director of nursing at our community hospital. I continued to work in nursing leadership positions until I retired from full-time work in the fall of 2000. Jay's support and encouragement for me in these challenging, fulfilling, and sometimes difficult positions has strengthened our marriage. My work in nursing leadership has also contributed to my increased confidence to speak out for justice in the church.

Fortunately, Jay's work in administration at the university gave him the opportunity to learn to know gay individuals and discover more about gay orientation. He shared information with me as he learned it and thus furthered my education. We also learned to know some other married gay men and their wives. The support group for wives of gay men was very meaningful to me. It was helpful to hear each other's stories and to learn more about this complex issue. While we did not find any solutions, it was reassuring to know that we were not alone.

During this time we were somewhat aware that the church viewed homosexuality as being sinful. *But why? If it was wrong, why was it so much a part of one's being? Why did homosexual persons report that from as far back as they could remember they were attracted to persons of the same gender? What truly is sin?*

Jay and I prayed about his orientation, but soon decided that prayer was useless to bring about any change. Then I learned about Rev. Troy Perry's book, *The Lord Is My Shepherd and He Knows I'm Gay.* It was enlightening and reassuring to learn that a Christian gay man had experienced God's love and grace in his life. His story was convincing and moving. It was a big first step on my journey to eventually believe that the church has chosen to misinterpret the Bible on this subject.

Another step was reading the stories by Bible translators who worked with the same organization that my youngest brother has worked with all his adult life. Stories from this organization about Scripture concepts or passages difficult to translate led me to a new understanding. It is quite possible that some of our scriptures have not been translated or understood accurately, given our limited knowledge of the culture and word meanings of that day. This seems to be especially true regarding the few passages now used to define homosexuality, which are meager in comparison to those about other concerns like greed, love of money, selfishness, abuse of power, wrath, and gluttony.

Although I was eager to attend the "Gay and Christian" conference, it was very uncomfortable for me. It was difficult to fit in, but it was very helpful. We met Christian theologians who also believed there was reason to doubt that the homosexual experiences referred to in the Scriptures would apply to committed, loving relationships between persons of the same gender. We were becoming more comfortable with our understanding that homosexuality per se was not on God's list of sins. We learned that other couples such as us were described as mixed orientation marriages.

During these years, we experienced some difficult times in our marriage and wondered if we could live with Jay's continuing homosexual attractions. At one point we seriously considered whether to stay married or to separate. However, we recognized that our love for each other was strong and that our marriage provided much happiness and satisfaction to both of us. Jay made it clear, emotionally and by his behavior, that his commitment is to me and to our marriage, and that he is not interested in having a gay partner. This commitment has continued to the present time.

We concluded that we did not have a good reason to give up our marriage and that we had many good reasons to stay together. We continue to be happy with this decision. Both of us are free to discuss and question each other about any issue. This has helped us learn from and build trust in each other.

An important source of support and information came from the gay and lesbian friends we learned to know through BMC. In the 1980s I was invited to be the first non-gay member of the BMC board. This service on the board with many fine committed Christian gay, lesbian, and bisexual persons gave me a very special and welcome opportunity to develop good friendships with them. It also put me in touch with the terrible pain that many of these persons experience as they seek to accept and treasure their orientation as a valid part of God's creation. The pain is often intensified by the rejection they experience from persons who are significant to them and by exclusion from their faith communities.

Serving as a board member was a special privilege. It gave me a greater understanding and desire to work to ease the pain that many GLBT individuals experience as they come out to themselves and to others. I treasure the board service for opening a very large window to a world I was struggling to understand and have found very fulfilling to be part of.

Jay and Ruth:

Over the years we have met a number of mixed orientation couples, often through BMC and mutual friends. Many of these couples eventually decided not to stay together after the gay, lesbian, or bisexual partner learned about and acknowledged his or her orientation. We did meet a few couples who, like us, wanted to stay in their marriage. Our support of each other has been very satisfying and important.

We have been asked occasionally to meet with other mixed orientation couples, many whose marriages are in turmoil over the sexual orientation issue. We quickly learned that each mixed orientation couple is different and will have their own way to work on their relationship. Sharing our story with other couples does not necessarily help them know what to do about their marriage, but sharing our stories has often been comforting to both them and us. It always helps to know we are not alone. It has been painful to see some of these marriages break up, though we realize some of the marriages were already cracking and the mixed orientation issue only made the break-up more certain.

We have become more courageous to speak up about the injustices we see in the church and in society toward GLBT individuals. Gradually we have shared our story with close friends, first in our small group at our church, then in other groups as well. As we considered telling our story for publication, we felt the time had come when we would have the courage to handle whatever negative reaction might come to us. We share our story humbly because we believe others can benefit from it. We even learned some new things about each other while writing this story! We believe we have been able to stay together by the grace of God and are very grateful for the life and love we share. We feel very cared for and supported by our loving Creator God and our church friends.

Ruth E.H. Martin was born near the town of Wakarusa, Indiana. She has lived in Lancaster, Pennsylvania, since 1988 and is now retired from full-time nursing in which she worked since graduation from Goshen College in 1956. After starting her nursing career in Indiana, she also worked in

California, Indonesia, and Pennsylvania. She has a master's degree in Nursing Administration from the Pennsylvania State University. Currently, she is a part-time relief nursing supervisor at Inglis House, a long term care, residential wheelchair community in Philadelphia for three hundred physically disabled adults. Retirement gives her the welcome opportunity to nurture friendships and her flower beds, among other activities.

Jay Martin was born in Gettysburg, Pennsylvania, in 1942. He grew up in Fairfield, Pennsylvania, just west of Gettysburg, where he was involved in the Fairfield Mennonite Church and was baptized there on April 1, 1956. He graduated from Bluffton College in 1964 and completed an MFA in organ performance at Pennsylvania State University in 1969. He has worked in middle-management and currently is conservation administrator at the Philadelphia Museum of Art. His father was the most significant and positive early influence in his religious thinking.

Other significant contributors to Ruth's and Jay's present perspectives include the therapeutic community of the Mennonite psychiatric hospital in California where they worked and met and the many special people in the Mennonite congregations they have been members of since 1968 in State College and Lancaster, Pennsylvania.

It seems to me that if we expend all our energy and attention on defining sin, we become the very evil we are trying to define. If instead we apply it diligently to acceptance of grace, to knowledge of God as a parent whose always-extended hand I can grasp and be led out of the swamp I may have become mired in, then we will ourselves become instruments of grace.

~ Lin Garber

~ *five* ~

The Terrain of Our Relationship

Josie Byzek with Virginia Rogers

"You have multiple sclerosis," said my doctor the night she called me at home. My first reaction was relief. For years doctors had insinuated that my various medical complaints were all in my head. In a way, they were right. MS is caused by errant white blood cells attacking the covering of nerves in the brain and spinal cord. It's kind of like having frayed wires in your computer's motherboard.

My partner, Ginny Rogers, unlike the cadre of rheumatologists, orthopedic surgeons, and other so-called specialists I have consulted over the years, says she never doubted my experiences with my body were real. She says she believes in me. She is like that.

Ginny also says that having a disabled partner – we have been lovers since 1988, and my disability has been part of my life since 1982 – teaches us both a lot about life and each other. First, it teaches us that disability is nothing to be afraid of; it is a normal part of the human experience.

As my mother approaches fifty-five, she is increasingly afraid that someday she might have to use a wheelchair or other equipment. I don't have that fear at all. I know from experience that I will use whatever tools are available to keep living, keep moving. I have already experienced the liberating power of a wheelchair, to suddenly be able once more to go fast and painlessly.

Ginny is right. Disability is a good teacher. Yes, it is scary when a new symptom just hits out of nowhere – like when I went blind in one eye – my strong, non-blurry eye – for months, but I have learned that, with time, I can adjust to anything.

Second, it teaches us not to take life so seriously – like the months when the most innocent of touches sets my leg bouncing like Thumper in "Bambi." Even though I am known for my irreverent sense of humor, when Ginny picked up the Thumper doll in the Disney store and said, "Hey, Josie, look, it's you," I wanted to die.

But that night, when I told the story to a friend of mine, who uses a power wheelchair for her MS, she said, "Do you think that's bad? I fell out of my chair today and had to crawl to the phone and call the paramedics. You know what I told them? 'Help, I've fallen and I can't get up!'"

I roared with laughter. My friend said, "This stuff *is* funny. Learn to laugh at it now." That is still the best advice anyone has ever given me.

Third, Ginny points out that my disability buys us membership into one of the most exciting social movements in the world: the disability rights movement. We have learned that all people matter, all people have a right to do and give what they can, and all people have a right to live free, rather than in a nursing home or other institution.

We have also learned that if it is built with steps, it can be built without steps. All people have a right to dine at restaurants, worship at churches, and take public buses. We have learned these rights are worth fighting for – we are members of disability activist groups such as ADAPT. I have had my belief in these rights tested in jails ranging from Harrisburg, Pennsylvania, to Atlanta, Georgia.

I have learned firsthand what I believe Jesus meant when he said we have to lay down our lives in order to pick them up again. If it were not for my body's idiosyncrasies, I may never have felt freedom at the cellular level as I do now.

And, I point out to Ginny, don't forget we have also learned – probably the most important lesson – that wholeness is not dictated by the body. Ever! Wholeness is something much deeper than limbs and organs, and so many people never even get to sense that deepness. I am so grateful that some of the times I have known myself to be the most whole are the same times parts of my body have been tingling, twitching, burning, or paralyzed.

I concede, it's not always like that. Sometimes it just sucks. Like when I was suddenly hit by fatigue in the Wal-Mart parking lot and insisted Ginny take me home *immediately* because "I'm not going to sit in the car like a pet dog." And, like those times when I'm so irritable with discomfort that if I were a pet dog I would be put to sleep.

Or, like the other week when I sliced my foot in a friend's bathroom. My leg just gave out and I slid into the toilet like it was home base. Once I could stand, I leaned against the door for a few minutes, bleeding, not knowing if I should cry because my foot hurt or laugh because for the first time in weeks I could feel my foot. Or, any of the many times I've peed my pants in public and we had to leave before anyone realized what had happened.

"You can't say watching me go through these things is easy," I insist to Ginny.

"Sure," she admits, "those things can be hard to watch, but they are not the defining factors in our relationship."

It's true. We communicate with each other better than most other couples we know. This builds an incredible level of intimacy between us. We have to talk to each other about some intensely uncomfortable topics just to make it through a typical month. It has made us stronger and closer in a society that increasingly sanctions weak and frequent relationships. We also have a level of physical intimacy that most people in their early thirties have no need of – to deal with off-line body parts. It spills over into our sexual relationship as well. We have learned to be forgiving with each other, to *take it easy* with the other's shortcomings.

Well, that last one is still a work in progress. But, given how well we communicate with each other, it is getting easier every day.

Speaking of communication, "It's now my turn to watch you deal with a disability," I say to Ginny. Fibromyalgia, in her case. She is learning some hard facts about communication that I alternately know and forget – mainly, that very honest and direct statements about what she can and cannot do at any given moment are crucial. I have relapsing/remitting MS, which means it comes and goes. When it goes, I move my body full speed ahead. Not too long ago I went for an early morning bike ride simply because I could, and I came home to find her still asleep.

"Still asleep?" I asked. "You should get up, it's beautiful outside." I think I even tried to become amorous.

"You don't understand," she answered, almost in tears. "You just don't understand. It's my day off. I want to sleep."

"Are you just tired?" I asked. "I can make some coffee to wake you up."

"Just go away," she begged, so I did, not understanding what I did wrong.

We talked about it later – much later – when she was up and about. Besides pain, fatigue is her main fibromyalgia symptom. She was fatigued, but did not tell me that. She just thought I would know. All I knew was that she said, "I'm tired." Being tired is very different from being fatigued. Most people can shake off being tired pretty easily just by taking a shower. Not even standing under Niagara Falls can shake off a bout of fatigue; you just have to wait it out.

It reminded me of all the times my body fritzed out on me, and I thought she would just know. Like when she angrily insisted I hurry up one morning, because I was making her late for work.

"It would go a lot faster if you would just come in here and button my pants," I answered.

She thought I was kidding, and it hurt my feelings. I realized later that I had not told her that a few days earlier my left hand curled up and lost its strength, and I was out of clean, non-buttoning pants. I thought she would just know somehow. I was wrong!

So I guess that is the biggest lesson disability has taught us about ourselves and our relationship: It's not possible to *just know* what is happening in someone else's body or mind – no matter how close you are to that person. After thirteen years, we are still learning how to clue each other in on what we can and can not do, and how we do or do not feel.

The terrain of our relationship includes the terrain of our bodies on a level not experienced by most people. Disability brings with it adventures and knowledge of myself and ourselves that I wouldn't trade for an Olympic gymnast's physique. "And that's how it should be," I say to Ginny.

"I agree," she says.

Josie Byzek and **Virginia Rogers** live in Harrisburg, Pennsylvania, with their eleven-year-old daughter Dawn. Friends since 1985, Josie and Ginny have been partners since 1988. The family attends MCC of the Spirit. Josie is associate editor of *New Mobility*, a magazine for wheelchair users. Ginny is coordinator of the Pennsylvania Transportation Alliance, an organization that focuses on obtaining rural transportation for persons with disabilities.

~ *six* ~

Together through Serendipity

Kara and Irene*

Prelude:

On July 9, 2001, we celebrated our six-year anniversary of being together as a couple. The past six years have been filled with many moments of joy and happiness for us as a couple. Our individual lives and careers have been continuing to evolve since we met, but our love for one another has only deepened and become more rooted.

Our hope is that as you read our story, some part of it will resonate within you. We come from very different backgrounds – and yet we have many similarities. Our journeys prior to meeting each other have been different. It feels like God intended for us to meet and be together because of the way we complement each other. Sometimes you just know that God had a hand in creating something good!

As a couple we find that our faith in each other, the support each of us gives to the other, and the continued presence of God's spirit enables us to live in unity and rejoice in our lives together. May you be blessed by reading our story as much as we have been blessed by living out our life's journey.

Kara:

I was raised in a traditional family with an older sister. Since my father was the primary breadwinner of the family, my mother was able to stay at home and raise my sister and me. I knew I was always the different one. I was the rebellious, adventuresome, squirrelly one.

---

* Names have been changed. In Greek, Kara means joy and Irene means peace.

I was a tomboy. I liked sports and the outdoors, camping and bicycling, softball, and working with my hands. I remember spending hours by my father's side helping him with household projects or working in his woodshop with the tools. My mother always tried to steer me back into the domestic activities that a young girl should learn like sewing and cooking, and even though I did those things, I never had a passion for them.

My parents were active in the church we attended that was affiliated with the United Church of Christ. Since they were involved with so many activities in the church, not going to church every Sunday was not an option for my sister and me. My parents had commitments to fulfill at church, and we attended Sunday school and church regularly.

As I grew older, I became active in the Youth Fellowship. It was a place where I got to see friends, and we always had a good time together. I remember learning the Bible stories and doing Bible study in Sunday school. When I was old enough to be confirmed and join the church, I was glad I could be in the same class as my friends.

I remember going to our church's Adventure Camp one summer. The adventure included canoeing twenty miles and backpacking twenty miles, each with an overnight stay. It was an experience I loved and one of my best church memories, for I always had fun and always learned something along the way. Outdoors is a place where I can sense God's love for me, and I am able to experience the beauty of God's creation. I can feel the breeze cool my face, be warmed by the sun, or walk along a sandy beach and sense God's ever-loving presence with me.

My teenage years were filled with lots of activities, such as field hockey, softball, Camp Fire, and the church. Even though I had a boyfriend on and off through high school, it still felt weird to date a boy. I loved to do the rough and tough kinds of things that are characteristic of tomboys. Since all my friends had boyfriends, I thought I should as well. I felt that I had to please my parents. I never wanted to hurt them by my actions, I only wanted to make them proud of me. So the thought of me being lesbian was never considered or explored.

Since I was from a small town in a predominantly conservative area, being gay was just not discussed. We never knew anyone who was gay. There certainly was not *anyone like that* who went to our church, so I had no exposure to what being gay meant or how a person knew that he or she was gay.

In my world, the expectation was that after you became an adult, you found a mate, got married, and began a family. You remained married to that person the rest of your life and that was it. No one ever talked about the "what if" factor. *What if you married someone you didn't love? What if you found out you were pregnant before marriage? What if you found out that you were gay, and you would never marry? What if you were gay, and there would be no grandchildren?*

Even though we had a secure and well-adjusted family, we never discussed our inner thoughts and desires. The more I am learning about my parents' childhood, the more I am able to realize why these kinds of things never got discussed. My parents' generation never discussed them either. So, even though I know my sister and I were loved a great deal, we could not talk about issues or concerns that we had, as that was forbidden territory. No one talked about one's inner thoughts or feelings. Areas of faith and love were just not discussed. Sad but true, that our innermost thoughts and feelings are kept silent and never allowed to surface.

When it came time for me to consider whether or not I would attend college, I really panicked. I had no idea what I wanted to do with my life and no direction in which to turn, except for the idea of becoming a physical education teacher. That was the only thing that came to mind. Since I loved playing sports with girls, and I loved the concept of building a team spirit with other girls, it made sense. But how could I ask my parents to pay for college for me, when I hated school and couldn't imagine being a teacher? The only reason I wanted to be in physical education was so I could continue playing sports and being with other girls, not that I wanted to teach children.

I also considered traveling and finding a way in which I would not need to have my parents pay for college if I decided later on that I wanted to attend. So, I contacted an Armed Forces Recruiter. After passing the ASVAB (Armed Services Vocational Aptitude Battery Test) and taking the physical, I decided to enlist in the United States Air Force at age seventeen. I always believed my motives for wanting to be a part of our nation's military were sound. I wanted to broaden my horizons beyond Pennsylvania and see the world, as well as get a college education. I accomplished that and more during the twelve years I was on active duty.

It was only after I left the area that my faith really began to take hold. I was able to build upon the dedication to the church that I had experienced as a child and call it my own. Since a good deal of my active duty time was spent overseas in places like Germany, the Republic of Turkey, the Republic of South Korea, and England, I had to rely on my faith to keep me going. In every location I was stationed, I knew that I was not alone, for I knew that God was watching over me. I knew God's love for me kept me safe and free from harm. I knew I was part of a bigger family beyond the Air Force family.

I also began to realize that no matter what I do or who I am, God loves me unconditionally. I am a child of God, who deserves to be happy and whole and filled with grace. For the first time in my life, I began to realize a calling to something much bigger than myself. I knew God had a much bigger plan for me beyond the Air Force.

In 1995, I separated from active duty and returned to Pennsylvania. I had nowhere else to go, so I returned to my home of origin. You have probably heard the saying, "Once you leave, you can't go back." Well, I definitely felt that was true for me! I returned to an area where the people had not changed; their priorities were the same, but I was a totally different person than when I left twelve years earlier. It was almost like going back in time to my childhood years. I certainly did not want to do that.

The summer of 1995 was one of transition and a greater awareness of my sexuality. I was experiencing great sadness leaving the military and returning from overseas. I was struggling with what I was going to do with my life and how I would transition into a new career. I was missing the military lifestyle and all of my Air Force friends.

Little did I know that only a month after I returned to the area, my life would be changed – forever! And, I would never have believed that of all places for me to meet the love of my life, it would be in my home church! The same church where I grew up, the same place in which many childhood memories were made, the same place where I prayed to God that I would find somebody to help make my life complete. Oh, how wonderfully God answers our prayers!

Irene:

Church was always part of my life, even before I can remember. My mother and father went to church every Sunday. I felt so grown up as I tried to read along in the hymnal as a three-year-old. The best part of church was at the end when it was time to get our coats on and go home, because we always went somewhere fun after church. This might include a place called Storybook Island with life-size characters from Mother Goose nursery rhymes or the lake or Mt. Rushmore or just to dinner.

I remember being part of the Christmas programs. My voice was lower than most of the children, so it was hard for me to sing along; but I did my best. After the program on Christmas Eve, I looked forward to the small brown paper bag filled with peanuts, hard ribbon candy with red and green stripes, and a tangerine. Even when we moved to Las Vegas, we still got the treats on Christmas Eve.

At that time there were no Wisconsin Synod Lutheran churches in Las Vegas, so my mother taught me the Sunday school lessons and my father taught my brother the lessons. Eventually a mission church was started. By the time my little brother was born, we had a small congregation meeting regularly. My brother and I actually helped build the church. I was good at dry walling and painting. We got paid with a free lunch, including tomatoes fresh out of the pastor's garden on a BLT (bacon, lettuce, and tomato) sandwich.

There were only two kids in my confirmation class. Students are not confirmed until after the congregation is satisfied that they have learned something about the church, so the entire congregation asked the two of us questions about the Bible, the commandments, and the creeds.

My faith was strong by that time. The summer when I was twelve, I went out for a walk in the park between church and Sunday school. I had a talk with God and asked that if God was really there, I would feel God's presence. I was immediately filled with an assurance that God was there and that God loved me. I am a very introspective person and sometimes feel quite lonely. God's presence has always been an important part of my life. The song "In the Garden" gives words to the feelings I experienced that day.

When I went to college, I discovered the fun of being sociable. However, I did not have much time, since I worked hard at my engineering studies. I soon began to recognize that my attractions and interests were for my female friends. My friend Scott said that I was a lesbian. I was vaguely concerned about this, because being lesbian is not a good label in our society.

I fell in love for the first time about the same time my mom was diagnosed with cancer. But my first love left me before school was out. I struggled with the pain of losing my first love and the pain of watching my mother lose her fight with cancer. Within six months of her diagnosis, she passed away.

I felt God's presence when it was time to find hymns for the funeral. I got the idea to get the Lutheran hymnal from the piano bench, and in the front I found a list of my mother's favorite hymns. One especially was circled. When I went to that page, her initials were on the song: "For Me to Live Is Jesus." This hymn is based on Philippians 1:21: "For to me, to live is Christ, and to die is gain." The song describes the way my mother died. She lived her last days with grace and beauty and was granted her prayer of dying before the cancer took her mind.

I eventually met another woman whom I loved, but she left me for the military. I was so depressed that my father had to have a talk with me one day. He said that it was like a divorce when she left me, and that I had to get over it and go on with my life. This was the first time we had talked openly about me being a lesbian. His biggest concern was that my heart would become hardened to God. He always loved me and accepted me as I was, and gradually I got over the loss.

My church did not often mention homosexuality, but when it was mentioned, it was listed as a sin along with adultery and fornication. I could not reconcile these good feelings of love with the church's teaching, so I avoided church for a while. I still felt God's presence, and I still prayed.

One day when I was feeling especially needy of the fellowship of other Christians, I heard of a church where gay people were welcome. I went to Casa de Cristo in Phoenix, Arizona, for the first time and heard the message that God loved even me. I kept going to that church for a long time. We had Bible studies on Wednesday evenings and church services on Sunday mornings and evenings. I found Christians with the joy of the Lord in their hearts and their worship.

Sometimes I think that gay people are blessed with more joy as Christians than heterosexual people are. In this society we are looked down on so much that Christ's love is even more precious to us. I reconciled my homosexuality and my Christianity by giving my whole self to Christ. I know God created me and that God knew all about me even before I was born. I have given over my feelings of attraction to women to God to either change or use for God's purposes. So far, my sexual orientation has not been changed.

All along, my sister-in-law continued to pray that I would meet a good Christian man to settle down with. I say that God answered her prayer because, after three years, I met the woman who is my permanent partner in life. I think God knew I needed to be with a woman.

Together:

The circumstances in which the two of us met were serendipity. After moving to a new area, Irene had been attending a local United Church of Christ church. Kara was stationed in England at the time. We had not met each other, but mutual friends, who knew us both, went to England and this is how we heard something about each other. Little did we both know that our friends had envisioned us meeting each other.

From the moment our eyes met that Sunday in the United Church of Christ, we fell in love with each other. We felt as though we had been struck between the eyes. We talked just outside the sanctuary as though we were long lost friends.

We have a great deal in common. Kara was in the military; Irene grew up on military bases. We both lost a parent to cancer around our twentieth birthday. We both share a strong love for the Lord and for the church and have both been active working to help the church.

Though we are very different in our personalities, we have had an easy time getting along. Early on, we found out what painful things we do to each other when we have disagreements, so we stopped doing them. We are so richly blessed by sharing our life together.

When we met, Irene had just been laid off from an engineering job of ten years and Kara was out of the military service.

One of the Bible verses that was very meaningful to us in the early days was Matthew 6:34: "Therefore do not worry about tomorrow, for tomorrow will worry about itself. Each day has enough trouble of its own."

Since we have been together, we both have changed careers. Being a teacher was a dream for a long time for Irene, so she went back to school and completed the coursework to become a teacher; she loves her work with children.

Kara is attending seminary to be an ordained minister in the United Church of Christ denomination. Because of the judicatory process involved with ordination, and the fact that gay and lesbian persons are still being questioned about their worthiness to be ordained, she wishes to remain anonymous.

In my mind the problem is not that there are gays and lesbians. They are not the problem. The problem is the church's refusal to extend grace and open arms to receive them.

~ Willis (Bill) Breckbill,
Welcome to Dialogue Series, #1

~ seven ~

No *IF* in Unconditional

Susan and Ann Reinhold

Susan:

Though we had met the year before, Ann and I began dating in 1965. In spite of many struggles, we have been together in a monogamous, committed relationship ever since. We have also been in business together, and we have faced great disaster and great joy. We have supported each other, and we have hurt each other. We raised two children together. In today's culture it is tough for *normal* relationships to survive. It is almost impossible for *special* relationships. Special relationships face pressures and lack of support from those around them.

We have been together for more than three decades, and there has always been *Love*. While participating in a recent panel discussion, Ann's response to the question "How have you stayed in this relationship?" really hit home. Her response was, "A long time ago we promised to love, not to love *if* the other met our expectations; we just promised to love." I have been the one to severely test the bonds of that love. While Ann is a heterosexual female, I am a lesbian – of sorts. I am more accurately a male to female transgendered lesbian.

The family that I was born into had a very significant impact on my life. Not only did my family go to church, but at a fairly early age I also realized that many of the most important people in my life seemed to have a relationship with God. This experience meant that I did not have to discover God on my own, nor did I have to assess the validity of this concept. *God* was a part of my life. For several generations, my family roots have been Church of the Brethren.

My first real struggle occurred before I started school. It had become apparent to me that who I was somehow did not fit the criteria of who I was *supposed* to be. If I allowed myself to be really *me*, I would somehow be gently nudged to where I was supposed to be. I came to believe that everyone struggled with sin of one kind or another. My particular sin was that my self-identification did not measure up to the norm. Regardless of my own discomfort, it was clear to me that I needed to be what I knew I was not.

I was just getting to the point of calling God on the carpet for making me feel like a girl (everyone could see I was a boy), when I had a great epiphany – I was sexually attracted to girls. Boys were supposed to be attracted to girls. At last, something started to feel the way it was supposed to.

Throughout junior high and high school, I went through several cycles of acquiring female clothes, wearing them whenever I could, feeling guilty, and eventually getting rid of all my female clothing. When I purged myself of the sin of being female, I would attempt to build on the remnants of my previous relationship with God. However, as time went on, the need to spend some time as *me* would overtake my relationship with God. I would start to dress as female and stop the relationship with God. Sometimes these opposing journeys would last for years. Each time the journey I set aside would call to me so strongly that I would once again change my course and head in the other direction.

In June of 1968, I took the *final cure*! I got married to the love of my life and knew that the real me would have to be laid to rest for good. By this time I was fairly good at *passing* as male. (Passing is a term in transgender circles referring to being able to move about in general society as a person of the opposite gender without being noticed.) I could fool just about anyone. I was not Superman, but everyone acknowledged me as male. Of course, *I knew* I was female.

The *final cure* lasted about one year. Then I knew that I either had to lie to Ann for the rest of my life or begin to somehow let her discover me. I also struck a deal with God. I acknowledged that who I was is a sin, but it was all I had; so God was just going to have to deal with that or abandon me. I was not going to abandon God anymore over this one deal. I figured if I was not good enough to sit at the table, at least the dogs and I could enjoy the scraps on the floor. Ann and I have discussed these years and neither of us really remembers how we crossed the line and began dealing with the real me. Perhaps we were just too young and too much in love.

A major event in my spiritual journey happened in 1997 in an Internet chat room. I had recently acquired a used computer and was on line for the first time. Ann had been putting up with my other self for some time in our home, but I was interested in finding out more about *me*. I discovered a transgender website and chat room where there were articles to read, definitions to try on, and people with whom to chat. In one of those conversations, someone asked what support group I attended. Without being *too-o-o* specific, I explained that I lived in central Pennsylvania and that surely nothing like that existed here. After all, I was nearly fifty and – until I got on the Web – had never conversed with another transgender person. While I was stating the facts of life, as I knew them, a message appeared on the screen: "RENAISSANCE – Meets first Saturday of each month at MCC of the Spirit, a church on Jefferson Street in Harrisburg, Pennsylvania."

"Surely, there is a mistake – a church in central Pennsylvania that would knowingly let people like me meet there!"

"No, no mistake."

"Well then, surely they want to get my name and address so they can send people around to *CURE* me."

"No, RENAISSANCE is a support group –" and so the conversation continued until I finally got the drift.

I had never heard of Jefferson Street. It was the Monday after the first Saturday, so I had missed that month's meeting, but you could "bet the farm" that I was going to find Jefferson Street the very next day. I think it was about the third – or maybe it was the fourth time – I had circled the block, when the pastor, Eva O'Diam, came out of the building and looked me in the eye. I had to stop! After all, remember – I pass okay as a guy. The building did not look much like any church I knew, but it was the right place. Not only did they allow transgenders to hold meetings there, I was welcome to attend the church as *me*! The following Sunday was the scariest day of my life. I think Ann was sure I had finally lost it. Here I was in the driveway in a skirt getting ready to drive to Harrisburg – on public roads – to go to church – as a woman!

When I first arrived at the Metropolitan Community Church (MCC), I had no idea how right my decision had been. For the first time, I found others who had struggled with their sexuality. I found a place where who I was – a child of God – was what I was supposed to be.

Oh, to be sure, there were some chilling moments as the new me explored my place in the world. After attending evening services for several months, I had one of my most difficult moments when I decided to attend a morning service and was confronted with children. All my old training kicked in. I headed for the door so I could get out of there before I created an embarrassing scene for Dawn's parents. Surely they would not let their daughter come in contact with the *unclean*! However, a strange thing happened. Josie and Ginny brought Dawn over to me to introduce their friend – *Susan*. I had never seen the possibility of being a friend that someone would want to introduce to children. At that point I had not considered myself worthy of being introduced to my own adult children.

"…to love and to cherish, from this day forward, until death do you part" has a familiar ring to it. I have been trying to think of an instance when I heard conditions added, like – unless you gain ten pounds, or unless I find someone better, or unless I get tired of you. In today's world it seems that is what is really meant when two people share that vow. Unconditional love is a rare thing indeed, yet it seems to have found me in many ways. The love that Ann shares with me is a gift more precious than I know how to express. Ann is still the love of my life!

Ann:

Perception is perhaps one of the most difficult concepts to grasp in life. I sometimes think that I had to be over fifty to understand that everyone sees things differently according to their own perception of the situation. Everyone brings to each situation in his/her life the total of his or her own experiences and knowledge. How, then, was I able to understand my partner's gender identity? We were married when I was twenty. I was so naive that I really didn't comprehend the *gender* situation at all. What I can remember was a feeling that *this* was just a passing phase and a way of dealing with stress or something similar.

Over the next thirty years or so, I devoted my time and energy to raising our two sons and starting my own business career. I admit that I really didn't pay much attention to the gender boundary crossing during that time. What I did not realize was that during those years of struggle to be a wife, mother, career woman, and my own person, I was also developing a faith in God that would give me the strength and grace to totally accept my partner as the person she really is.

When Susan first discovered and began attending the Metropolitan Community Church of the Spirit in 1997, I did not foresee the changes that would come to our life together as a result. Because of the experiences of the previous four years, Susan left the Church of the Brethren and joined the MCC while I have remained at the Church of the Brethren. Difficult situation? YES!!! However, not an impossible situation to overcome. Since the people in my church do not know Susan, they have arrived at many unusual and incorrect perceptions about why my partner chose to join another church.

I have come to realize how much *open-mindedness* is needed to understand that diversity relates to gender issues as well as to race, ethnicity, lifestyle, occupation, and wealth. The majority of people with whom I come in contact are not aware that there is a *spectrum* for gender as well as the other facets of each person. Society at large has accepted most diversity among race, ethnicity, religion, age, and economic status; however, alternative identifications of gender (other than strictly male and female) are something very few people understand or even want to consider.

Our social life has changed also. Since most of our friends with whom we interacted socially do not know Susan or are not aware of the gender spectrum, it has become more comfortable to spend time with people who do know and accept her. I have one very close friend in whom I have confided. When I first *told all* about my relationship with Susan, her reply was "WOW! You are so lucky! You have a partner who really understands how you think and feel and can also fix the car when it doesn't start!" Actually, when I looked at it from that perspective, I realized that I had gotten a pretty good deal.

A question Susan and I are often asked is: "Does your family know?" The answer is "Yes." The natural follow-up to that is "How do they feel about it?" Some are accepting and some are not. Susan's mother, brother and sister-in-law are supportive while still struggling to understand the unique gender identity of someone they thought of as a son and brother. Our two sons are less accepting, but continue to love us anyway. They struggle with the idea of how *Dad* can be a female. The remainder of Susan's family know about her, but have never met her as a woman, so their perceptions are somewhat distorted.

My family is mostly deceased and sharing our unique journey has never been an issue. Through the family's struggle to understand the *Susan persona* of my partner's character, I have seen my own struggle mirrored a hundred times. However, the greatest miracle has been that of observing God's hand and guidance in teaching me one of life's greatest lessons: Love others, whoever they may be, just as God has loved and totally accepted me.

Sometimes we do not immediately realize or understand the unique gifts God has given to each of us. When looking at other people's lives, most individuals wonder how others manage to deal with what they perceive to be tragic or difficult circumstances. It is those same circumstances that help teach the lessons God wants us to learn. Although most people I know would see having a transgender partner as an insurmountable problem, it has actually been a gift. It has been an almost five-decade process for me to recognize how very blessed Susan and I are to have found each other.

We are very different in physical appearance and characteristics. Susan is an extrovert, while I am the introvert in the family. Yet, it has been through the struggle to overcome all the differences previously mentioned, that I have come to realize my greatest gift – the ability to find my authentic self and the willingness to share what I have discovered about that knowledge with others. I now share Susan's joy of life's amazing lessons that can be learned from each other, thanks to the knowledge that we are here to help one another in our faith journeys. The pathway begins with gratitude for what we have been given and continues with knowledge that we are not alone, but are helped by the Creator every step of the way. Knowing this does not make life's problems disappear – just easier to handle when they come.

Susan's Epilogue :

When Ann and I originally consented to write our story, we were afraid that my job would be in jeopardy if *Susan* became public knowledge. However, I made a decision at the end of 2001 that I would seek a career in my female identity, and on January 15, 2002, I made that intention known to my employer.

Up until this time, I was known at work as a male. During the next three weeks, many things occurred. My coming out to my employer caused much distress and misunderstanding.

During that same period of time, I had an opportunity to attend Robert Schuller's "Church Leadership Conference" in Anaheim, California. I experienced the week together with my pastor and five others from my church. On the flight to California, I was awake while the others around me were sleeping. Alone with my thoughts, I began to consider the events I had set in motion and the impact they could have on my life.

My contemplation turned to prayer, and I shared my fears with God as I had many times in the past. I tried to express my desire to submit to God's will and not try to force my will into prominence. I listed the questions that had plagued me from my youth. *Is this female identity the real me or something I have created? Is it my will or God's will that I live in this identity? What difficulties will this bring to my family? How will my children deal with this decision? Why am I so afraid if this is God's plan for me? How can I tell if the answers I think I hear are from God?*

In my arrogance, I told God I was aware that Christ had told the Pharisees they should not ask for a sign – and I did not need a burning bush – but how was I to know if I was choosing the best way without some sign from God? The answers I thought I had were answers that agreed with my desires. I wanted to *hear* the answers and *know* that they were God's answers for me and for my family.

To say that the week was a startling spiritual journey for me would be an understatement. Throughout the week, answers rained in on me – from speakers at the conference, a pastor in a church service, Marsha Stevens in a concert, and a homeless man on the beach. I listened to these voices because, in each case, I felt awareness that while the person speaking may not have known I was there, what they were saying was meant for me to hear.

The doubts I had in the first hours after asking for God's guidance disappeared on Monday evening, the first day of the conference. I had earlier received several of the answers I was waiting for. When I walked out of the restaurant after dinner, it was completely dark, except for the moon. As I looked up, a bit of cloud touched the edge of the moon and for a moment there was a burst of a rainbow. Not a burning bush – but a rainbow in a night sky!

As I looked down, a voice within me said "Look up!" I thought, *"I already saw it – I saw your rainbow at night."* As the voice kept insisting, I looked up. In those few intervening moments, a cloud had covered the moon, and there was now a full circle rainbow in a completely dark sky surrounding the moon. As I stood watching God's sign in the sky, others from the restaurant came outside and looked up. To them it seemed an oddity – a rainbow at night. To me it was a statement that I had better be very intentional about what I asked of God in the future.

I returned from California and on February 7, 2002, was terminated from my job. Now it is April, and I have accepted a position as an independent representative for a professional association. I will begin my new career as *the real me*. I do not know what lies ahead for Ann and me but I *do know* that life is full of miracles.

Susan Reinhold was born and grew up in Lancaster County, Pennsylvania. She graduated from Elizabethtown College in 1970 and has been self-employed much of her life. Until the early 1990s, she was a life-time member of the Church of the Brethren. Susan has been active in many organizations including Rotary Club and various Chambers of Commerce. Today, much of her time is spent in various ministries at Metropolitan Community Church of the Spirit in Harrisburg, Pennsylvania.

Ann Reinhold was born in a small town in south central Pennsylvania and lived her entire life within a fifteen-mile radius of that town. She went to college, graduated with a BS degree in Elementary Education, and taught elementary school for two years until Susan and Ann started their family. She began her career in the banking industry when their oldest son was six months old, and she has been in numerous positions (bank teller to vice president) within several banks for more than twenty-five years. In 1999, Ann was diagnosed with multiple sclerosis. She continues to work full-time, but has curtailed her extra-curricular duties to that of church treasurer, personnel committee, and the local Rotary Club. Her hobbies are reading and traveling (when she gets the opportunity).

> What Jesus gives us is a critique of domination in all its forms, a critique that can be turned on the Bible itself. The Bible thus contains the principles of its own correction. We are freed from bibliolatry, the worship of the Bible. It is restored to its proper place as witness to the Word of God. And that word is a Person, not a book.
>
> ~ Walter Wink,
> *Homosexuality and the Bible*

~ eight ~

Complementary Diversity

Julie A. Lichty and Mary C. Rhodomoyer

Julie's story:

When I look back on my childhood and adolescence, I get the feeling that I was a typical Mennonite. My parents were Mennonite schoolteachers, and my father became a pastor when I was in high school. I attended a Mennonite church, and my education – elementary through college – was in Mennonite schools. It was only after I finished college that I began to see life as more than what existed in the Mennonite bubble in which I had lived.

I remember having feelings that I might be gay as far back as fourth grade. Sexual development can be difficult for anyone growing up in a religious environment. The church typically did not make sexuality a priority. So, for me, these feelings of being different were scary, because in the religious world in which I lived there was no room for homosexuals. There was not even room for discussion on the matter. Homosexuality was considered wrong, and anyone who was gay could not be a Christian. This is what stuck with me all the way through college and beyond. These are the feelings that I suppressed until I was able to see that not all of what is taught in church is truth.

Meeting Mary was so insightful because it allowed me to see a normal everyday person who just happened to be a lesbian. We met while working in a group home for mentally retarded adults. Mary went to work, spent time with her family, and seemed to enjoy life. She had an abundance of friends. Mary is the type of person with whom everyone wants to be friends. She is full of ideas and energy.

Once we met, we became instant friends. It was not long afterwards that I knew I had fallen in love. It was also the time that I realized I could no longer be in denial over who I was. It was time to accept myself as gay and move on with my life.

Moving on meant a real struggle, because I was going against everything that I had been taught in school and church. I did not feel any different as a gay Christian than I did as a straight Christian. I did not even feel different as a person in general. All I felt was that I was more me than I had ever been. I needed to resolve the conflict inside of myself. What I found was that God loved me even more once I accepted who I was. When I was in high school, I used to pray to God to make me be straight. God never did that. God's answer to me was that it was okay for me to be gay. That answer was Mary.

Mary's story:

My childhood was nothing like Julie's. My spiritual development came from outside of any religious institution. My family never went to church. I remember my grandmother taking me once or twice and the preacher shouting something about fire and damnation.

I sometimes battled with extreme feelings of being alone. When my loneliness got to be unbearable, I learned to talk with God. It was not like I was praying for a better life or different circumstances. I was simply sharing myself with God. This developed into a wonderful relationship. To this day, I know that God has always taken care of me. I have had some terrible experiences in life, but nothing that God did not help me to overcome.

Sometimes I find myself unable to find the words to pray. This often happens when I am feeling especially down or hopeless. Then I turn to Julie to provide the words for me. She prays aloud to God and asks for the peace that I am seeking.

I suppose I began to know I was gay in elementary school. It was not a horrible discovery for me to make. I think I was just too young to really know what it meant. In high school I dated guys and did drugs as my way of overcoming the feelings of being different. After I left high school, I began to be open to my sexuality. I even knew that my parents were open to it, because they liked the girls I brought home much better than the guys!

When I met Julie it was like a breath of fresh air. Her smile was consuming. I was drawn to her structured way of life and attracted to her caring personality.

Our story:

Remember the saying, "opposites attract"? In the beginning of our friendship and even as our relationship progressed, we thought we were so much alike. We would talk for hours on end about a multitude of subjects. We also would spend entire afternoons together, playing a range of sports and recognizing our equal abilities. We even shared similar lifelong goals. We considered ourselves far from opposite. How wrong we were!

The more we discussed topics and got to know one another, the more we realized that we did not agree. It became painfully clear that our diverse backgrounds caused us to have very different views on life. The two of us together make for an interesting conversation. The satisfaction of being together comes when we are able to see issues from the other person's perspective and broaden our own views.

We continue to play sports together, although it is not always as fun as when we first met. We realized that our abilities came to us in different ways. Julie played organized sports since she was ten. She grew up with a father and brother who watched sports every day on TV and consequently taught her the finite rules to any sport imaginable. To this day, Julie plays sports with a combination of natural ability and an intense knowledge of rules and strategies.

Mary does not always know the rules. She plays with natural ability and a desire to play well and do whatever it takes to win. She grew up with three brothers who did not care that she was a girl. She had to survive against them all. If you could combine us into one person, you would probably get an excellent athlete. When we play against each other, we usually end up throwing tennis rackets or shouting obscenities. Neither can stand to let the other win.

When we met, we were working in the same job. Our life-long dreams appeared similar. However, that, too, went to the wind. Mary has since become an artist/photographer, with a bachelor's degree in fine art. Through her work she uses surrealistic photography to express the spirituality of nature and self-realization. Julie is a child welfare social worker who is pursuing her master's degree in social work. The two could not be more opposite. However, the combination is powerful and creative, with a structured sensitivity to the earth and all things in it.

Our differences are what draw us to one another. We enjoy the discussions, competitions, and debates about life. What keeps us together are the things that we share in common. We are both deeply affected by any sort of suffering. This sensitivity goes beyond that of humankind. We share a love of nature and the preservation of animal and plant life. It is not often that you find someone who complements you so well. We consider it a blessing that we found each other in 1996 and have been able to maintain a loving, caring relationship to the present day. Both of our families have welcomed the other as a member of the family. Their acceptance is the ultimate way that we have felt God's love.

Julie A. Lichty is a foster care caseworker for a county child welfare agency. She is also currently in a Master's of Social Work program at the

University of Pennsylvania in Philadelphia. In her free time she enjoys walks with her dog, Frankie, and spending time with family and friends.

Mary C. Rhodomoyer recently graduated from Temple University's Tyler School of Art in Philadelphia with a Bachelor of Fine Arts degree in Photography. She is a manager in Tyler's bookstore and also a part-time instructor of photography at the school. She is pursuing freelance portrait and artistic photography as well. Ms. Rhodomoyer plans to begin graduate school at Tyler in the fall of 2002.

Jesus said, "You shall know the truth, and the truth will set you free." If that's true then much of the church doesn't know the truth, since it is often a place of bondage.

~ A South African missionary

~ *nine* ~

Our Vision of Healing and Hope

Larry Miller with Stephen Wilcox

The current vision statement of the Mennonite Church states: "God calls us to be followers of Jesus Christ and, by the power of the Holy Spirit, to grow as communities of grace, joy and peace, so that God's healing and hope flow through us to the world." Surely our ability to become "communities of grace" requires us to learn to know and understand one another. It is with that goal in mind that we decided to share our story.

I (Larry) was the second of four children born to my mother, a full-time homemaker, and my father, a truck-driving former Old Order Amishman, who "jumped the fence." Ours was a loving home, and we children never lacked any of life's essentials. I do recall, however, from a fairly young age, feeling somehow different from my brothers and other male friends. By the time I was twelve or thirteen years old, I came to the troubling realization that I was attracted to members of my own sex.

I remember, as a seventh grader, searching through texts at the Orrville (Ohio) Public Library to find some explanation for my feelings. What little information I found was frightening. My affections were described as deviant, perverse, inverted, and disordered. I determined at that point not to share my feelings with anyone. Author and lecturer Brian McNaught describes the dilemma for gay and lesbian teens this way: "having a secret that you don't understand and that you can't share with anyone for fear they won't love you anymore." That was certainly true for me.

At age fourteen, I made the decision to be baptized into the Orrville Mennonite Church. My understanding of the Christian faith was perhaps somewhat immature, but I was sincerely drawn to Jesus along with his teachings and his example. Our denomination's emphasis on peacemaking was also particularly important to me. I hoped that my commitment to Christ would somehow replace my sexual attractions. However, as I moved into my high school years, these feelings only became more intense.

My response was to keep myself busy. I was actively involved with our local Mennonite Youth Fellowship. All of my closest friends were other MYFers, and I found our emphasis on group functions provided a comfortable social setting. Even so, I was aware that my parents were wondering when I would begin dating. In an attempt to meet their expectations and maintain their approval, I once asked a girl from a nearby congregation to accompany me to an MYF-sponsored Halloween party. All I remember about the evening is how phony and uncomfortable I was. I felt ashamed to have involved another person, without her knowledge, to maintain my secret.

Throughout my teens, I spent many nights praying that God would change me and take away my unwanted desires. It was not to be. I could only conclude that God wasn't interested in answering my requests in the way I had hoped. My prayers for change became less frequent and eventually ceased altogether. Instead, I put my efforts into making sure that my behavior conformed to what my parents and church taught. I continued in this pattern after high school while I worked on my grandfather's dairy farm, did a two-year term of voluntary service with MBM (Mennonite Board of Missions) in Phoenix, and completed a degree in respiratory therapy at Hesston College before moving to Washington, D.C., to take a position at the Washington Hospital Center.

Over the next few years I went through a period of intermittent church attendance at various congregations in the Washington area. I gradually developed a group of friends, mostly other young Mennonites living in the area. We shared many good times. I felt comfortable with these friends except on those occasions when our conversations broached the subject of romance. My responses were always guarded and deflective of any specifics. I hoped my friends would draw their own *incorrect* conclusions about my sexual orientation. As one by one my friends married and started families, I found it increasingly difficult to repress my own desire for a loving companion.

I also wanted a closer connection to my faith tradition and thus decided in January of 1988 to formalize my membership at Hyattsville (Maryland) Mennonite Church. I was aware that the congregation had already gone through a process of discernment regarding the membership of gay and lesbian people and had concluded that sexual orientation per se would not be a consideration in anyone's request for membership. I joined quietly, without identifying myself as a gay person.

Later that spring, at age thirty-four, I developed a friendship with a hospital coworker who eventually shared with me that he was gay and that he found me attractive. I was both excited and nervous as we began a relationship that would last five years. From the very beginning, however, we had the ill-conceived notion that we would be closeted about the nature of our relationship. As I look back now, I wonder how we ever thought we would be able to maintain such a pretense, but I think it speaks to the amount of fear and shame with which I was still living.

I grew more emotionally distant from my family and friends to avoid discovery. The stress involved in constantly describing each other as friends or housemates became burdensome and destructive of the relationship itself. Without a mutually shared faith or external support system, things began to unravel. When it became apparent that the relationship was ending, I also became acutely aware that there was *no one* from whom I could seek advice or support. I felt more isolated than at any other time in my life.

However, I did know that my isolation was self-imposed, and I decided to risk self-disclosure. I phoned the only openly gay couple in our congregation one evening and explained my situation. The guys were wonderfully supportive and referred me to a therapist, whom I saw regularly over the next year. With her encouragement, I came out to my family, friends, and my church family at Hyattsville.

During this same period, I attended the 1993 assembly of the Mennonite Church in Philadelphia. There I made my first contacts with the Brethren/Mennonite Council for Lesbian and Gay Concerns (BMC)[1] and have found the organization to be a wonderful source of friendships and support.

I began to read a number of books by gay or gay-friendly writers and theologians and came to the realization that God really does love me as I am created, and that my sexuality is a gift, not a mistake or a sin.

In the fall of 1994, while in Ohio visiting my mother, I paid a visit to a gay couple I learned to know through my involvement with BMC. Jonathan Sprunger and Steve Berg are gracious and hospitable guys who host occasional backyard cookouts at their home near Winesburg. At one such barbecue, their neighbor Steve Wilcox came by, and we had a chance to converse for a while.

That was the beginning of a long-distance courtship with many phone calls and weekend visits. I discovered that we had each been praying for a life partner with similar values related to the importance of family, faith, and personal integrity. I was delighted to learn that he was a skilled chef! And, I began to hear his personal story.

Steve grew up in the small village of Benton in Ohio's Holmes County. As the oldest of four children, and also the old-

---

[1] Brethren/ Mennonite Council for Lesbian and Gay Concerns, PO Box 6300, Minneapolis, MN 55406-0300.   Phone: (612) 722-6906.   Fax: (612) 343-2061
E-mail: BMCouncil@aol.com   Web:www.webcom.com/bmc/

est grandchild in his family, he was frequently the caretaker for his younger siblings and cousins. The family attended and was actively involved in the local Lutheran church (ELCA).[2] Steve was baptized into the congregation as an infant and subsequently confirmed in the faith during his early teen years. He sometimes attended the vacation Bible school program at nearby Martin's Creek Mennonite Church.

He recalls sensing that he was somehow different from his peers at a very young age, and he was frightened when he began to recognize his same-sex attractions. He sought refuge from his thoughts by keeping busy with chores and family activities.

Steve did not doubt that God loved him, but could not understand why he was created as he was. He always enjoyed a close emotional connection to his grandmother and was comforted when she confided her belief that "We are who we are when we are born, created in God's image." In later years, he was one of her primary caretakers until the time of her death.

At age twenty-two, Steve informed his parents he was gay. They were not surprised by this information and were open and accepting of him from the very beginning. Steve and his first partner Allen were welcomed in their home and even came to live with Steve's parents for a period of time. Steve and Allen lived together in Phoenix for four years. They separated when Steve moved to San Francisco to work and to complete a degree in interior design, but remained close friends until Allen's death from AIDS-related complications.

Following his father's untimely death from a ruptured cerebral aneurysm, Steve moved back to Holmes County to be nearer to his family. Thus it was that our paths first crossed some years later at the home of our mutual friends.

Since Steve's move to the Washington, D.C., area, our love for each other and for God has grown and so has my own sense of self-worth and self-confidence. In the fall of 1995, I attended

---

[2] Evangelical Lutheran Church of America.

a management retreat along with about a dozen of my peers and supervisors from the hospital. As a team-building exercise, the facilitator asked each of us to share a synopsis of our personal lives. Each person in turn began to relate information about spouse, children, hopes, dreams, etc. As my turn approached, I felt my pulse and breathing begin to quicken. There was an initial look of surprise on some faces as I began to describe myself as a gay man. But when I shared that I had found a loving soul mate in Steve, the group broke into a round of applause. I was the one with the surprised look on my face as my boss spoke about his gay brother and the facilitator about his gay son. It was as though the others had finally been given permission to speak.

Now, many of my coworkers have learned to know and like Steve. We are invited as a couple to work-related functions. This same sense of goodwill, acceptance and inclusion characterizes our interactions with Steve's coworkers in his job at Bloomingdale's department store. We feel especially thankful that my hospital employer provides health insurance coverage for the same-sex domestic partners of its gay and lesbian employees. This insurance benefit was a lifesaver for us three years ago, when Steve required surgery for multiple coronary artery bypass grafts.

Steve and I regularly visit our families in Ohio. We maintain a second home there that Steve built some years ago on a corner of his grandfather's farm. Steve is an avid bird watcher and enjoys the wooded setting. I have been welcomed and embraced by Steve's siblings from the very beginning. It so happens that one of his sisters is lesbian and his brother is gay, so I anticipated at least a certain level of acceptance in the family! Steve's mother is also a lot of fun and can be counted on to stimulate some major belly laughs. I have come to love her. However, our visits to her home are usually kept short, because Steve's Southern Baptist stepfather prefers that she minimize contact with us.

My own mother has always shown love and acceptance for Steve and me, even as she continues to grow in her understanding of issues that affect us. Each spring she travels with us to Pennsylvania for "Connecting Families," a weekend retreat for Mennonite and Church of the Brethren families who have LGBT (lesbian, gay, bisexual, and transgender) members. The weekend has become the spiritual and emotional high point of our year. She has also found the local Wooster, Ohio, chapter of PFLAG to be a welcome source of nurture, support, and education in a community that is largely characterized by silence regarding the lives of LGBT people.

Likewise, my sister and brother-in-law, along with their two young children, are very close to us. We felt honored when Barb asked if we would raise their children in the unlikely event that both she and John become unable to do so. Unfortunately, we only see my two brothers and their families on an occasional basis. I would describe their attitudes toward us as superficially cordial, but condemning.

In addition to that offered by our families, we are thankful for the welcome we have received from our congregation at Hyattsville Mennonite. Our active participation is encouraged in fellowship groups, committees, worship, service projects, and other church functions. Most recently, I served as a congregational delegate to the General Assembly at Nashville and continue as a delegate to Allegheny Mennonite Conference. I'm looking forward to serving a term on the pastorate (board of elders) beginning this fall (2001). A commitment to being inclusive of gay and lesbian people of faith seems to be shared by most members of the congregation. The congregation recognizes that this makes it vulnerable to criticism and perhaps disciplinary action from the wider denominational conference, but has chosen to live with this tension.

On the home front, our life as a couple seems pretty ordinary. Jobs, errands, home and yard maintenance, cooking, laundry, and other activities of daily living consume much of our available time. Steve is a great cook and this summer he has been canning his signature tomato cocktail. His interest in design and decor has added much warmth to our home. I love to read and enjoy following local, national, and church politics. We both enjoy gardening, long walks, restaurants, art gallery visits, occasional movies, and informal gatherings with a few close friends, gay and straight. We look forward to our monthly evening potlucks, one with our small group from church and the other with our local BMC group. We want our home to be a place where guests feel welcomed and at ease.

The emotional and spiritual benefits of living together as a couple are considerable. Our relationship offers us companionship and mutual care taking. We have supported each other through serious illness and periods of unemployment. We love to laugh together. (Just the other day Steve labeled my attempt at weight loss our version of "the heifer project.") His little quips buoy my spirits!

We are committed to each other and are secure enough in our relationship to be able to argue and banter at times. We challenge each other's inconsistencies and offer each other encouragement in the face of disappointment. We frequently offer and receive forgiveness from each other for our shortcomings. We have promised to be faithful, and we trust one another implicitly. We confide our fears, hopes, and joys to each other. In our love for each other, we occasionally get a glimpse of what *God's* unconditional love for *us* is like.

Thus, we have much for which to be thankful. Our professional, social, family, and congregational lives are well integrated. However, the denomination of which we are a part continues to view our love for each other as sin. We would like to have our relationship blessed in the Mennonite Church USA, but we are not willing to ask any pastor to risk his/her career and credentials to perform our covenant ceremony. We often discuss the possibility of relocating permanently to our home in Ohio, but are uncertain we would be able to find a nearby Mennonite congregation that would welcome our involvement in its life and mission.

Obviously, our vision of healing and hope has not yet been articulated and embraced by the Mennonite Church USA. We hope for the day when no young people growing up in our congregations will be given the impression that God's love does not extend to them because of their sexual orientation. We wish that more LGBT people of faith could find a church home in which they can be open, honest, and safe from Bible abuse. We long for a day when the many spiritual gifts of women and LGBT people in our churches will be acknowledged and appreciated, and we will be welcomed in both pew and pulpit.

Finally, we pray that some day, our denomination will articulate and communicate a loving, realistic, sexual ethic for LGBT Christians, rather than abandoning young people to find their own way through the maze of choices in our society. This would include provision for the recognition, blessing, celebration, and support of committed gay and lesbian relationships, recognizing that we are *all* God's children and need love in our lives in order to grow to our fullest human potential. We believe that genuine Golden Rule love requires us to do no less.

We will do what we can to hasten the arrival of that day, through prayer and by being open about our lives, so that *all* the members of our body – gay and straight alike – can experience a Mennonite Church that is truly transformed.

Larry Miller and **Stephen Wilcox** celebrated their seventh year together in the fall of 2001. Larry is employed as a clinical supervisor of respiratory care in the Department of Pulmonary Services at Washington Hospital Center. Stephen uses his interior design training in the visual merchandising department at Bloomingdale's. Both men enjoy the cultural and ethnic diversity that living in metropolitan Washington, D.C., affords them.

~ ten ~

Unconditional Love

Martha and Nina Joy Montgomery

Martha:

Joy and I feel honored to be invited to share our story in this book. My part of the story begins with my birth in 1950, long before Joy and I met. My mother and I lived with my grandparents until I was four years old. Throughout my childhood, I did not like the way boys played and would play with neighborhood girls every chance I could get. Everyone saw me as a boy, but even at a very young age, I knew I was different. Because I was perceived to be different, I was the victim of a rock throwing incident that caused blindness. Doctors did not expect me to ever be able to see again, but God healed me!

All through my life, something did not fit. No matter how hard I prayed and asked God to remove my conflict or to change my body, nothing happened. I learned very early in my school years to pretend to be what others expected me to be, or I would get beaten up continuously. No one knew the secret that lived deep inside me – I felt like a female! Wearing dresses felt very normal for me. During competitions, I would internally cheer for the girls, even if it meant my team would lose.

From about the age of eight, I almost always had a hidden stash of female clothes somewhere. When I was almost sixteen, my parents found my clothes. They didn't understand any more than I did why I felt the way I did. All they could comprehend was that I must be gay. So they sent me to a therapist, who said he was a Christian. He gave me some tests and, just from the results of these tests, proclaimed that I was *Gender Confused.* He explained to me that the treatment for this disorder was shock therapy.

I went to the library to learn what shock therapy entailed and was horrified that anyone would do such a thing to any other human being. No way was I going to give this therapist enough information to ever do that to me! I became adept at lying.

After I graduated from high school, I worked part-time at a toy store, but decided I wanted more out of life. So I enrolled in a Christian college, about twenty miles from home, for the spring semester and lived on campus. I wanted to take as many religion classes as I possibly could. In my first semester, I took "Old Testament," "New Testament," and "Introduction to Christian Religion," plus some other classes. I was sure that if I worked hard enough for God, surely God would remove my conflict.

The following summer I worked in the kitchen of a summer youth camp. However, no matter how hard I tried or how much I prayed for my conflict to go away, there was no answer to my problem. Therefore, I gave up trying and transferred to a junior college. I moved in with my grandparents rather than return home. My grandfather was a jack-of-all-trades. He worked at many odd jobs. I was able to make a little money by helping him with some of those jobs.

During this time, I began visiting different churches in the area. The first Sunday that I visited Joy's church, I sat next to one of Joy's girlfriends. After the church service, I joined some others who were talking together in the parking lot. An usher interrupted us to ask me if I could take a man to the Veteran's Hospital. I was surprised to discover the man was one of the kitchen helpers from the youth summer camp of the previous summer. There was no way I could refuse.

I hoped there would still be time for me to attend the youth group singspiration service later that evening. When I knocked on the door to join the group, everyone gave me a big cheer for helping the man out. They did not realize that I knew him, because we had worked together during the summer.

Joy and I actually got introduced to each other about a month and a half later. Five days after I was introduced to her, I asked her for a date. When the time for our first date arrived, my car broke down, so my grandparents took me over to her house, and we played parlor games instead.

It was only a matter of a month or two until we realized we were meant for each other. I was certain that if anyone could cure my internal conflict, surely she could. However, I kept my conflict a secret from her. After we were engaged, I joined the military service in order to provide for us.

Eight months and a day after entering the service, we were married in the same Baptist church where we met. After our marriage, I needed to report to the Seattle, Washington, area for assignment. We found a sister Baptist church and began attending services there.

Joy:

My story began more than thirty-one years ago. When Martha and I met (she was Mark then), it didn't take long to know that God had brought us together. We could see God's hand in the timing of lots of things in our relationship. When we married, I knew that this was the *one* God had chosen just for me!

Early on, however, mysterious things began to happen. I thought I had married a man, but this man started wearing my underwear underneath his military uniform and blamed me by saying that "the laundry wasn't done." I carried this guilt for years – needlessly.

Life went on, and we had two children – a daughter and a son. When our older child was six, a relative passed away. I took the kids and went to be with my family for a few days while Mark stayed at home. When we returned, there was my spouse – all dressed up and having a blast as a housewife. I was furious! Through clenched teeth I blurted out the name *"Martha!"* Who knew it would become her name of choice years later!

As time went on, our kids became aware that their dad was wearing a dress or dressing androgynously most of the time at home. I remember one time coming home from church with the kids (at that time Mark was refusing to go with us) and finding my spouse lying in bed, happily wearing full makeup. I wanted to throw up – I was so revulsed! I had to leave the house for a while. I drove to a shopping center where I could be alone in a crowd and just walk around and pray. Later, I remember forcing him to take off my muumuu before I went to bed with him. As the kids grew older, the tension grew.

Martha:

Our kids could not bring their friends home from school, because they were not certain how I might be dressed. It was not an easy time for any of us, but in spite of the conflict at home, they both did rather well in school. As time went on, my internal conflict grew much stronger. By the time our kids were graduating from high school, I could hardly breathe while wearing male clothes. I became almost half paralyzed. I felt certain that my medical problems were just a side effect of my internal conflict.

I searched page by page through our telephone book, trying to find something to explain how I felt. One day I was able to find a support group on a computer bulletin board system and get a referral to knowledgeable doctors to help me with what I now knew was *Gender Identity Disorder*. But Joy wanted to keep the status quo and refused even to read books on the subject. She kept hoping that if she ignored my dilemma, it would just go away. She did not want to give up on having a man in her life.

This was a very difficult period in our marriage. Both Joy and I considered suicide, each feeling it would make life easier for the other. I felt that life would be easier for the entire family if I did not exist. Joy did not believe that two women could be married to each other; if she were not in the picture, I would be free to be myself.

Joy:

Mark talked in his sleep. At first it was, "I want to be a woman," but eventually it became, "I am a woman." I did everything I knew to stop this; however, I was in a no-win situation. I felt that I was losing my husband. I could see no way that we could be happy continuing in this direction. I thought this was a choice my spouse was making, and I felt it was a wrong choice.

After all, Mark had a wife who adored him and two children who loved him, plus brothers and sisters on both sides of the family who thought he was a pretty terrific brother. My parents thought they had the world's best son-in-law. Mark's stress was growing and taking a toll on his health. So, now I was threatened with another way that I might lose my husband.

I had kept this secret inside of me for a very long time. One night, when someone I trusted asked how I was, the truth bubbled out in tears and sobs. Finally, I had someone to pray with me! She suggested that I take advantage of the counseling that our church provided. It sounded good to me.

Later, my spouse joined me for two sessions. The therapist convinced Mark to try to be a man again. Well, that was short-lived! But I pounced on the opportunity and got rid of the clothes that I saw as a hindrance to my *miracle.*

When Mark reverted back to Martha again, I was instructed to present an ultimatum: "Be the man of this house or get out!" Well, that was the wrong thing to do, and my spouse spent a couple of nights elsewhere. When she came back, she slept in a different part of the house. The tension was unbearable!

Martha:

The therapist from our church, who Joy talked me into seeing, had been trained in a way similar to Exodus Ministries. After only two visits, I found myself ready to end my life! Without divine intervention, I am certain I would not be alive today.

The church therapist talked Joy into using what he called *Tough Love*. One night when I came home, I discovered that my family had prepared a very special dinner. After the meal was over, they all got up and informed me that I was no longer welcome in my own home. They had packed my bags and now told me to leave. They no longer wanted me to live with them. For me, that was hardly love at all! They told me they wanted me to live out on the streets, thinking that if I was desperate enough, I might allow God to take over and help me overcome my desire to be a woman.

Through all of this difficult time, God never left my side. Even though I had no money, and the only credit card I had was already at the maximum credit limit, I decided to try for a motel anyway – and my credit card was accepted. At least I had a place now to spend a couple of nights.

The next morning, I called someone from work, who informed me that Joy did not have the right to throw me out of my own home. Therefore, the following day I managed to get back into our house again, but we slept at opposite ends of the house and never even spoke to each other.

I eventually moved into an apartment complex. Within a week or so, legal separation papers showed up at my door. Now I had to find money to hire an attorney. I scraped enough together and turned the separation into a full-scale divorce. If she could not stand me as I was, I figured there was no use in even trying any longer to keep the marriage together.

Joy:

At this time, my parents were wrapping up the final affairs of my uncle who had recently died. They were planning to move in with us for a short time before moving on to California to live out the rest of their days. Even though I didn't really want them to move in with me, I felt I had no choice.

Consequently, they were living with me when I filed for legal separation. I did not think I could be married to a woman. I knew I still loved my spouse, but a lifetime of being raised in conservative Christian churches was ringing in my ears. When Martha turned the separation into a full-scale divorce, my world fell apart!

Martha:

During this stressful time, God led me to a wonderful church. After attending for over a month, I decided to officially join the Seattle First Christian Church (Disciples of Christ). Because of the changes that were going on within me, I felt that I wanted to be baptized as my true self, and the church granted my request. I became an active member, singing in the choir and helping in the kitchen for special dinners. I even became a deacon in the church.

Some other churches had made it clear to me that they would rather I did not attend their services, and I honored their requests. I am thankful for the church that took me in and accepted me as part of the family. I am certain I am where the Lord wants me to be at the present time.

The divorce proceedings continued for seven months. While all this was going on, I never felt more at home with myself. I was now able to give expression to the female inside that I always felt myself to be. At last, I was not needing to pretend to be other than myself. I began estrogen therapy, and the many physical problems I had been experiencing just disappeared. My health got better – not worse! Even though there are many medical conditions that could have stopped my transition, not one adverse thing happened to change my course of action. I could finally see light at the end of the tunnel! I just kept moving closer and closer to that light.

But things were not going well on the home front. Joy chose to listen to people who told her that my condition was all a choice. While we were separated, we could not even talk on the phone to each other. I told Jesus that if I could not take care of Joy, I wanted God to send someone to her who could. This was a very lonely time for me. Everyone I had known before turned against me – family and friends. Only my brothers and sisters in my new church stood by me.

Joy:

Our younger child joined the military and was off to boot camp in the same month that the older one moved to a dorm on a university campus. Three weeks later, my parents moved out. I was more alone than I had ever been in my life.

On the rare occasions when my spouse and I would talk on the phone, the calls would be brief and would normally end with one or the other of us slamming down the phone. The poor phones needed to be healed! During this time, I cried *a lot!* And I prayed *a lot!* And I just existed.

I also attended a "Divorce Care Class" that was being offered at my church. It was the first time they had ever offered such a class. The group was small. During the thirteen-week course, we were shown a series of videos and given a workbook to read and fill out. The one line that stuck with me was, "You have to accept reality for what it is, not for what you want it to be." Hmmm….

All this time, I still believed God for a miracle – specifically, that my spouse would call and say that being the man in our relationship was the right thing after all. After a quiet Christmas with our young adult children home from their new routines, a new year began.

Early in January, I was watching a TV show on TBN (Trinity Broadcast Network). They had a guest who had SRS (Sexual Reassignment Surgery), but for the wrong reason. This man had become a woman because he wanted to be loved by men, but he was now sitting there dressed as a man. He regretted having the surgery. What I heard was that God loves people like this unconditionally just as God loves all of us unconditionally! Oops, I had put conditions on my love for my spouse. I cried through the whole program.

Shortly afterwards, I got a phone call from my former spouse, and I realized that it wouldn't kill me to call her "Martha." The wall began to come down. After another phone call, we began to talk to each other – each resisting the urge to slam the phone down when our ideas were challenged. I offered to bring the controls of the electric blanket to her since she had the blanket, and she invited me to have dinner with her.

When I arrived at Martha's apartment, we gave each other a hug – the first time we had touched in months. As the evening progressed, we talked, we cried, and we realized we still loved each other. After that it became a time of "your place or mine?" with the understanding that each of us could ask for a time-out if need be. There was only one night after that when we chose to be alone. However, I was still holding out for my *miracle*, believing till the last possible moment that God would change my spouse. (I had at least four hundred people praying!) But, lo and behold! I am the one who changed.

We had a little counseling just to reassure each other and to make sure that both of our needs were met. Then we called off the divorce. I still had to cry an ocean of tears as I mourned over every *thing* that was my husband and all that I was giving up. But, I had peace from God. I knew that God had brought us together to begin with. I also knew that God hates divorce and the Bible says, "What therefore God has joined together, let no [one] put asunder" (Matthew 19:6, KJV).

I knew that the two of us together would not be welcome in our old church and decided it was time to consider finding a church where we could both worship together. We visited some churches near our home, but we were not welcome in any of them.

I was concerned that if I attended Martha's church, it might affect how the people there viewed Martha. I did not want to make it difficult for her. However, I did not need to be concerned. The people at Martha's church welcomed me with open arms just as they had previously welcomed her, and this church became my church home also.

Because our house was in need of some repairs, we lived temporarily in the apartment Martha had been renting. She was having difficulty at her job and took a leave of absence, so she could work on repairing our house. About a month before her Sexual Reassignment Surgery was scheduled, we moved back into our house and gave up the apartment.

I stayed at home when Martha traveled to Montreal for her surgery. However, our son joined Martha in Canada, hoping to talk her out of the operation. His efforts failed, but his parting words to her were reassuring. He said, "No matter what, our family will stand behind your decision."

Would I go through this again? *I don't know.* Was it worth it? *Yes!* Would I change places with any of my girlfriends? *Not a chance!* There is a special adoration I receive from my Martha that is priceless to me. It was worth hanging in there through all her transition.

Martha:

We have kept our commitment to each other "till death do us part" – not until gender surgery do us part. On July 16, 2001, Joy and I celebrated our thirtieth wedding anniversary. We renewed our vows to each other in a wonderful ceremony while attending our denomination's General Assembly. We are so grateful that our renewed commitment to each other could be blessed by our church.

Martha and Joy Montgomery were born in Southern California. Since their marriage, they have lived in the Pacific Northwest. Martha is an electronics technician, working for the Boeing Aircraft Corporation. Joy is a clerk for Rite Aid Pharmacy. Both Joy and Martha are active in their church, Seattle First Christian Church (http://www.seattle-fcc.com), a congregation in the Disciples of Christ denomination (www.disciples.org). Joy teaches in the elementary Sunday school.

Martha and Joy have two grown children, a daughter and a son, and are proud new grandparents. Other interests include attending live musical theater, and they love the Mariners baseball team.

On March 17, 2002, their congregation and Pilgrim United Church of Christ voted to merge into one congregation. Much work remains, but the new church will continue to be welcoming to all people.

A person's feelings are part of that person's core being. It is unspeakably cruel to dismiss such feelings lightly or to run roughshod over them. "I had always heard that homosexual feelings were evil," said one gay Christian. "But then, when I would think about my feelings for the person I love so much, I couldn't understand how such deep love could be bad."

~ Letha Dawson Scanzoni, "Can Homosexuals Change?"
Christians & Homosexuality: Dancing Toward the Light
Special issue of *The Other Side*

~ *eleven* ~

Traveling United

Roger Snyder and Kevin Johnston

We have been in a committed relationship with each other since June of 1988. We met at church, where Kevin "always wanted to meet my life partner, as God and my spirituality have been an integral part of who I am as long as I can remember. I needed to share my life with someone with whom that aspect would also be important." Not only do we share this point of view, our backgrounds and upbringings are also similar.

Roger's parents were married in September of 1957, Kevin's in October of the same year. In February of 1959, Roger entered the world; Kevin was born thirty days later. Both of us grew up on farms, and church life played a large part in our lives almost from the beginning. Roger has two brothers and one sister; Kevin has one brother and one sister. Both sisters are the youngest siblings. Roger's country home was just outside Kitchener, Ontario, Canada; Kevin grew up in and around Wallaceburg – about two and a half hours away. However, the first twenty-nine years were very different for each of us.

Roger:

I was raised in a very loving Mennonite family on a beef farm not far from the city of Kitchener. I have always been aware of a loving and gracious God as a sustaining and reassuring presence in my life.

Sexuality seemed to be off-limits for discussion in my growing up years. It was something that I gradually learned about. I remember, in grade two, being devastated when my best friend, who lived on a neighboring farm, moved away. I cried myself to sleep for many a night, and I remember my mother trying to console me.

As a member of the local village Scout troop, I began to have deep emotional feelings for another boy in my troop. I remember telling him that I loved him, but I know at the time I had no knowledge of what that word meant. Shortly after this revelation, I became aware of a very real, intense, and personal salvation. I joined the church at thirteen and believed that my feelings for other young boys would disappear. High school brought new knowledge about the evils of being gay, but my attraction to other young men about my age only intensified through my teen years. I struggled considerably with God about my inner feelings.

After grade eleven, I decided to finish high school at Rockway Mennonite High School and was sure I would find the perfect Mennonite girl to settle down with. Instead, I fell hopelessly in love with my best friend, with whom I carpooled to school. We hung out constantly for several years – went to church youth group together, worked together, and became very close. My friend did not share my intense feelings, and I ended up being totally sexually frustrated.

We double-dated so that I could be close to him. I had terrible guilt about what this was doing to the young women I spent time with. I prayed about my unresolved sexuality and decided that I would escape this situation by entering the Voluntary Service program (MVS) sponsored by the Mennonite Board of Missions of our denomination. Since that time, I have become aware of quite a number of young men in the church who did exactly the same thing for the same reason.

During my MVS assignment in Los Angeles, I prayed for strength to face and overcome my attraction to other males. I became stronger in my faith and studied my Bible a lot. I realized that my God was loving and accepting of us if we allow ourselves to submit to his will. I reveled in Christian rock and gospel music and my involvement in the church.

At the same time, I began a relationship with another young man in my MVS unit. We became inseparable, but my need for fidelity and commitment frightened him. He broke off our relationship abruptly after I repeatedly told him how much I loved him. In devastation, I left my MVS assignment several months early and returned home to Ontario. I sought the help of my parents (whom I had told about my sexual attraction to men several years earlier) and my local Mennonite pastor. I received unconditional love and support from them.

I enrolled in travel school in 1982, and later that year was placed in my first travel agency as a junior apprentice. In 1985, I moved to London, Ontario, since I had begun a relationship with a young man from that city. We were both very actively involved in the local Metropolitan Community Church and with the small Ontario chapter of Brethren/Mennonite Council for Lesbian and Gay Concerns (BMC) that I had founded the year before. I also began attending Valleyview Mennonite Church, where I was a member of the midweek Bible study group and sang solos in church.

I confided in the local pastor that I was gay, but she was not supportive of me. She set strict parameters on my level of involvement and refused to consider a transfer of membership from my home church in the Kitchener area.

During this time, I relied a lot on emotional support from my parents. The three of us served together, telling our stories in a number of speaking engagements in adult Sunday schools throughout southern Ontario. We were even invited to address a seminar at the biennial General Assembly of the Mennonite Church (MC)[1] at Purdue University, West Lafayette, Indiana.

Therefore, it was with a heavy heart and lots of tears that I left the Mennonite Church and sought spiritual nourishment

---

[1] In the General Assembly at Nashville, TN, in July of 2001, the final vote was taken to merge the Mennonite Church (MC) and the General Conference Mennonite Church (GC) into Mennonite Church U.S.A. (Mennonite Church Canada had been formed at the St. Louis Assembly in 1999.)

solely from the local Metropolitan Community Church, where I was soon chair of the local board of directors. Early in 1988, our pastor resigned to pursue other interests, and I was asked to be the interim lay pastor.

During this time, I became aware that I was beginning to have deep feelings for Kevin Johnston, who was also very involved in the congregation. We seemed to have many interests in common. Throughout 1988, we fell in love and began to spend a great deal of time together.

Kevin:

I was baptized in the United Church of Canada, where my parents were married. When my brother was born two years later, my grandmother took me to Sunday school at the Baptist church. Apparently I liked it, so I stayed and grew up there.

My father worked for a farmer. When I was four, we moved to the country from town, living along a river road. The farmer eventually relocated a small house onto the farm so my father would be closer to his work.

I knew from the age of four that I was *different*, and also knew deep inside that it was wrong for me to be that way. I remember wishing I could have been born a girl – just so it would be okay to like boys the way I did.

I always wanted to play the piano; however, I began taking accordion lessons at age nine since we could not afford a piano. I studied accordion until age fifteen when I had reached grade nine level and have since taught myself to play the piano. I often played in church, accompanied the junior choir, and appeared as resident musician for a TV children's programme our church produced on the local cable network.

Church life became my life – Sunday school, junior choir, and cub scouts. I eventually joined the senior choir, Wednesday evening Bible study, and young people's group, where I served as president for a couple of years. This was on top of attending worship services Sunday mornings and evenings.

All through school, I was involved in music and drama in one way or another – singing in choirs, participating in school plays, or playing clarinet and alto sax in the band. As I progressed to high school, I remained involved in school bands and drama groups, often playing lead roles. In grade ten, I was asked to play sax in a stage band, "Brass with Class." This was good for me socially because I never felt I fit in anywhere other than the church. During my years with the band, I also began writing music.

Throughout high school, I dreamed of pursuing a career as a child psychologist. However, all that changed in May of 1977 when I attended a youth retreat and met God in a way I have never since experienced – a call that would haunt me for the next twenty some years. When I returned home from the retreat, my father told of a dream that he had when I was young, where I was a preacher. This was the confirmation I needed. So, all my plans for the future were out the window, and I began to prepare for what I was told I was to be.

That June I finished grade twelve and participated in a youth programme, "Katimavik," that took me east and west. Before the programme ended, I returned to Ontario. On the train a young man returning from Bible college in Saskatchewan befriended me. He encouraged me to consider this venue, so in September of 1978, I began to work toward a five-year bachelor of theology degree at a Bible college in Toronto.

All my life, romantic interests and crushes were on other guys, although I tried to date girls. Hailing from a small town, I thought Toronto was heaven! I had no one to stick his or her nose in my face, so I began to explore this *thing* I had been struggling with ever since I could remember. Although I knew deep inside that it was bad, and I could never be a minister and gay, *it* would not go away!

After two years in Toronto, I reasoned that a more structured setting was in order and transferred to a Baptist college in London. That summer provided time to reflect and evaluate life, and I realized I had to get out of school – now! This completely devastated my parents, but I had no choice. Worst of all was the fact that I could not tell anyone the real reason why. The best answer was that I had to find myself.

Avoiding anyone or anything affiliated with God, church, or anything church-related, I ran as far and fast as possible. But a "still, small voice" ate away within me, and eventually I knew I had to return to church. I contacted the local Metropolitan Community Church and began attending with minimal involvement.

In May of 1983, I met a vice-principal in another city, who convinced me to relocate in September. *Not a good move*, for I landed in the local hospital two weeks later, not expected to live. He had beaten me as I slept.

Now, my parents discovered the truth about me! I had often talked of a gay cousin in London, but they were not receptive to such conversation. I knew that there was no way I could ever disclose who I was. However, now, they knew! – and the reception was pretty much what I expected.

My parents would not discuss it, so I found solace in their next-door neighbors, who introduced me to the local Pentecostal assembly. I could not return to the Baptist church, yet still yearned to be part of a congregation. For two and a half years I was very involved in this church. At the same time, I connected with a local family, who had a ministry. I traveled with them to churches throughout Ontario, ministering in music and word. In June of 1985, we journeyed to Guyana where we held revival services for a week. I saw God work in ways I had only read and heard about before and was profoundly affected.

In February of 1986, the local pastor found out about me. I had been secretly dating a young man for several months and the word had traveled. My resignation from the church was requested. If I "repented and turned from my ways," gradual reintroduction would take place. I obliged him and never returned.

While I was visiting my parents' neighbors several months later, the pastor remorsefully confessed to them that he had wrongly handled the situation.

Finally that June, I reestablished in London, Ontario, and immediately returned to the MCC, where I became involved as music director and coordinator of worship and music. I also served on the board of directors and the pastoral search committee. There I met a young man with whom I would become friends and eventually establish a life-partnership.

Again that "still, small voice," that had been calling out since May of 1977, kept at me – to no avail. There was no way that God could want me to be a preacher. I had finally accepted being gay, but I thought that gay and preacher were like water and oil. They didn't mix. I could not yet see that God always gets his/her person in due time!

Since 1988:

In the next month, personal circumstances in both our lives brought us together for the first weekend in June. Pouring out our souls, we both admitted that we had developed more than friend feelings for each other, but as Roger was in an almost four-year-old relationship that was in its winding down stage, things were slow in developing. His ex-partner was also a very involved member of MCC and a friend of mine as well. The last thing either of us wanted to do was to hurt him, so we kept our relationship closeted for a while until Roger was able to talk with him.

As one would expect, things became quite uncomfortable for all three of us and for the congregation as well. Because Roger needed to deal with the breakup, and we were unsure as to what the future would bring, we dated only, for about a year and a half. In January of 1990, we moved in together and began sharing living space.

That fall, we both began to realize that we had more or less outgrown MCC and were also quite burnt out. I was cast in a second show with a theatre company in London and had become friends with one of the producers. After several conversations, she invited Roger and me to check out her congregation as it seemed to offer what we were both seeking. The first Sunday in January of 1991, we worshipped at First St. Andrew's United Church and were at choir practice on Thursday evening. It has been one of the best moves either one of us has ever made.

From the beginning, people presumed that we were together as a couple. In fact, if we were not together at a church function, people questioned, "Where is Roger?" or, "Where is Kevin?" We wore no placards, but were just ourselves, and people learned to know us as *people* first. From the beginning, we felt total inclusiveness. We both transferred our membership that November.

Both of us have been very involved at First St. Andrew's in the choir and serving on the archive, membership, music, and worship committees, and we are both elders. In the late spring of 1999, Kevin was interested in and encouraged to apply for the position of church school coordinator (he had been teaching in the church school for a while). He was appointed at the end of April and has also been involved in ministry to seniors and conducting worship at several area facilities.

Since then, Kevin has said "Yes" to God's call to full-time ordered ministry in the United Church of Canada and he is currently attending Emmanuel College in Toronto in preparation for ministry.

On April 30, 1994, after much encouragement from our minister, we celebrated our relationship in a covenanting ceremony in the chapel at First St. Andrew's. Approximately 110 guests joined us, most of whom were from the church, as well as members of our families (mainly Roger's). It was a groundbreaking event as the first ever same-sex observance in the congregation. Since then, one other couple has celebrated their relationship (women), and we were honored to be their witnesses.

Although we would both love to be parents, this joy in life is not ours to experience. However, we are proud of four nieces and six nephews: Mike and Amanda (from Roger's brother Neil), Stephanie and Bill (from Roger's sister Colleen), Jason and Derek (from Roger's brother Dan), John (from Kevin's brother Fred), and Jenny, Eric, and Allison (from Kevin's sister Jane). Roger is also godfather to Jenny, and Kevin is godfather to Eric. We believe these ten people are more special to us than they would be if we had children of our own.

One of Roger's passions in life is travel, and we have been fortunate to enjoy many trips during our thirteen plus years together. Probably the most memorable one for us took place in February and March of 1999, when he arranged and co-led a pilgrimage to Israel, and Mom and Dad Snyder joined us. For some time, we had wanted to share a journey with them, and what better place for that to happen than the Holy Land! Twenty-seven people (mostly from our church) made up the tour, facilitated by Roger and our former minister.

Other interests in Roger's life include exploring, history, stamp collecting, and the outdoors. Kevin enjoys reading, cooking, performing in musical and theatrical productions, and composing music. Last year he wrote a play with original music that the children presented at our Christmas Eve family service. Together, we enjoy music, theatre, travel, and the many special children in our lives.

Even though we have both been deeply hurt in the past by our respective churches of origin, we each continue to have a strong faith and commitment to God and are very involved in our present congregation. We believe that life's challenges and trials occur for a reason in order to build character, strengthen the inner spirit, and dare us to grow. Though our future will not be without its difficult times on the path we are called to follow, our faith and our God will not let us down. We know this. And it will be an exciting adventure to discover what God has for us as, united, we proceed along our way!

Kevin Johnston and **Roger Snyder** currently reside in London, Ontario, Canada. Roger continues his successful career as a travel agent and is very involved in their home congregation, First St. Andrew's United Church. Kevin is on staff there and is also studying toward ordination in the United Church of Canada at Emmanuel College, University of Toronto.

Our pain is no longer that of having a gay son, it is a deep disappointment over the church's attitude toward our gay sons and lesbian daughters . . .

Our journey has led us into a deeper understanding of our faith. We have also come to realize that it is our Christian duty to help in some small way to dispel the ignorance of our churches.

~ Paul and Martha Snyder,
From Wounded Hearts

~ twelve ~

Simply in Love

Sandy Manne and Starla King

Sandy:

Growing up, I did not have a strong sense of self. Not many people I knew did. My family lived on Long Island and later in upstate New York. Both places were lands of conspicuous consumption. Friends and neighbors were consumed by materialism, constantly outdoing one another by buying the latest in fashion, electronics, cars, vacations, and whatever their fancy desired. My family did not have a lot of money. We were not poor, but many of the trends of the time were just not attainable. Thus, trying to "keep up with the Joneses" was difficult for us – and for me. All I wanted, like most any teenager, was to fit in – be a part of the crowd.

I was Jewish, I was overweight. Oh, I did have Jewish friends. But their families were more religious than mine. My parents forced me to join a youth group at our synagogue, but I hated every minute of it. Since my family did not study or actively practice religion in the home, I was clueless as to the religious elements of the youth group and their gatherings. It was easy for the members to just shove the fat kid aside.

In spite of the lack of a spiritual upbringing, I somehow managed to develop a sense of God and the role that God played in my life. My concept of God was quite simplistic. Although I was not religious and did not live my life to the prescribed way a Jew should live, I believed that God saw me from the inside out and knew darn well what a good, caring, loving, hardworking person I was. To God, that was much more important. And, I would forevermore be judged by God according to those criteria.

Around that same time, I began to suspect I might be gay, although I certainly would not have used that specific term in conjunction with the feelings I was having. After all, *gay* was not a word one would want to be associated with. Besides, I did not want to be pushed further into that dreaded social fray. I began to see that my capacity to bond emotionally with women far exceeded my capacity to connect with men. I would never have acted upon these feelings, nor would I ever have communicated this to my parents. I merely hoped that over time perhaps these feelings would disappear, and I would someday be normal.

Throughout college, I tried to be "normal". To my circle of friends, I was just like every one of them. I talked about how cute the college guys were. I talked about who I envisioned marrying one day. But deep inside, I knew I was kidding myself. Sure, I could easily marry a guy, but I would truly never be happy. I was effectively living a charade.

After graduation, I had to get away. Far away. Away from the influences and expectations of my family and friends. I knew I needed to be somewhere that allowed me to finally develop that sense of self that I never had growing up. I decided to relocate to Washington, D.C.

Developing my sense of self took a while; it was much harder than I expected. After five years and two boyfriends, I finally found the courage to date a woman. The relationship was an unbelievable awakening for me. It allowed me to experience and learn what I needed to fulfill *me*. I thought God was quite okay with this because God saw how happy and complete I finally was. (Actually, it never dawned on me until I met Starla that God might not be okay with it). When I realized this relationship was no longer fulfilling, I ended it. About that same time, I also decided it was time to go back to school for my master's degree. So, on the heels of ending a three-year relationship, I took on the stress and strain of graduate school. Having never been much of a student, I knew I was in for quite a ride. Of course, I had no idea that Starla would be part of that ride!

Although we had the exact same classes for weeks, Starla and I didn't utter a word to each other. She thought I was aloof (I preferred to think I was shy). About thirty days into the first semester, during a break from class, I announced to my classmates that I was "taking a walk down to the bookstore; would anyone like to join me?" Starla responded that she needed something from the bookstore. Thus began the first conversation we ever had. In the ninety-second walk to the bookstore, we learned that we lived around the block from each other and frequented the same places. Starla was a writer, I was learning to play guitar, Starla played piano, I played sports, and the list goes on.

We entered the bookstore and both headed to the same section of the store. We bent down to pick up the same book from the same shelf, and BAM! I was smacked over the head with crazy, smitten glee. Throughout the following week, Starla and I carried on a voracious e-mail exchange. The tone of the exchange started as friendly, getting-to-know-you type stuff. By the end of that week, the tone of the exchange was decidedly different. At that point, I was ninety-nine per cent certain there was a mutual attraction. But the missing one percent would not afford me complete certainty that *something was there*. Not until we met face to face in class the following week was I able to validate, by asking Starla point-blank, if there was a mutual attraction.

Starla:

I'm not sure when I first really knew I was gay, but I knew it long before I admitted it. I grew up in a Mennonite family, immersed in the Bible, church, prayer, and God. I went to a Mennonite high school and a Mennonite college and found great strength in my beliefs. My friends and I had regular Bible study meetings, prayed together, and left encouraging notes and Bible verses in each other's lockers. I remember those days fondly, but I still remember the angst I felt about so many of my close friendships – female friendships.

I made friends easily and got to know people quickly and deeply, so I could not understand why I kept feeling unsatisfied with the friends I loved the most. Actually, part of me probably did understand, but would not admit it. How could I? The one thing I was *always* sure of was that homosexuality was a *sin* and a perversion. It was just plain *wrong* no matter how you looked at it, and the Bible clearly said so. So, I pushed it all far back in my mind, hoping it would just go away and I would be satisfied with having really good female friends who would hug me sometimes.

Then college gave me an experience I could not ignore. I got to know another female college student, and my reaction to her was so strong that I could no longer convince myself that it was typical. I still remember the day I stopped lying to myself. I was hanging out with a group of students, and I went to sit on my friend's lap (which was actually quite typical behavior for students at my college – we were a pretty affectionate bunch). What I wasn't prepared for was the rush of emotions and the way my stomach flipped. It was so strong that I remember being both thrilled and horrified as I thought to myself, "I must be gay. I'm really attracted to her. I must be gay!" Okay, so I had admitted it to myself, but I certainly wouldn't *ever* admit it to anyone else. It was *so wrong*, and I was a good Christian who certainly would not do something wrong!

She and I were best friends for years, then drifted apart for a variety of reasons. We had not been in touch for a while when she called me and told me her news: "I'm gay... I love women." With that announcement, she opened the door for me to talk openly about my longing for the emotional and physical connection with other women. We even considered dating each other, but the decision came down to whether or not I would be okay with doing something that I still believed was wrong. I thought I had to choose between her and God, so I chose God. And, for the next few months, I fell into the deepest, darkest depression I have ever known. For the first time in my life, I had made a decision that I wholly and completely regretted, even though it was supposedly the right decision according to my Mennonite beliefs.

For months, I fought the longing for an intimate relationship with a woman. And for months, I felt as though I might as well stop living, because I was not allowed to have the one thing that I needed so deeply. The emotional pain was so intense for so long that I finally just wore out and stopped fighting it. I decided that if I ever had a chance again to be in a relationship with a woman, I would take that chance, no matter how wrong I had been taught to believe that was. I could no longer ignore my need.

I didn't have to take that chance until a few years later when I was accepted to graduate school in 1996. Little did I know that it would completely change my life, my beliefs, and – in many ways – my world.

During an orientation meal, I noticed one of the other new students because I was almost sure she was gay. I watched her curiously for the next few days and quickly decided I didn't much care for her – I thought she was unfriendly and perhaps even unfeeling. Then one day during a break, we went to the bookstore together to buy books for our classes. On the way back, we started talking about where we live, and discovered we lived less than a mile apart – near the same lake. I mentioned how beautiful that lake is, and that I had spent time just writing about that lake. Sandy listened closely, very interested in my writing and the lake, and I started changing my mind about her. My writing is such a sacred thing to me, and to have her affirm and respect that made me think that perhaps I had misread her. That conversation started a week of e-mails back and forth to each other.

We started out talking about school things; then the questions became more and more personal. I would check my e-mail over and over, hoping for a message from Sandy, just so I could feel my heart skip a beat and my hands start shaking, as I realized that perhaps something *real* was going on between us. We saw each other again a week later after class, and I just had to know what was going on between us. Sandy claims she was the first to ask, but I still believe I was the one to clarify, "So, is this...are we...is...this what is going on here?" Sandy grinned and said, "Yeah...yeah, I think it is!" I almost passed out – I was in a relationship with a *woman*!

Sandy and Starla:

Soon after that, driving back from school together one night, we both agreed that we weren't interested in casual dating – if we were going to be together, we would want to try to make it last for a very long time. We talked about how different our backgrounds were and especially about Starla's struggles with her Mennonite understanding that homosexuality equals *sin*. Sandy knew there was great risk in dating someone who was unsure of the *rightness* of it all, but took that chance anyway.

The next year was very intense and rocky for both of us. Although Starla felt more whole with Sandy than she had ever felt before, she also felt as though she had lost the very foundation of her life – the church and her closest Mennonite friends who believed her lifestyle was wrong. The one place she had always turned for support and comfort became the place that condemned and rejected her the most. "Hate the sin, but love the sinner" was a great-sounding motto until she was the *sinner* and the only real feeling was the hate. Love with such huge conditions (that you not be who you truly are) surely did not feel like love to her.

Sandy, on the other hand, had such a different understanding of God that most of her anxiety came from dealing with Starla's pain and confusion. While she was able to offer endless emotional support, she didn't have the understanding of Mennonites that would allow her to support Starla in the way that she needed spiritually.

One day in a bookstore Sandy was browsing a book about top websites and saw a listing for the BMC Listserv (Brethren Mennonite Council for Lesbian and Gay Concerns). She was eager to tell Starla about it. Starla immediately joined the listserv (anonymously) and soon sent an introductory message to the several hundred people on the list. Too late, she realized that her automatic e-mail signature had her full name and Internet address of her personal website. Ooops! Turns out that was the best thing that could have happened. Some people who knew her and her family sent her supportive e-mails and began proving that there are people out there who believe that God affirms and loves gay/lesbian/bisexual/transgender people too.

While this outside affirmation was quite important to Starla's healing, Sandy's simple view of God became the foundation for a shared understanding of a loving, supportive God. After one particularly painful and hopeless-feeling day, Starla was crying to Sandy about feeling as though God didn't love her any more now that she was no longer denying her homosexuality. Sandy's response was: "God still loves you."

In frustration, Starla responded, "Yes, but how do you *know* that?"

Sandy looked her directly in the eyes, put her hand on her heart, and said, "I...just...*know.*" In that moment, Starla began a whole new understanding of God, away from the judging, critical, love-with-conditions God toward an unconditionally accepting, nurturing, Loving Godde. The change was so powerful that she even changed her preferred spelling of *God* to *Godde* to signify a different perspective and a gentler Being.

Today, five years later, we share an important basic understanding and belief in a God/Godde who not only honors our life together, but also *gave* us our life together. Although Jesus has little significance for Sandy, she shares Starla's belief in following the example of treating others with respect and Love – not judgment. We both believe life is sacred and each day a gift, and we both see and feel God/Godde in life's little miracles of nature, relationships, and each other. We light the Hanukkah candles and decorate the Christmas tree together and enjoy the surprise of learning about each other's significant rituals and beliefs. We have gone from the fears of focusing on each others' differences to the joys of discovering the core shared similarities and the different ways we express the same beliefs and understanding of God/Godde.

God/Godde is Love, and we are in Love – God/Godde's Love. It really is that simple.

Sandy Manne and **Starla King** live in Ashburn, Virginia (outside of Washington, D.C). They have been together since 1996 and are happily committed to a lifetime together. They both have an M.S. in Organizational Learning and work in technology communications. They enjoy spending time parenting their three cats, co-creating their home environment (inside and out), and dabbling in gardening, photography, and cooking.

~ *thirteen* ~

Our Life Together

Twila Chaloupek with Jackie Keown

Our story as a couple begins with our individual stories. Both have great similarities though are different due to our individuality. I was born into a Christian family that has a long Mennonite tradition. Both my maternal and paternal family have been Mennonite for several generations. I was born in Newton, Kansas, and grew up in Goessel and Hesston. These towns are right in the heart of the Kansas *Mennonite Belt*.

I am the oldest surviving child of my mother and father. My mother died when I was scarcely three years old. I have a sister who is almost two years younger than I. She was only fifteen months old when our mother died. Dad remarried in just about a year. This union was blessed with two more children.

We all grew up in the Old Mennonite Church tradition. The faith community of my youth is now known as Whitestone Mennonite Church. I remember the older country church that decided to move to town and has become a much larger church. I was baptized at approximately age twelve in the first group of those who were baptized in the new church building. I remained active at Whitestone Mennonite Church through my college days at Hesston College

Jackie's family moved to Wichita, Kansas, from Arkansas City, Kansas, when she was almost twelve. She grew up in a less church connected family than I did, but remembers some old-fashioned revival services in the church of one of her grand-mothers. However, no one in the family regularly attended church. Each of the five children went to church wherever they wanted *if* they wanted to go. Jackie relates going to church with a few neighborhood kids on a church bus several times.

As an adult, she has attended several different denominational groups. At various times, friends asked her to attend church with them. Some of those churches were of a Pentecostal nature. Many of her beliefs are similar to those of the Mennonite church, though more in line with the more liberal Mennonite thinking. In her family, all her brothers have served in the military. Jackie tried to enlist in the Air Force in her early twenties, but was not able to, due to educational requirements.

Jackie has known since her early childhood that she was different from most girls. She states that she knew men were to be friends only – not for intimate relationships. She knew that one of her mother's sisters lived with a woman. By exchanging letters, she discovered why she always liked her Aunt Sylvia so much. Jackie and her Aunt Sylvia both were/are lesbians. Aunt Sylvia told her she knew from the time that Jackie was small that she was *like her*. Unlike Aunt Sylvia, Jackie did not engage in hard drinking.

After I graduated from Hesston College with my associate degree in nursing in May of 1976, I moved to Wichita and worked in one of the major hospitals. All my life I knew that I was different. I did not feel comfortable with a man. I dated some young men in late high school and for a short time after college, but it was never fulfilling.

Later, I met some new friends and started going to church with them. One of these friends was a student at Hesston College. She was living with another female, and I soon came to know that she loved this woman. I learned to know them as a couple. And, finally, I figured out why it was that I had always felt different.

I had never heard about homosexuality until that point. In the 1960s, parents and church groups were the primary providers of sex education, and homosexuality was not on their agenda. I do not remember that we covered diverse sexualities in nursing school either. After I moved to Wichita, I discovered a group who were gay and were still accepted as Christian. I just missed being a charter member of this church, the First Metropolitan Community Church of Wichita, in 1977.

During this time, I was in and out of several lesbian relationships, one of which lasted for almost two years. It was like my other close personal relationships – miserable and problematic. During that time, I lost my job at the hospital because of some of my own personal problems, no doubt due in part to my difficulty of self-acceptance.

I became a problem drinker and drank in excess from time to time. I sank into a deep depression that only got deeper, the more and longer I drank. After a short time, I began working for a large well-known humanitarian organization. When I became honest with my supervisor, we both agreed that I needed to check into Prairie View Mental Health Center.

I will always be grateful for the support that my church friends gave me and for my family who still loved me in spite of my sexuality. My parents did not approve of my lesbian relationships, though were not vocal in their disapproval. They all seemed to be more concerned about the alcohol problem and thought that if I were to quit drinking all the *other problems* might go away.

In the early 1970s, I worked part time at a restaurant for an owner who was lesbian and employed many of my gay and lesbian friends. This woman happened to be Jackie's ex-partner! Jackie and I did not have the opportunity to cross paths at this time, though we may have seen each other in the clubs and bars. Jackie moved on to other relationships – some of which took her to Colorado on several occasions – for several years at a time.

For approximately ten years, Jackie worked for her younger brother at several of his A & W Root Beer restaurants in Wichita and in Oklahoma. This allowed her to become more financially secure and enabled her to purchase a house in the early 1970s. After the business franchise was sold, she started her long work history with the food service group (and its long succession of successors) at Boeing Aircraft Corporation in Wichita. She has worked as a line cook, a baker, a short order cook, and now is the cook/server in one of the seventeen satellite kitchens at Boeing.

Though Jackie has never been able to be open about her sexuality with most of her friends, especially at work, her immediate family knows. None are openly approving, nor do they make known any disapproval.

After leaving Prairie View Hospital, it seemed that everything changed for me. During that time, I attended Alcoholics Anonymous and was around many *straight* persons. It was very important not to drink, as I did not want to return to the severely depressed state of mind. I began to wonder if my sexuality was not a part of my drinking story. I even mentioned that possibility to some of my AA friends and sponsors. One sponsor agreed that many times drinking allows for more promiscuity. Although she did not feel I was truly an alcoholic, she acknowledged that I did have psychological problems that made the drinking more problematic.

It was almost two years after beginning AA that I met my soon-to-be husband, Eric.* He was in and out of AA as well. I was honest with him about my being with a woman for several years, but he did not seem to have a problem with it because it was a thing of the past. Eric made some rather bragging statements about when he was in prison he was the *strong man* and

---

* Name has been changed.

used weaker men for sexual gratification. It seemed there were a few skeletons in both of our closets!

Our marriage was troubled even before it started. Eric was unable to maintain any length of sobriety, and continued to have problems with the legal system. He found it difficult to sustain a monogamous relationship. We moved every year or two during much of the marriage. We lived in many small towns in remote places in the Oklahoma and Texas panhandles as well as in western Kansas.

For the last three years that we lived together, we lived near his family. These were years that I again grew restless and began to doubt that I really was meant to be straight, especially when one of Eric's cousin's wives came out as a lesbian. However, I wanted to remain in my marriage because I felt that maintaining a marriage was important, as marriage is meant to be "until death do us part."

In late 1990, I was injured on the job. I was able to continue to work for several more months, though this injury would take its toll. In early 1991, the pain from my back injury became so severe that a long hospitalization resulted. After release from the hospital, we came back to central Kansas. This was Eric's decision, one I don't regret, though not the one I particularly thought was the best. Eric remained with me for much of the following four months, but left when I was again hospitalized for surgery. After that, he did not come back for more than a week at a time until I finally had enough and filed for divorce.

Not long after I filed for the divorce, I began an intensive biblical search into the truth about sexuality and what the Bible says. I read a book, *What the Bible Really Says about Homosexuality,* by Dr. Daniel Helminiak. I carefully read the passages of Scripture that he reviewed and the entire text from which they were excerpted.

I also called and arranged a meeting with a pastoral friend, and we went through the Scriptures together. We used the

Greek and Hebrew dictionary and found that the statements made by Helminiak in the book were correct. I began to realize that I was not bound for eternal damnation, and I felt a tremendous relief.

About the same time, a person in my Sunday school class came out as a gay man. I felt a new freedom and realized it was only a matter of time until I, too, had to become honest with myself. However, I felt sad because I knew I could not be as open with my truth. In response to John's[*] disclosure, our class did an intensive study and review of our own feelings surrounding sexuality. It became obvious to me that in order to maintain a friendship with many of these people, I had to live as though I were straight.

It was near this same time that I realized the need to return to school to finish my bachelor's degree in nursing. I completed all the paperwork for student loans and the admission paperwork for the nursing program and for admission to Bethel College of North Newton, Kansas. At the same time, I kept looking for someone with whom I could build a relationship – another woman.

One Sunday afternoon, on my way home from work, I saw the ad that brought Jackie and me together. Some people say that meeting someone from a newspaper ad is risky, but we both feel God used this way to bring us together. We knew soon after we met on September 3, 1995, that we wanted to be together for life. I worked hard in school and spent many of my nights with Jackie. After my first year in school, I sold my mobile home in Hesston and moved in with Jackie to stay.

In 1997, I graduated from Bethel College. While in college, I learned to know other lesbian and gay people on campus. Many of us knew we needed a support group. Late in that school term, a group was started with the help of the student outreach representative from BMC International (Brethren/Mennonite Council

---

[*] Name has been changed.

for Lesbian and Gay Concerns). I knew my gay friends on campus would have a good support system. Jackie and I remain active in the Kansas BMC group.

On September 5, 1998, just a few days after the third anniversary of our first meeting, we shared a commitment ceremony at First Metropolitan Community Church in Wichita, Kansas. John, the man from my former Sunday school class, was the pianist for our ceremony. Many of our Kansas BMC group were there to share the special day with us.

One of the newest members of the group played the piano at our reception as a gift to us. In June of 2001, Lowell passed away. His passing saddens us, though we believe he has become a pianist in God's reception room.

We knew at the time of our commitment ceremony that our spiritual journey was leading us to move on. The first three years of our lives together, we attended First MCC of Kansas in Wichita. Later we worshipped with a small Mennonite church, which seemed somewhat inclusive. We both enjoyed the fellowship, though this group is like many others in the Mennonite church. The division along the lines of inclusiveness concerning sexuality was apparent. We both came to realize that this was not something we could deal with at this time in our lives, so like many of our Kansas BMC friends, we intermittently attend an inclusive United Methodist church. God remains a leader for us as we continue to learn and grow.

There have been events in our lives that have tested us. In late 1999, I became disabled from Reflex Sympathetic Dystrophy. The treating physicians feel I have had RSD since the fall of 1990. The illness causes a lot of pain, both of the muscles and nerves. The medications given do not take care of much of the pain. The physicians feel that if the spinal column stimulator or the medication pump takes care of fifty percent of the pain, it is successful. (Two sites for information regarding RSD can be found at http://www.americansocietyforrsd-crps.org or http://www.rsds.org.)

RSD is a disease of the sympathetic nervous system. The immense pain is due to a short-circuiting in the sympathetic nerves. The pain does not go away and is frequently resistant to medications. Many persons, myself included, take a high dose of one of several anti-seizure medications. These drugs are supposed to decrease the pain by enhancing the effects of the pain medications. The drugs, in addition to different spinal blocks with a long acting Xylocaine derivative, are standard methods of treatment. Frequently, spinal nerve stimulators or medication pumps are required. Also, there are circulation, nail, and hair changes. Many times depression which is quite resistant to treatment occurs.

I was treated with lumbar sympathetic blocks. As too much scar tissue developed and the blocks became increasingly difficult to do, my doctors decided to try the insertion of a spinal nerve stimulator. After the insertion, the symptoms became more severe on my left leg and the insertion of the third wire was attempted. This was not possible, so my doctors decided I needed the medication pump. The doctor has chosen to use morphine in my pump. Consequently, I have to return to the hospital as an outpatient every five to six weeks for refills.

Jackie and I are learning that physical limitations can hold blessings as well. We struggle to meet the changes that disability can mean to a couple. It is difficult to realize that changes in mobility and function can change our images of the future. However, we enjoy the time we spend together. We like to spend time with friends and enjoy fishing and camping.

In the summer of 2001, we took a trip by bus to Boise, Idaho, and enjoyed the scenery. The trip took us through the mountains in Colorado, through Berthoud Pass, Steamboat Springs, and Craig. In Utah we traveled through Park City, Vernal, Salt Lake City, and Ogden. Preparation for the Olympics in 2002 was seen all over the greater Salt Lake City area.

Immediately after that trip, I was able to go to Elkhart, Indiana, for the First Annual RSD Retreat (www.rsdretreat.com). This retreat is the fulfillment of a dream to bring at least three or four persons with RSD together. There were over seventy-five persons, including the caregivers, who came to the retreat.

Even though we have needed to change some of the sleeping accommodations, we still enjoy camping. We both enjoy many things that God has created and the pristine beauty of nature. We enjoy searching for new places in Kansas where we can spend time doing things together while pursuing our hobbies.

Twila Chaloupek and **Jackie Keown** are faithful in their commitment to each other in spite of the physical disabilities that limit their activities. Jackie continues to work for Aramark Food Services at Boeing Aircraft Corporation in Wichita, Kansas. Twila is keeping busy several days a week with a friend's new business. Otherwise, her disability prevents her from engaging in full-time employment.

Someone told me that for years he had had a friend with a homosexual orientation. Before becoming a Christian, the heterosexual man had always accepted his friend fully. But when the homosexual friend learned of the heterosexual's conversion to Christ, one of his first questions was, "Can you still love me – now that you're a Christian?" And the man wasn't able to answer affirmatively for many months.

~ Letha Dawson Scanzoni, "Putting a Face on Homosexuality"
Christians & Homosexuality: Dancing Toward the Light

~ *fourteen* ~

"Not Under the Law, but Under Grace"[1]

Arthur Martin-Chester with Stevie Martin-Chester

Introduction:

We are members of many organizations. The two we are most active in are Metropolitan Community Church of Philadelphia (MCCP) and Men of All Colors Together/ Philadelphia (MACT/P). One time when we attended a potluck at a MACT/P member's home in West Philadelphia, I made a Crock-Pot full of a marinated chicken dish with rice on the side. Others brought vegetarian stew, hot wings, salad, and much more.

The evening went by quickly, and we were soon packing up to head home. There was still a half Crock-Pot of chicken left. The host didn't have room in his refrigerator for the leftovers, so we decided to carry it home. I packed up the rice, Stevie took the Crock-Pot, and we headed for the stairs. As a friend and I arrived at the bottom of the steps, we heard a yell behind us, then a crash, and turned to see Stevie flying down the stairs, landing on his back at the bottom. At first he didn't move. "God," I said, "I hope he's all right!" As we tried to find out if there were any broken bones or sprains, thoughts flashed in quick succession through my mind. *God, what would I ever do without him? He completes me. I would be lost without his wisdom, his bubbly personality and his touch. Thank God, he is all right.*

---

[1] The title comes from Romans 6:14, *RSV Bible*. New York, NY: Thomas Nelson and Sons, N.T., 1946.

Stevie:

We live in the Philadelphia area of Pennsylvania now, but are transplants from Connecticut. Stevie was born and raised in a middle-class neighborhood of New Haven. He was raised by his mother and grandmother, strong African-American women. By the time he was nine, both mother and grandmother had died. That left his grandfather to raise him and his sister.

Stevie's grandfather, whom everyone called *Grandpa*, impressed upon him the kind of life he would have. Being a young African-American man living in a world of white privilege and *isms* – especially racism – was going to be hard; but if he kept Christ in his life, he would always have a friend.

Being of a Baptist tradition, Stevie went to children's Bible school for three years. He was always questioning and challenging the teachers. They thought he was a troublemaker. Grandpa's answer to that was, "There is nothing wrong with questioning old ideas, because that is the way you can get new and better ideas."

Stevie never accepted things for the way they were, and that kind of attitude sometimes got him into trouble. When he went to church, he expected to be fired up – not to have his fire stomped out. It seemed like there was always something or somebody who was trying to put out his fire. Therefore, at age twelve, he made a decision. He talked with his grandfather and told him he didn't want to continue going to church and wanted to quit Bible school, because he did not like the hypocrites there. His grandfather agreed, and Stevie almost forgot about that institution.

He kind of knew that he was gay at the age of eleven, but did not have a name for it. Being gay never seemed to be an issue in his family. His grandfather was a man of few words, but he always got to the point. Stevie truly loved his grandfather, but what he really loved about him was his wisdom. Grandpa would say, "Stevie, no matter what you do, there is always going to be somebody who is not going to like you. Don't try to please everybody. It's hard enough trying to please yourself. Do the best you can with what you got. That's all you can do." Stevie is still living by those words today.

The year after Stonewall[2], at age twenty, Stevie decided to get political and became very public about being gay. He was very proud and excited about it as well. He remembers telling his grandfather about his first boyfriend. While riding a city bus on their way home, Stevie was groping for words to cushion the shock for his grandfather. Not knowing what to say or how to say it and stumbling over the words, he finally told Grandpa that he was gay. At first, his grandfather acted like he didn't hear him, so Stevie repeated it. Then Grandpa said, "Stevie, I knew it all along." That revelation gave new depth to their relationship and a whole new perspective on life.

As the years went by, Grandpa became Stevie's best friend and biggest fan. Stevie says, "We talked about everything. I was in the Connecticut Gay Men's Chorus for six years, and my grandfather came to every concert." Although his family was small, they were always supportive.

Stevie remembers seeing two angels when he was younger, one in the likeness of his mother, the other looked like his grandmother. Always, the visions of the two angels assured him that everything in his life was going to be all right. Stevie believed that God had a plan for his life, even though he did not always understand it.

Something his grandfather told him when they talked about the facts of life has always stayed in his memory. Grandpa said, "Stevie, in your life you are going to take many roads. The road might go to the left or to the right; it might be rocky or smooth; you might come to a detour and have to start all over again. It

---

[2] Refers to the Stonewall riots, which were named for The Stonewall Inn, a gay bar in New York City's Greenwich Village. Police raided The Stonewall on June 27, 1969, as they had often done before, but this time they met with resistance from gays and lesbians. The riots became a turning point in the struggle for gay rights.

doesn't matter what road you take, and it doesn't matter how long it takes for you to get home – just get home." That philosophy has helped Stevie through some troubling times and always gave him strength to go on. Stevie lives his life every day with Grandpa inside.

In the early 1980s, Stevie met a guy and started dating. Unknown to Stevie, his friend began attending a church in New Haven. One Sunday evening, Stevie asked him where he had been. The friend told him that he went to a church called Metropolitan Community Church of New Haven. He said that it was a Christian church with a special ministry for homosexuals. Stevie said, "Oh, really! Interesting." The friend suggested that Stevie visit the church also.

In the back of his mind, and in his heart, Stevie knew that there were gay Christians somewhere out there. This was a golden opportunity to find out about them. Stevie thought to himself, *"Where is this road taking me now?"* He decided Easter would be a good time to visit the church. He got all dolled up with a nice new suit and tie and went to church for the first time in a long while.

When he walked in, he received a program, sat down, and looked around. What a surprise! Out of about thirty men and women who were there, he discovered that he knew about twenty of them. Stevie wondered why they never told him about this church. It felt just wonderful to be there, and they even had a little choir! When it was announcement time, they welcomed everybody. They asked everyone visiting for the first time to stand up and introduce themselves. When Stevie introduced himself, everybody applauded.

Later, they talked about membership and Stevie thought, *"Lord, this is it."* He enthusiastically asked, "What time is the class? Where is it? Can I take it right now?" When they gave him the information, he quickly agreed to join the class. In the class, he learned what the Bible really says about gay people. He heard the true story about Sodom and Gomorrah and the true story about the Metropolitan Community Church. He loved it all.

Stevie began working in the church, singing in the choir, and going on radio and TV to talk about the church. He remembers his first introduction to TV. Yale University, like most colleges at the time, had a celebration called GLAD Day. This was simply a gay week at the university. TV cameras were there reporting on the event. Stevie says, "There I was, sitting on a bench with my pastor and wearing a pink triangle on my lapel." That was his first time on TV; there have been many more times.

Arthur:

I grew up the oldest of six children, in a middle-class, mostly white, suburban town outside New Haven. In high school, I felt the touch of Christ in my life and dreamed of preaching the Word. In my late teens, with the Vietnam War heating up, I decided to join the U.S. military, so off to the Navy I went. The Navy taught me many things. The one thing that stuck with me over the years was *how to be a man*. "A real man does not have limp wrists or talk with his hands the way you do," I was told.

I learned to close myself off from those around me to make sure no one, not even myself, could see the real me. It was a rule of life that would stay with me for more than twenty years.

After the tour of duty in the service, my intentions were to go home to Connecticut to stay with my family for a short time and then move to California. I discovered that my Mom had become a born-again Christian, and her convictions about Christ were ever-present in our home. I decided not to move away. My mother's apron strings were just too hard to leave behind.

I considered myself a Christian even though I wasn't going to church often. I felt that established religions were not for me. As a Christian, I did what was expected of me; I got married and started a family. My wife and I have three wonderful children, two boys and a girl.

For most of our marriage we had problems. Sure, money was always tight, but there were other problems. Although I was convinced that I loved my wife, there was something keeping us apart. We would often go for months without being intimate. This was frustrating to both of us. I tried everything I could to find out what was wrong with me. After all, it was *my* problem that kept us apart. I felt it would become *natural* if I could just get over the fear of having more children. So, after talking about the ways to prevent pregnancy, I decided on a vasectomy. After the surgery everything would be okay – but it wasn't!

As our children grew up, we started attending a local Full Gospel Pentecostal church. With prayer and the help of our sisters and brothers in Christ, I thought we were making progress in our relationship, but in time it was not to be. I began seeing a therapist to help me sort out my problems. This, too, was not the fix for our marriage. For many years, I prayed for the answer, but God did not seem to hear or care.

Finally, my wife could not take the emotional neglect any longer, and she walked out. I could not blame her, for I was only caring for the financial needs of the family and not the emotional and physical needs of my wife. I was depressed, lonely, and still looking for the reasons for our marriage failure.

After all those many years, the only thing I could come up with to account for my lack of intimacy with my wife was that I was gay! I had often struggled with that thought, but pushed it aside, because I thought it was against God's law and I was a Christian. Now, with my wife gone and the kids grown, I was alone and fearful. Could being gay be the problem?

I had come to this crossroad many times before, but always made a turn in another direction. *"There is no way I could be gay,"* I thought. Now I was at that life intersection again, and it was time to look down that road and explore the possibility.

Other things were happening in my life also. My mom, who had been sick with emphysema for years, had just been diagnosed with lung cancer. My dad was in denial, and the family was shaken to the core. Watching my mom struggle day to day as she was consumed by this malignancy was not easy. It took a toll on all of us. My questions of self-worth and sexuality had to wait. "The family needs to come first," I said. Saying good-bye to my mother, the mortar that held our family together, was hard.

After her passing, I realized how frail life is and that no one is promised more than this moment. God has promised that those who believe in Christ will live an eternal life in the presence of our Creator. I knew where my mother had gone, but would I ever see her again? The struggle with my sexuality and my fear that I might be gay was the problem. If that was my choice in life, then I felt I was condemned to hell for the sin of homosexuality. There had to be another answer, but where could I find it?

It was months before I could bring myself to say out loud the words, "I'm afraid I'm gay." My therapist was the first person to hear them from me. When I was finally able to say them aloud, they became real. *I was gay!* How could God have made this mistake with me? I needed to find answers.

As I searched, I found the Metropolitan Community Church of New Haven. The advertisement in the paper said they had "a special outreach to gay and lesbian people," but I did not want to be gay. I wanted to be Christian! There was no way I could be both. Perhaps they could tell me how God could have made this mistake.

The first time I went to the church was difficult because I had no idea who or what to expect. I sat in the back, knowing that if I felt too uncomfortable, I could slip out the door. When the service started, I could feel the presence of God. *"How can that be?"* I thought. *"This is a gay church! God couldn't be here!"* I cried openly for the first time in months.

I felt a need to be honest with my family and friends about my sexuality and had to find a way to tell my mom. I went to the cemetery to talk with my mother. *"I have to tell her I am gay*," I thought. Her gravesite was still barren. It was winter, and the grass had not started to grow. I knelt in the soil next to her grave, with a rose in one hand, and started talking to her. All I could manage was to say how much I loved and missed her. I placed the rose next to the stone and went home.

Weeks went by, as I continued to work toward answers in my life and where it was going, now that I could finally say I was gay and know it was true. But I had to find a way to tell my mom about being gay. I wished there was a way she could have been told before she died, but that had not happened. I found myself at her grave once again.

With a rose in my hand, I knelt in front of the stone that represented my mom's life and confessed the sin of homosexuality. "Mom," I said, "I'm gay!" At that moment, there was stillness in the air and then a whisper of wind. I could feel her presence and her touch. Within my spirit, I heard her voice. She said, "I know you are gay, and God loves you. I have seen the book and on the last day, when the seventh trump sounds, your name will be called. Today, all of heaven is rejoicing because you have finally confessed to be the person you were born to be."

Tears rolled down my cheeks as her voice faded. At that moment, I knew I was not a mistake. I kissed the rose and laid it down. There was still so much to learn, but now I knew I could be a Christian and gay. I sat and cried. The joy was overwhelming!

The next Sunday at church, I stood and gave witness to my newfound freedom in Christ. I had been freed of what religious organizations had taught me was sin. The Metropolitan Community Church of New Haven became my hiding place from the world, a sanctuary where I could be my whole self. I could not get enough of the teaching and music.

Our Lives Together:

The first time I saw Stevie, he was singing a solo in church. I was impressed with his voice and the feeling he put into the music. I was not looking for a relationship, but I was drawn to Stevie. The following Sunday, I decided to ask him if he needed a ride home. I didn't get the chance, because Stevie left right after the church service.

I became more involved in the church and sought involvement in the gay community as well. I joined a group that was active in combating racism and homophobia, Men of All Colors Together/Connecticut (MACT/CT). Reading through the literature, I noticed a name – Stevie Martin. Could this be the same Stevie I saw at church?

After the service the following Sunday, I quickly moved across the room to catch Stevie before he could disappear. He was not leaving immediately because he was selling raffle tickets. As I approached, he offered one to me. My question was answered when I saw the ticket – it was a fundraiser for MACT/CT. Stevie was surprised when I said, "Oh, so you are Stevie Martin."

Stevie had always been a busy person. As a community leader, he worked to start an AIDS organization to fight homophobia and racism, plus he took care of his grandfather, so he had not noticed that I was interested in him. After purchasing a ticket from him, I waited for a time to talk. Stevie suggested we go somewhere else because the church was too busy, and it was hard to have a lengthy conversation. We decided to go to a diner nearby. Our conversation was as if we had known each other for years. Coffee and tea led to sharing a chef's salad, and the time flew – one hour became four and more.

Stevie remarked that dinner was wonderful, and he couldn't believe he was having a conversation with a man who was so up front about everything. It was late when we left the diner. I drove Stevie home. Since he lived with his grandfather, we stayed in the car to continue talking. A good night kiss brought feelings neither of us expected. Stevie knew we were falling in love, but I was feeling confused about my feelings. We both knew we were becoming best friends.

The only time we could see each other, because of my work schedule, was after church, but we talked on the phone every day. I was finally able to adjust my work schedule so that we could see each other more often. At Christmas time, we became engaged, and a few months later, I asked Stevie to move in with me.

Soon after that, I was laid off from my job, and the prospects of finding a job near our home were looking dim. God's promise to those who believe is that all their needs will be provided in God's own time. Our money was running low, but just in time a job offer came for me out of nowhere. If I accepted the position, it would require relocating to Pennsylvania.

During the job interview, I felt God was saying to me, "This position is yours." All I needed to do was believe. Not only did God give me a job with an employer who would provide same-gender health benefits, but God led us to a home in a neighborhood of wonderful and accepting people.

Time moves so quickly. Before we knew it, a year had passed in the Philadelphia area. We were making plans for a Holy Union ceremony to be officiated by the founder of the Universal Fellowship of Metropolitan Community Churches, the Rev. Troy Perry. Rev. Perry was coming to Philadelphia on the twenty-fifth anniversary of the denomination to celebrate the joining of twenty-five couples.

At the ceremony, we were asked to gather in a semi-circle near the base of the steps to the Philadelphia Art Museum. Before the celebration, Rev. Perry explained how the exchange of vows would take place. Stevie doesn't remember the others involved. "It was as if Art and I were the only couple there," he said.

Stevie told me how much and why he loved me, and I did the same. We exchanged rings and were pronounced a couple. Then we sealed our vows with a kiss. Stepping forward, we asked Rev. Perry to bless our union and a broom we had brought with us. He gladly complied with this African-American tradition from Stevie's heritage. Then we placed the broom in front of us, and with feet planted together on one side of the broom, we jumped – landing flat-footed on the other side.

It was then that we realized there were others watching. "There must have been sixty people standing around, cheering for us," said Stevie. The following day a co-worker of mine gave me a video tape of our ceremony from Channel 29 news. Now, we have documented proof that our commitment to each other has been affirmed and blessed by a minister of the gospel in a public ceremony.

Arthur J. Martin-Chester and **Stevie Martin-Chester** live in Norristown, Pennsylvania. Arthur works as a technical service representative for a machine manufacturer. He enjoys photography and cooking. Stevie works as a sandwich and salad cook at a local café. His hobbies are cooking, music, and art.

Let us make our intentions crystal clear. We must and will be free. We want freedom – now. We do not want freedom fed to us in teaspoons over another hundred and fifty years!

~ Martin Luther King Jr.

~ *fifteen* ~

"But the Greatest of These Is Love"[1]

Tom and Jean Zook

Jean:

On a foggy November night in 1983, my husband Tom and I began a long journey of truth and discovery. Tom had planned a getaway for the two of us at an inn in the North Carolina Blue Ridge mountains. We were in marriage counseling at the time – one of several times in our twelve years together. Although we loved each other deeply, we had not been able to achieve the level of intimacy we desired. I was very anxious about the trip. I feared that my husband was going to admit that he had found another woman who more completely fulfilled his needs – that he wanted to end our relationship.

Tom:

I needed to get my wife away for the weekend. I knew the revelation I was about to make needed to be made away from our home, because it might forever color the place where it was revealed. After checking into the inn, we spent the afternoon walking and talking in the mountains. The inn was adjacent to an old Episcopal church that had a beautiful fresco of the Last Supper.

After dinner we sat for a long time in the church, contemplating the fresco covering the wall behind the altar. Seldom have I felt so close to my wife as I felt that night. Never had I needed so much her trust! How much I identified with the figure of Judas pictured slinking from the door of the Upper Room! Yet I

---

[1] 1 Corinthians 13:13 b. *RSV Bible.* New York, NY: Thomas Nelson and Sons, N.T., 1946.

could also identify with the image of the young John, looking upon Jesus with total trust.

Jean:

The silence of the church was very spiritual; the fresco seemed almost alive, as if the gaze of Christ was directed at us. I remember thinking that he was probably looking at me in disdain, fully aware of my inadequacies and my fears about my marriage. I felt lost to him.

Tom:

Through quiet darkness we returned to the inn where, during the night, I began awkwardly to reveal to my wife that she had married a gay man.

Jean:

Oh, what a sense of relief I had! He hadn't been having an affair with another woman. *He's just gay. I can deal with that. He's not leaving me – the love of my life is not leaving me for another woman. God does answer prayer. Thank you God!*

But wait! Did I really hear what I thought I heard last night? *He's gay! Oh, God, he's gay! And he has been in a love relationship with **OUR** best friend. I really do love him. How will we sort this out? How does this make him different? Two people I thought I knew – now what? I don't have any past experience that helps me with **THIS**!*

I grew up in a small coal mining community that was a mixture of immigrant families. Although my community was not racially mixed, its ethnicities made religion an important factor affecting community life. I attended the Evangelical United Brethren church, but my home life was based on the rigid Calvinist values of my mother's upbringing. Ironically, I was often sent to church with my grandmother because my parents did not attend regularly. It made no sense to me that I was required to join the church, but was not allowed to go on outings with the church youth group because my parents did not approve of the lifestyle of one of the leaders. By the time I went away to college, finding a church home was not a priority.

I was poorly prepared for college; between struggling with academics and continuing conflict with my family, there were times I felt very alone and desperate. To my amazement, somewhere in my rocky and conflicted religious adolescence, I had developed a strong personal relationship with God that re-emerged in the form of a ritual of daily prayer in a campus chapel. That feeling of closeness to God was my salvation, sustaining me through the stress and guiding me onto a more positive path, as I made the transition to adulthood.

After graduating from Temple University, I chose to remain in Philadelphia. I moved into an apartment, endeavored to make new friends, and started life anew. The first friend I made is the best friend I will ever have. We have not only been best friends now for thirty years, but husband and wife.

That was such a wondrous time in my life. I had never felt such joy and hope. I felt that God was fulfilling a promise to guide and protect me and was rewarding me for enduring the struggles of adolescence. My fiancé and I were deeply in love. Several months after we met, he asked me to marry him. I remember his disappointment when I gave him a qualified "yes," stating that I felt I had a lot of growing up to do and that I might end up being a very different person. My answer to him was, "Yes, if you are willing to take the risk." I now find it ironic that at the time of the proposal, the man I was saying yes to was already a different person than the one I thought I knew.

My fiancé had been living with his friend Joe,* who soon became my friend as well. By the second year of our marriage, the intimacy Tom and I had shared seemed to be diminishing. I was very sexually inexperienced and worried that our problems were my fault. In this new community, the only close friend I had was Joe. On several occasions, I drove to Joe's house to ask

---

* Name has been changed.

for advice. Each time Joe was not home, and I kept my feelings of desperation to myself, afraid to talk to Tom and have him confirm my fear that I was the problem. At the time, I had no idea that Joe would have been the least able to help me.

Although the level of intimacy in our relationship was not ideal, Tom and I had a strong bond of love and continued to plan for our future together with anticipation. Our efforts to have a baby resulted in a year and a half of frustration. Tom decided to enter graduate school in North Carolina. Our first child, a daughter, arrived on the morning of his first big exam, marking the beginning of a very difficult time in our relationship.

We had moved to another state where we knew no one. My husband was a full-time student. I was unemployed and unable to find a job in my profession. We had no local support system, no experience with infants, little money, and – with all the stress – no intimacy. As time progressed, I found work, and Tom found part-time work, so our situation improved. Life took on some of the old joy and hope for the future that we had lost.

Our second child, a son, was born four years later. With his birth, the stress cycle started again. Tom was still in school, and I worked several jobs to keep us afloat. The next years were a mixture of great family times and diminishing intimacy.

The trauma of a gunpoint robbery at his work seemed to emotionally paralyze Tom. He quit his job and withdrew from me, becoming increasingly angry and hostile. I felt I had little power to change anything in the relationship. I made contingency plans for the children and me to have a safe haven if that became necessary.

One day he simply announced that he wanted out. I did not know what to think, but I distinctly remember feeling panic and fear. I could not admit that it was the end of our family. We had enjoyed many good times, but I was afraid to let the chaos escalate. I could not understand his hostility and how we had come to this point.

Tom:

I grew up in a small farming community in the Midwest, the youngest of eight siblings. My parents were active members of the local Congregational Christian church. As a teenager, I chose to join my parents' church. That church family contributed greatly to my development.

The recognition of my homosexuality began to clarify during the first two years of college. In my earlier teen years, I had uncomfortable feelings about my sexuality, or more precisely, the objects of my sexual attractions and fantasies. Though there was not a lot of open discussion about homosexuality as I was growing up in the 1950s, I was familiar with the words "fairy" and "fag" and knew that, for my well being, I should not be identified as such.

In my teen years, I engaged in same-sex experimentation with friends on several occasions. I enjoyed the excitement and the sexual release I experienced in these encounters, but I felt a great deal of guilt afterwards. I do not know what precipitated the guilt, because I was not taught in church, in school, or at home that sex with other males was wrong.

During adolescence, I read the Bible every night before going to sleep, and I was familiar with the condemnation passages that continue to be cited as judgment of homosexuality. Growing up on a farm, I had ample opportunity to observe the sexual behavior of a variety of domesticated animals. Since I had no other *sex-ed* exposure, I assumed the sexual behavior of animals was normative to human sexual experience. I often observed farm animals in same-gender sexual activities: young bulls in mounting activity with each other and heifers running to sniff the urine of another heifer in heat. Therefore, it would seem that human same-sex activity should not have seemed abnormal to me or have been a cause for guilt. I suppose I can attribute the guilt feelings that I experienced when fantasizing about being with other boys or enjoying looking at male bodies to the understanding I received from my Bible reading.

In my second year of college, I became very depressed. As I became more aware of my homosexual orientation, I also became more intent on keeping it suppressed. I dated a girl at college and was quite attracted to her, but I knew that I did not experience the same girl-obsession that other college guys seemed to experience.

I had always been put off by sexual jokes and did not see what was so enticing about the *Playboy* centerfolds that some of my friends smuggled into their rooms. Near the end of my second year of college, I decided to quit school. My future seemed a shambles – totally without direction. The faith that had sustained me throughout my youth had vanished, replaced by grave doubts about the existence of God and, most certainly, of a God who would possibly love *me*. I decided to join the Air Force.

In those days before "don't ask – don't tell," I was asked to sign a statement denying homosexuality when I enlisted. Though I had been taught the importance of truth since childhood, I could not admit and confirm with my signature that I was homosexual. Furthermore, I could not imagine what path in life such an admission would determine for me. I did not know another homosexual. I only knew that this would be something that I could never explain to my family and friends. I boarded the plane for Texas with the knowledge that I was a liar and a cheat, who would some day surely be unmasked and then face some unimaginable and terrible consequences.

Several months later I arrived at my permanent assignment in Europe. I was totally lonely – totally depressed on my first day in Germany, as I sat in the day-room awaiting my room assignment. Suddenly, the door opened, and there he stood – a big smile setting off the twinkle in his green eyes, the high-collared white medic uniform in stark relief to his black hair. He had been reassigned from Tripoli, and his well-tanned face bore evidence of the North African sun. He was extremely amiable and conversation came easily with him.

We shared very good adventures during our time together in Europe, from hiking in Switzerland and Norway and driving from village to village on wine tasting excursions along the Mosel and Rhein to visiting as many museums and cathedrals as we could on weekends and passes. Joe became my first and only male lover; our relationship lasted for nine years.

At some level, I suppose that both Joe and I knew that our relationship could not last. We each dated girls occasionally; neither of us felt at all threatened by that. My family thought the world of him, never imagining that we were lovers. I was also loved by Joe's family and soon became as a son and brother to them.

However, no paradigm existed in the '60s upon which an open same-sex relationship could be modeled. I could no longer live in this false world, and I could no longer accept being recognized only as Joe's good friend. I loved Joe deeply. It was becoming extremely difficult to keep my love for him hidden. I knew that it would only be a matter of time before the true nature of our relationship would become apparent and then all bets would be off. I greatly desired to live in an open manner in a relationship that I could celebrate with my family and friends – one that society around me would accept as valid and would affirm.

In my final year of college, I met Jean. We soon became very close friends, spending many pleasant times together. We seemed to have so much in common: our lives, our goals, and our values. A close bond formed between us easily. We both have happy memories of those early days together in which I grew to love Jean, even as I love her still.

We were married in a Methodist church ten months after we first met. Although my sexual relationship with Joe ended shortly after I met Jean, we maintain a close friendship still. Jean, too, developed a bond of friendship with Joe. Since he lived near us, Joe often spent time with us. We picnicked, skied together, and double dated when he was seeing a girl.

Jean was not aware of the nature of our previous relationship. I had succeeded in escaping from one lie into another. Our married life was good. I thought that the sex was good or, at least, had ultimate faith that it would grow better with time, but my homosexual drive was at times extremely hard to contain. I continued to fantasize about men, and though Jean would always be the sole focus of the intimate time we shared together, my private times and thoughts were often consumed with the desire for intimacy with another male.

I continued to have a great deal of guilt and stress around this issue, knowing that my sexual attraction toward men was not going to go away, and yet I did not know how to deal with it. I could not discuss my feelings with Jean – or rather elected not to do so. I felt Jean idolized me. I could not face the prospect of having her respect and love for me compromised. How could she possibly continue to love and respect me if she knew the truth about me?

We shared many happy times, but the stresses upon our marriage began to escalate. I became increasingly unsettled and unfocused. On an outward level, our lives and our marriage seemed so ideal (one friend still comments that she always viewed us as an example of what a good family should be), but internally I was becoming more and more "a basket case." At one point I nearly abandoned my graduate studies, but commitment to my advisor compelled me to continue. I did very well in the graduate program; nevertheless, I ultimately gave up all attempts to continue on to a post-graduate position that would lead to a good teaching job. I lost much faith in myself and seemed to be a total fraud!

The tension in our marriage continued to increase. I did not feel sexually fulfilled, and I am sure that Jean at times felt totally used. Two children increased our visibility as a family, but also added to the stress upon our relationship. I started to contemplate suicide, imagining ways that I could accomplish the act so that Jean would still receive insurance compensation. I began to stash a secret supply of lethal drugs so that I would be ready when the time came. My life was in a downward tailspin.

Jean accomplished the one thing that saved us all: she sought professional counseling for herself. Soon I recognized that it was I who was in need of professional help. Jean had become my scapegoat. Standing in my garden one overcast afternoon, I was overwhelmed with knowledge I had been unwilling to admit before. I screamed aloud, "I am a homosexual! Oh, God, I am a homosexual!"

Then I put down my shovel, went into the house and called family services for help. A few days later, I sat in a therapist's office, pouring out truths about myself that had previously been spoken to no one. A few weeks into my therapy sessions, I knew that, ready or not, I had to open myself up to Jean. I reserved a room in the mountain inn where I planned to come clean.

Jean and Tom:

In our journey toward understanding and acceptance, the one thing that has become clear to us is that there is no magical formula for making relationships work. We have learned that neither of us is perfect and it is imperative to allow each other freedom to be who we are. A love relationship will not work if either partner is living a lie. We feel that process is more important than product. The patience and struggles that go along with resolving relationships can be a very long road that we have to learn to enjoy traveling, or the arrival at the destination will not be worth the trip. As long as we are comfortable with our commitment to each other and the way our relationship works, others will have to take responsibility for their own uncomfortable feelings with our marriage. We cannot allow those who are uncomfortable with us to destroy our peace.

Jean:

I will not say it has been easy to accept and process the new *gay* man in my marriage. He gives me full permission and encourages me to ask whatever I want to know, but it is a little like asking me to converse in a foreign language for which I have little fluency. Tom's coming out to family, friends, church, and community has been freeing for him. I have enjoyed seeing his self-confidence, natural ease with people, and passion for life re-emerge to strengthen our relationship. I know in his heart that he knows I accept him and love him. I support his active involvement in GLBT advocacy and am thankful that he has found his voice.

Jean and Tom:

We know that our marital strength lies in the fact that our love is abiding and that our commitment to each other is total and unequivocal. Moving our relationship back on track has taken a lot of therapy, time, faith, and introspection. It has caused a lot of pain for both of us. We are not totally sure how we have come to where we are now in our relationship. For each of us, perhaps, it is a matter of not knowing how to unlove a very special and integral part of our being. We realize that our relationship will continue to change as we become more adept at using a common language to share our thoughts and feelings from our different perspectives.

Jean:

Although many positive changes have come out of our acknowledgement of Tom's homosexuality, I sense that there is a long road ahead of us. I realize that I do not truly understand what being gay means to him, how he really thinks and feels about his sexual orientation, but I am committed to continuing the journey together.

Tom:

I have determined to never again lie about my sexual identity. I now easily identify myself as a gay man. I cannot deny that identifying myself as gay while remaining in a mixed-orientation marriage has been difficult for many people, both gay and straight, to find credible.

Some of the conservative members of the local Mennonite congregation, where Jean and I had previously been members, preferred to believe that I was not really gay, because if I were, I could not be married to a woman. In some gay and lesbian circles, I have been censured for *hiding* in my marriage or appearing to be a poster child for Exodus International (an ex-gay organization). However, close friends and family accept me as I am and, though they may not understand the dynamics of our mixed-orientation marriage, do not make lack of understanding a hindrance to individual relationships.

I advocate as I can for GLBT folks, sometimes publicly, but most often as just a quiet gay presence. I have been active in Soulforce, an interfaith group of GLBT folks and their supporters that continues nonviolent advocacy for justice and truth in the context of several major denominations. I have outed myself in the workplace in support of homosexuals who face abuse from co-workers.

Anticipating probable public exposure anyway, I have outed myself to the entire local community through an editorial piece in the local newspaper. If the e-mail responses that I have received after the editorial piece was picked up on the internet are indicative, I am out also in Hawaii, Indiana, and Florida. I understand my coming out to be a process that I know will continue as long as I breathe.

Tom and Jean:

In the final analysis, all we can ask of ourselves is to live our lives with integrity and to harbor love, compassion, and mercy for all who journey this earth with us. We are sustained by the unfaltering trust that we are loved by our Creator just as we are created, just as all of this wonderful creation is loved – no more and no less. That is enough for us. We anticipate growing old together, grateful for the most wonderful gift God has given us – each other.

Tom and **Jean Zook** live in Winston-Salem, North Carolina. Tom is a pharmacist at Wake Forest Baptist Medical Center and Jean is an occupational therapist working in the North Carolina school system with severely handicapped children. The Zooks are active in Parkway United Church of Christ, an open and affirming congregation.

O Lord, open my eyes that I may see the need of others, open my ears that I may hear their cries, open my heart so that they need not be without succor, let me be not afraid to defend the weak because of the anger of the strong, nor afraid to defend the poor because of the anger of the rich.

~ Alan Paton in
Instrument of Thy Peace

~ *sixteen* ~

Overcoming Differences by Relying on the Cornerstone

Manuel R. Diaz with Eric Yurkanin

Both Eric and I were raised Catholic. However, each of us was involved in church in very different ways. The differences in all aspects of our being is what attracted us to each other, but it is the cornerstone of our common belief in God and the salvation through Christ which drew us into relationship with each other.

This cornerstone in our relationship is also why we seek a stronger, more holistic relationship with our Creator. Our holistic approach includes reading and studying the Word (Bible), sharing it with others, allowing others to share their views with us, and living out the Word in every aspect of our lives. Are we successful? *No, not always.* Do we continue to struggle? *Yes, absolutely.* Do we maintain our faith in all ways? *Yes, definitely, yes!*

Eric's faith journey was always full of a certainty – he knew the Creator loved him. His faith was challenged in college when he expressed feelings for his same-sex best friend. After he found himself rejected, he questioned where his life was taking him, especially as a Christian and as a gay man. He attempted suicide because he could not find the answer on his own. But thanks to the people who cared for him – including his mother – and his belief in Christ, he began to see that God created him to be exactly who he was – a gay Christian man.

He continued to nurture the belief that God, our Creator, planned that he would be gay, but he sensed this knowledge had to be kept silent. As he became more involved with the Christian organizations on his college campus and other organizations after graduation, he found very little acceptance for this seemingly contradictory belief – you can be a Christian and also be gay.

My journey was less straightforward. I participated in church and did all the things I thought were expected of me. I was an altar boy and was involved in the Holy Name and the Knights of Columbus organizations at my parents' church, but I was merely going through the motions. I never really felt like I belonged. However, I knew I loved God and believed in a Greater Power. It just seemed life was not that simple.

For me, the signs of a Higher Power had always been present. When I was six months old, I had staph pneumonia. The doctors had given a prognosis of my imminent death. My parents and extended family had a stronger faith than the doctors. They changed hospitals and began praying. I believe both actions saved my life, but I believe that it was the power of my family's faith and their prayers that played the larger part in my survival.

In my teen years, I gave up my involvement in church. Later, in college, I met a girl who helped me to accept Christ into my life. The struggle between my sexuality and my spirituality was not so easily set in balance. I became involved in a local Baptist church, Campus Crusaders, Navigators, and other organizations. I thought if I were actively involved in these different organizations, God would be able to take away my attraction to other men. However, what I found was hypocrisy – and people like me, who were struggling with homosexuality or other issues. I again stopped attending church.

In 1988, I graduated from Texas A & M University and moved to Dallas, Texas. My sexuality and my faith came together when I accompanied a friend to the Cathedral of Hope MCC in Dallas. I still remember crying through that entire first service and many after that. I had finally found a place where I

belonged! I had found a place to worship God where I did not
need to be ashamed or hide the fact that I was gay. I truly believed that God accepted me for who I was, scars, faults, and
all. My Creator's grace and salvation were offered freely and
without expectation.

In May of 1997, I relocated to Allentown, Pennsylvania, in a
work-related move. I had no idea what a gift God had in store
for me, nor did Eric. We first met on August 30, 1997. I had
just returned to the place I called home at the time – a room I
was renting from a friend. I had been out all day with my parents, taking in the local sites and looking at houses. Eric happened to be visiting our mutual friend Charlie, who lived in the
same building.

Eric's corps had just won first place in a drum and bugle
corps competition. Eric was so cute, with his boyish face and an
innocence that beamed. But there was something else – something pure and honest about him. I was attracted to him and
flirted with him, but he appeared less than interested.

A few days later, and very much to my surprise, Eric called
me on the phone. I had invited a friend over to my place, and
we were watching movies and eating pizza. Being the friendly
and not so shy individual that I am, I invited Eric to join us also.
He accepted my invitation and soon appeared at my door. As
before, I was very much attracted to him. In fact, during *The
Mirror Has Two Faces*, I ever so coyly brushed his hair and
bumped my leg against his – not in a sexual way – I merely
wanted to touch him. As the evening neared its end, my friend
Mike indicated it was time for him to go. Eric agreed that he
needed to go also because the next day was his first day back at
work.

As Eric was leaving, I knew I wanted to spend some more
time with him. There was something about him that drew me to
him. At this point, I still did not know if he was attracted to me.
When he lingered a bit at the door, we had our first opportunity
to talk alone. He came back in, and we ended up talking late

into the night, sharing very openly about our past, our faith journey, and our dreams for the future. I know I tried to use some corny line to see if I could get him to touch my skin or to kiss me, but Eric stayed strong.

From that point on, we began to court each other – and it was truly a courtship. This was so different from dating any other guy or girl I had ever been in a relationship with. We were taking it very slowly. Eric had ended a relationship a few years before in which he was engaged to a guy. I found this to be amazing since two people of the same sex cannot marry – right?

We began to spend every possible minute together, sharing stories about ourselves and talking about the future. We also incorporated a spiritual aspect into our relationship very early on. Initially, when we lived three houses apart in Allentown, we got together to pray every morning before setting off to our respective jobs. We also finished our day with prayer together. After I bought my home in the suburbs, we prayed over the phone.

We attended several churches in the Allentown area, trying to find a place of worship where we both felt comfortable. We were searching for a church that would be as welcoming as possible to a gay couple. We enjoyed the worship and music at several churches, but none of these were places where we could be open about our relationship. I had attended Metropolitan Community Church of the Lehigh Valley (MCCLV) before, but it was much smaller than the Cathedral of Hope that I had attended in Texas. I was not sure if Eric and I would fit in. For a while, we attended another church in the morning and then attended MCCLV in the evening.

Although MCCLV was very welcoming, we were younger than most congregants, and we felt a little out of place due to the age difference. The church had a very *family* type feel to it that offered some positives and some negatives. This was different from some of the other churches we had visited.

We liked the people at MCCLV. Moreover, during the service, Eric and I were able to worship together with our arms around each other, and we especially enjoyed taking communion together – this was something we could never do at any of the other churches we attended. We began to attend MCCLV regularly, but we still attended other churches occasionally.

I think we both concluded that our search for a church home was ended when we attended worship at one of the other churches and heard a sermon on homosexuality, citing some of the infamous clobber passages from the Bible. I remember feeling like the pastor was speaking directly to us, and I think Eric felt the same way. It was then that we decided to only attend MCCLV. We needed to be with other Christians who believed as we did – that you could be gay *and* Christian. At MCCLV, we felt welcomed to bring our entire selves before God and the Body of Christ with whom we worshiped.

I am writing this story about our lives in November of 2001. Eric and I have been attending MCCLV for over four years. We both became members on the same day. Initially, Eric served on the board of directors, and I became involved with the congregational care ministry. We have also served in several other ministries of the church – sometimes together, sometimes on our own. Our unique differences are apparent through the ways we are involved in church ministry.

We continued to pray together daily, or as much as possible. But between our workload and our involvement at church, we began to experience some relationship issues. Consequently, we sought counseling to try to improve our relationship and read a book about gay relationships.

We are different from each other, not only in our personalities, but also in our faith journey. Eric's faith is very strong; however, because he is an introvert, sometimes people do not get to benefit from the depth of his faith. This faith is evidenced in his commitment to God, his commitment to our relationship, his commitment to serving God's people at MCCLV, his dedication to teaching his students, and in his concern for the community at large.

This past year, Eric marched in the local Gay Pride Parade. To some, this may not seem like much; but Eric is a teacher and is very fearful of losing his job. He has shared his faith as a gay Christian by speaking at public events such as the Gay-Straight Student Alliance at Liberty High School and at a workshop at Moravian College.

The Holy Spirit propelled Eric into action through the words of one of his former students, who attended MCCLV one Sunday. Although the young man probably does not know it, God used his words to give Eric courage to be more open. The essence of what the student said is: "Mr. Yurkanin, I wish I would have known about you when I was in school. It would have made my high school days much easier."

I, too, have grown in my faith. I came out to Eric when I first met him, not only as a gay Christian, but also as HIV positive. This was hard for me – others had rejected me because of my status. My faith in God and our love for each other have proven to have a very positive effect on my health. In 2001, my quarterly blood results have continued to come back *normal*.

I have come out at work and have spoken in front of over a thousand people about being a gay man in a corporate environment. In recent years, I have had many opportunities to share about my life. I have shared my faith journey and God's grace in dealing with my HIV status with my church and individually with those who struggle with the issue of their sexuality and their spirituality. Recently, I came out to several of our company chauffeurs, not only as a Christian, but also as a gay man. I share my faith openly. Also, I continue to explore the Creator's diversity by worshiping with Jewish and Sikh friends at their holy places.

Eric and I joined a small Bible study group in order to further nourish ourselves in God's Word. This greatly helped us in developing a new appreciation for each other. It also gave us an opportunity to minister to others and to be ministered to by others. As in most groups, there are dynamics that affect the nature of the group and bring changes. Although the group members have changed, we continue to go whenever possible.

We are also in the process of looking for a small Bible study group for gay couples. We would like to continue to fortify ourselves in God's Word and at the same time learn from the successes and struggles of other gay couples. Perhaps others can learn from our relationship as well.

Eric's upbringing as a white Slovak American in the rural area of Hazelton, Pennsylvania, has been very different from my upbringing as a Mexican-American in Houston, Texas. His family nucleus is made up of his mother, Geraldine, and his two sisters, Georganne and Jennifer. This is very different from my family, which consists of my parents, Johnny and Hope, and my four brothers and sisters, Johnny Jr., Lupe, Cindy, and Vincent.

We have celebrated various holidays at our respective homes, where the size of the family gatherings, the style of the celebrations, the foods, and the interactions are very different. In all our interactions with our families of different cultural background, Eric and I have tried to embrace some balance and variety. He has eaten many Hispanic dishes and has become a very good cook of Spanish meals. I am not as good a cook, but I have eaten many Slovak delicacies.

We also have a small family – it's a queer family, but it is our family. We have two dogs: Missy, a dachshund, and Butch, an English springer spaniel. They were my dogs before Eric and I began our relationship; the *kids* (meaning, dogs) love and recognize Eric as a parent figure. They cry when he is gone, and they get excited when he comes home.

Furthermore, our family extends beyond our biological family. We have friends from both inside and out of our church to complete our family of choice. We pray for them and they pray for us. We are blessed to have friends who support us in prayer and with their love.

Being a Mexican-American and growing up in Texas, I have experienced prejudice. I have been called names like "wet-back," "fag," "spic," and more. Eric says he has never experienced or seen that type of prejudice. I think being with me and meeting people of different nationalities has opened his eyes to this injustice.

I am very blessed. I had a good education and now have a very good job. Because of this, I think some people find it difficult to treat me with the same disrespect that was previously shown to me and to my family and is still shown to many marginalized individuals today.

Eric has only experienced this feeling of being different since we began to travel, or perhaps at some of my family gatherings back in Texas. It is not because they have made him feel like the odd person out; it is just that our family dynamics are different than those of Eric's family. We discuss loudly and passionately, and we also tend to be more physical than Eric is at his family gatherings. My family does ask about him regularly, and Eric's family also asks about me. They know we love each other very much.

Eric and I will celebrate our anniversary of five years together on September 1, 2002. We have experienced many challenges in our relationship because Eric is an introvert and I am an extrovert. But, we both have many gifts to offer to each other and to the lives of those we touch.

Like most couples – especially gay couples – Eric and I have struggled with our differences. However, we always seem to be able to turn to our faith. Our faith in God and the belief that the Creator brought us together for a reason helps us to resolve the issues that arise; hence, the cornerstone of our faith serves as the cornerstone of our relationship.

When dealing with family, I am a bit of a dissident. If any one in my family speaks of a wife, husband, boyfriend, or girlfriend, I talk about Eric. There was a time when I would not recognize their anniversaries, because I felt like they did not give as much value to my relationship with Eric. However, as I was writing this story, I allowed my family to read the initial draft, and they became aware of my feelings. Now, some of them have asked about the date of our anniversary.

Since I have come out at work, I have Eric's picture on my desk. I have a jigsaw puzzle in my office and proudly announce that my partner Eric made it for me. On the outside of my office door, I have a *safe space* magnet and gladly talk to people whenever and wherever possible about the need to be tolerant and to embrace God's creative diversity.

In October of this year (2001), I received the offer of an opportunity to live out a lifelong dream of living and working abroad. Earlier in our relationship, this would have been a cause for great consternation and, maybe, even possible talk of ending our relationship. However, after prayer and acknowledgement of the gift God has given us in each other, we decided that I could pursue this opportunity.

One of the benefits of being out at work is that my employer recognizes my relationship. The company will be flying Eric to Germany to be with me over the holidays. I am sure this would not have been possible if I were still in the closet.

I want to urge all who are reading this story to seriously consider coming out and living openly with the truth of who you are; and when you do, encourage others to come out also. Not only am I talking about individuals who are gay, lesbian, bisexual, or transgender, but also people who are allies to this group of marginalized people. The more people come out as GLBTA, the more people will realize intolerance is not acceptable.

Eric and I continue to grow, and we continue to be challenged. We continue to pray that the cornerstone of our faith that also serves as the cornerstone of our relationship will continue to be on solid ground. Both of us are still very much involved in MCCLV because we believe in our church's Vision statement of "Bringing God's hope and sharing Christ's love with the Gay, Lesbian, Bisexual, Transgender, and Allied community by the power of the Holy Spirit through bold and courageous action."

Will our lives together end "happily ever after"? We surely hope so. But, even now, Eric and I pray together over the long distance between Germany and the United States. Someday, when death parts us, we will have to pray together across eternity, but we will still be together, even if we are not together physically.

Manuel R. Diaz is realizing his lifelong dream of living and working abroad as a chemical engineer in Work Process Optimization in Germany. This is a short-term assignment, after which he will return to the United States. He hopes to continue traveling with his work, although a bit less, and he hopes to travel more often with Eric on fun vacations.

Eric Yurkanin is an instrumental music teacher in Pennsylvania. He plans to return to college to complete a third degree in mathematics in pursuit of a new career in Actuarial Science.

Ultimately we need only to fear the dangers of our turning away from God for the sake of social conformity.

~ Ted Grimsrud in *Triumph of the Lamb*

~ seventeen ~

Believing in Miracles

Christen Chew and Deborah Becker

Christen:

I was born in Honolulu, Hawaii, and was the youngest of nine children. My nationality is Asian Pacific Islander. My father was a very open and loving person, and my mother was the greatest mom a kid could have. I was raised in a Mormon family. We were taught to believe in God and the teachings of the church. My father told me that one day when I was old enough to understand, I could make my own decision concerning baptism and church membership. I attended Bible school as a child, but other than that I was not very involved in church activities. I always felt that there was something different about me, and I questioned the doctrines and practices of the church.

One day our church building burned to the ground and all the church records were destroyed. Because they had no records of who was baptized and who was not, the church elders encouraged my father to have his entire family rebaptized. He strongly disagreed with them. My father felt that once you were baptized, it was final. Because of this disagreement between my father and the church, my faith journey faltered. I attended different denominations, but never felt at home. I was searching for answers.

Deb:

I was born and raised in a Mennonite family with all the traditions and history of faith that are associated with Mennonites. I can trace my roots to some of the earliest Anabaptists who came to America. Growing up, I somehow acquired the sense that the faith journeys of my ancestors had formed the foundation for my own unique personal faith journey. When I was twelve, my grandfather, a Mennonite preacher, baptized me into the church. My life revolved around my family and the church. We attended all church services, and even as a teenager I was involved in the leadership of the church. After four years of study at Lancaster Mennonite High School, I received a small scholarship to attend Eastern Mennonite College (now Eastern Mennonite University).

Even though I was heavily involved in the church, at some point during my growing up years I began to realize that the teachings of the church were very narrow. I began to question why I had to shape my life and my beliefs based on what the church taught. I decided that instead of attending a Mennonite college I would attend a local state college so that I could broaden my views and beliefs.

Christen:

When I was sixteen, my father died from a massive heart attack. As a result, my mother moved four siblings and myself to California. I went to high school in California and continued to search for answers to my questions. To add to my confusion, while I was in high school my feeling that I was different began to intensify. I realized that I felt more comfortable around girls than boys. When one of my best friends "came on" to me, I was frightened. I remembered that I had been taught in Sunday school that homosexuality was wrong. Yet, I felt comfortable around her and enjoyed her company. I began to understand that I was a lesbian, but I kept it a secret – especially from my family because I was afraid of how they would react.

When I went to college, I was able to accept who I was, and I came out as a lesbian. It was liberating to be honest about my identity. When I came out to my mother, she was upset for a few days, but soon changed her mind. She said, "You are my daughter, and I love you. So, when are you taking me to a gay bar?" Well, I did take her, and she had more fun than I did!

Deb:

In college, I exposed myself to new people and new teachings and began to learn more about myself. One of the things I learned was that I am a lesbian. I had no problem accepting this, but knew my family and friends from church would not be as open. I separated myself from the people that I cared about for fear that they would discover my secret and push me away. I also separated myself from the Mennonite church, knowing that my being a lesbian would not be tolerated, and unless I *repented* I would be treated as a sinner.

I especially feared what would happen if my parents found out. At that time they were very rigid in their beliefs. There were some things that they just would not accept. I knew that my being a lesbian was one of them. I distanced myself from my family and made up excuses to stay away from family activities. However, as the years went by, I grew more confident in my belief that God loved me – even as a lesbian.

I came to a point in my life where I had to be honest with my parents about who I was. When I did tell them, I got a mixed response. My father said that I would always be his daughter and that he would love me no matter what. My mother was unable to say that. I felt like I had put her in a dilemma. *What would she do with this new information about me? Would she close her mind and treat me according to the teachings of the church? Or, would she open her mind to the possibility of changing the beliefs she had held all her life?*

Fortunately, she chose the latter. Along with my father, she decided that they would learn all they could about homosexuality and what the Bible did and did not say about it. They studied. They dialogued with new friends. They attended a Connecting Families weekend, and they became more and more open and accepting. Sadly, during this time my father passed away. My mother has continued this journey on her own and has fought her share of battles on our behalf.

Christen:

I began to feel that something was missing in my life. There was a void that needed to be filled. One day a friend asked my partner and me if we wanted to go to church. I questioned whether there was a church that would accept me as a lesbian. My friend assured me there was such a church. The next Sunday we accompanied her to the Metropolitan Community Church in Pomona, California, where she was a member. I felt at home! Finally there was a place that accepted me the way God created me! I became actively involved in different events and soon started a praise band with five other women. We traveled to different churches and sang praises to the Lord. I could feel God's presence with me everywhere I went. It was awesome!

As the years went by, I could feel my life changing. I knew that God was calling me to something more. What was it? What did God want of me? I began to feel a strong calling into the ministry. I went to seminary and was ordained as a pastor in the Metropolitan Community Church. I started a women's prison ministry and became a part-time pastor at Sunrise MCC in the High Desert in Lancaster, California.

Things were going wonderfully until my relationship with my partner of ten years came to an end. It was a tough time, but God saw me through it. During my quiet time in prayer, I asked God to show me the way and what I was to do. I felt that God wanted me to start over. God showed me that I would be called to a new church in a different state and showed me the faces of some of the people I would meet and some of the experiences I would have. God even showed me a picture of the person I would meet and fall in love with. Starting over was frightening, but I trusted God for guidance.

I met my partner Deb when I was a candidate for the position of pastor at a Metropolitan Community Church near Lancaster, Pennsylvania. She was the vice-moderator of the church. There was a strong connection between us immediately – I recognized her as the person God had revealed to me while I was still in California. We talked and talked and discovered that we had a lot in common. It was a match made in heaven and a gift from God.

I served this church for four years and five months. The ministry was Spirit-filled, and I believe that God used me to bring many to Christ. Through some unpleasant circumstances, I felt God calling me to take a break. So I resigned my position as pastor and gave up my pastoral credentials. I began to attend Grace United Church of Christ, an open and loving congregation, and became a member on October 14, 2001.

Deb:

In the years before I came out to my parents, while I was searching for acceptance, I was introduced to the bar scene and found friends there. I found people who were like me. I was not alone. However, there was still something missing. There was emptiness in my life. It was during this part of my journey that I found the Metropolitan Community Church (MCC). I felt at home. I found new friends. I learned that it was okay to be a Christian and a lesbian. In the years since I found MCC, I have been able to incorporate some of my Anabaptist heritage with my newfound beliefs that God loves and accepts all God's children.

As Christen has already said, we met at MCC. Since she was applying to be our pastor, she was obviously on her best behavior! I was immediately drawn to her, and when she sang, I knew she was the one. When she accepted the position as pastor, she moved to Lancaster, Pennsylvania, from Lancaster, California. If she had not been chosen to pastor our church, I think I would be living in California instead of Pennsylvania.

For a little more than four years, I was a pastor's spouse with all the unique joys and stresses that go along with the territory. After some very trying circumstances, Christen decided to resign as our pastor in May of 2000. During that time of transition, many of our friendships were tested. Some survived and some did not. It was very stressful on our relationship also. Christen was unemployed for a while. She had to deal with all the emotions that accompanied resigning a pastorate. Time and prayers have healed many of the wounds, and Christen now works for a local printing company.

Christen:

Like many couples, we have our ups and downs, but through it all God is with us. Our God is the core of our existence and the creator of miracles in our lives. On November 5, 2000, I had a heart attack. There had been a blood clot in an artery, which caused major damage to my right ventricle. I woke up in the Intensive Care Unit at the hospital, not quite sure of what was happening. While I was in the Catheterization Laboratory having a stent placed in the blocked artery, friends and family began showing up at the hospital. There were at least twenty-five people in the waiting room. A prayer chain was started. People changed their schedules so they could sit with me while I lay in my bed. Friends even sat with me at nighttime during the first week. Deb was with me every single day. I was in the ICU for seventeen days and spent an additional three days in the Cardiac Unit before being discharged two days after Thanksgiving.

The following February I had a setback and went back to the hospital. I had congestive heart failure. I was retaining fluids and swelled up like a balloon. My doctor believed that I might need a heart transplant. It was frightening news for both Deb and me. I was transferred to Hershey Medical Center, where I underwent dozens of tests to see if I was a candidate for a heart transplant.

Miracles do happen! I didn't need a transplant! The new drugs that they tried at Hershey kick-started my heart into healing. God is awesome! It has taken almost a year for me to heal. My life is back to normal – except that I still take about nine pills every day. I believe in prayer and know from personal experience that prayer does work.

My life is a miracle. It has been a difficult time, but with prayer and the support of family and friends we have made it through. There isn't a day when I do not thank God for being with me and for bringing Deb into my life.

Deb:

Christen's major, life-threatening heart attack was the most frightening experience in my life. I stood by helplessly while the paramedics and doctors fought to save her life. In the hospital, they immediately installed a stent to open the blocked artery, but her heart had been severely damaged. On day one, she was given only a ten percent chance of survival. She spent a total of seventeen days in the ICU. With each passing day, her condition improved a little bit, far exceeding the expectations of her doctors. After twenty days in the hospital, she was allowed to come home. She spent three long months struggling with illness and depression.

When she was hospitalized again in February, it was frightening to be told that she might need a heart transplant. At Hershey Medical Center we were assured that they would do everything in their power to avoid the need for a heart transplant. Fortunately, they were successful. They fine-tuned her medications and changed her life.

Throughout this experience, we were blessed to have family and friends who stood by us on a continuous basis. They gave me some of their strength so that I could pass along my strength to Christen. Through the miracle of the Internet, we were able to ask people all over the world to pray for Christen's healing. She is living proof that prayer changes things.

Christen and Deb:

Our daily life is uniquely our own. Deb is self-employed and works days and evenings. Christen works the third shift at a printing company. We have adjusted our lives to this schedule to accommodate time together, time with family, friends, and household chores. Our family situations are also rather unique. Both of Christen's parents have passed away. Except for a sister, who lives in the same city as we do, her family is scattered all over the United States. Distance keeps them from being very connected. Parts of Deb's family are also not very connected. Because of divorces and remarriages, there is separation and tension between some family members. We are not allowed to see two of Deb's nephews because we are a lesbian couple. This gives us great sorrow, and we hope that one day a miracle will cause this situation to change.

Deb's mom is always there for us and is a strong supporter of our relationship. She is truly a mother to both of us. We daily thank God for being in our lives and for the miracles God has performed in not only bringing us together, but also in keeping us together.

Christen Chew has lived in Lancaster, Pennsylvania, for the last six years. She served as pastor of Vision of Hope Metropolitan Community Church in Mountville, Pennsylvania, for four and one-half years. Presently, she is employed by a local printing company as a bindery operator. In her free time she collects WNBA (Women's National Basketball Association) cards and watches as many women's basketball games as she can. Christen also loves to sing and play her guitar and is learning to play the piano. She and her partner, Deb, have been together for six years.

Deborah Becker has lived in Lancaster County, Pennsylvania, all of her life. She spent sixteen years working for a local tourist attraction in retail marketing and is currently self-employed, creating one-of-a-kind crafts and furniture and cleaning professional offices. She loves gardening and has transformed her backyard into a productive vegetable garden. Deb also enjoys running, walking, and just about any activity that takes her outdoors. She and Christen spend as much time as possible with their two godchildren, and they enjoy spending time with and entertaining friends.

~ *eighteen* ~

The Seasons of Our Love

Jo A. Longenecker and Laurinda Beckstead

Those who know us well are aware that we have long been warriors against stereotype packaging of people in all walks of life. It is imperative that one be able to identify the human reflection of one's self in another. Without this vantage point, projected faceless, nameless, stereotyped images form vestibules for hatred and dissociation. Identification of *them* intrinsically requires delineation along contrasting features. The whole process starts to crumble if similarities are brought into focus. Those qualities we hold most sacred and touch us at our innermost souls are the essentials that draw us together as human. To view within the eyes of another a gentle all embracing love, sweet simple joy, heart wrenching sorrow, and the tattered remnants of dreams is to discover another's wholeness as an individual.

We have long been concerned that the invisibility of committed same sex couples has contributed to the ability to project the impression that we do not exist. This, in turn, contributes to an arsenal aimed to project GLBT folks as nonhuman, immoral, and *not like us*. We acknowledge that we have contributed to this process in the past by seeking and benefiting from our anonymity. Even warriors require a growth period wrapped, at least, in a sense of security to nurture inner strength and maturity. Our journey through many varied life experiences has aggressively chiseled, firmly molded, and gently polished our individual concepts of self as well as our unity as a couple.

Roberta Showalter Kreider shares our concern that stereotyped GLBT images predominate the landscape and our sense of need to provide the world with an intimate glance into the lives of committed same-sex couples in order to facilitate fracture of these projections. We have been active in supporting her vision to compile and edit a selection of life stories. Requested to include our own story, we have consented.

The fabric of our lives and love, fourteen years in the weaving, is a pattern breathtaking as it is inscrutable: one with all colors and textures, but ultimately for all seasons.

We each had visions of entering into a lifetime relationship with someone – of the opposite gender, that is. Then, our paths crossed one dreary November day in 1986 while Jo was interviewing at the family practice residency program Lauri was already enrolled in. The following summer, we quickly became good friends, Lauri in her second year of residency and Jo in her first.

One of the enduring mysteries of life is how mutual attraction can surmount the most daunting of obstacles. With our minds firmly set on heterosexual paths to happiness, we met with disbelief the message of our hearts: we were in love. What to do with such a turn of events? Convention never held much sway with Lauri, and thus, she did what she does best: she followed her heart. Jo, on the other hand, began an arduous battle through a maze of internal and external constructs in an attempt to have *reason* prevail. But love, being stronger than reason, is here to tell the rest of the story.

A dream come true, Lauri opened an office in a semi-rural area in need of medical care. She flew *solo* the first year, then was joined by Jo. It was a good match. We discovered that working together complemented living together. It allowed integration of both our personal and professional lives. There are moments when business and medicine seem diametrically opposed. When applying harsh realities to lofty ideals becomes a poignant proposition, our shared values and priorities facilitate navigation of these obstacles.

One of the unique benefits of family practice is the opportunity to know people within their multigenerational context and over the course of time. It is humbling to realize the number of people who granted us such an intimate place in their lives. This aspect of family medicine has sustained and enriched us.

Over the years we received mailings at our office with numerous permutations of our names. Our favorite was *Longstead*, which has become our informalized mutual name.

What we did not anticipate was an inexorable decline in Lauri's health necessitating her retirement three years ago. For years, she has persevered with the unpredictability of lupus, an autoimmune disease with many faces, most of them ominous. The most recent and least negotiable battle line has been her brain. The learning curve for us has been bittersweet. We are facing issues typically ascribed to later life. Undoubtedly, of her numerous life challenges, this certainly eclipses them all.

Lauri's religious background is one of rich diversity: her relatives were primarily Episcopalian or Mormon. In youth she became familiar with the Mennonite tradition and as an adult has found expression in the Catholic faith. Throughout her life though, she has lived a faith not limited to any one organized institutional dogma. Her spiritual life is firmly grounded in a personal relationship with the Lord and his/her creation.

In contrast, Jo is a descendant of multigenerational Mennonites, grew up in a Mennonite church and attended a Mennonite high school and college. Following years of active participation in the life of the church, there came a period of intense scrutiny and rancorous contention regarding homosexuality.

This larger than life specter snatched the focus of many a congregation away from the crux of its faith and redirected it towards a crusade to restore homogeneity. Even the churches of

Jo's childhood and most recent belonging were caught up in the fray. In the fallout, people emerged from unlikely places. God spoke in new voices. Although not currently official members of a church, we have found our faith nurtured through prayer, music, reading, meditation, friends, and a variety of places of worship. This otherwise fatal course of events ironically opened new doors of insight and deepened our life spirit.

We have each been blessed with wonderful families (dysfunctional elements not withstanding). Each wended their own journey to their current place of support and acceptance of our love. With varied degrees of angst and ease, they have mirrored many of our own steps. They have fashioned breaks in the wall of silence that so insidiously forms around GLBT individuals and their kin. Lost is the innocence that the church, let alone the world, is safe and welcoming to all. In a sense, they have come to shoulder this blessing and burden with us.

Lauri's maternal expressions began in adolescence with her sister, sixteen years her junior, and continued in her relationships with many pediatric patients. Due to the perils intrinsic to her health and requisite medications, childbearing was not an option. Jo's maternal instincts have found outlet at work and home. Our bevy of animals currently numbers three horses, two dogs, and a cat. They range in age from five to seventeen years. Their unerring love and affection has been a great source of joy and satisfaction.

Also rewarding are the unfolding lives of our nephews. Each, in his own precious way, affirms us as individuals and as a couple and inspires us with hope for the coming generations.

We recognize the substantial lack of the societal sanction of marriage as well as frank hostility toward the sustenance of a long-term committed relationship. This calls for creative alternatives. One such was a tenth anniversary weekend celebration we had with family and friends. Other highlights include retreats sponsored by Connecting Families[1] and BMC[2]. As friends, peers, and family relate to us as a *couple*, and in a manner universal in application, they nurture the foundation which sustains us. This growing tide of conventional confirmation sweeps us from the eddies of isolation into the enriching waters of community.

Honesty coupled with trust is the *sine qua non* of this relationship. Anything less and things begin to unravel, as our periodically frayed edges attest to. To be patient with one another's seasons of the soul, to nurture each other's dreams, to celebrate our differences, to bask in each other's gifts, this is the stuff that love is made of.

Stronger than our foibles is God in us beckoning we enter this sacred space called home. Home, where joy and heartache meet, where the mundane merges with the sublime. It is here that we can flourish in each other's spheres and be the women God's grace and love fashioned us to be.

We have chosen to share with you, as we did with our family and friends during our tenth anniversary celebration, our journey as it is depicted through selections from our personal journals. May it provide a window into our world.

Where we have been
    is indeed important,
        for it forms a part of where
        and who we are.

---

[1] A group of Brethren and Mennonites who are committed to providing mutual support for families with gay or lesbian members. For more information or to receive the CF newsletter, contact Ruth Conrad Liechty, 1568 Redbud Court, Goshen, IN 46526; e-mail: rliechty@juno.com.

[2] Brethren/ Mennonite Council for Lesbian and Gay Concerns, PO Box 6300, Minneapolis, MN 55406-0300. Phone: (612) 722-6906. Fax: (612) 343-2061 E-mail: BMCouncil@aol.com   Web:www.webcom.com/bmc/

Yet let it not cast shadow
  on what we may become.

For in the potential obtained,
  the growth achieved,
    lives the hope
      of tomorrow.

LRB

Presented to me with caring hands and tear-filled eyes, hand written on a single piece of paper, folded into a small square and carefully placed in a simple box. A gift like no other for a daughter to receive, and carry with her always in her heart and soul:

My Most Darling Lauri –

Seventeen years ago an Angel came to me on silver wings and gave me the most precious gift – you. You have always been very special to me, as I watched you as an infant, grow to a tiny child, to a little girl, to a young lady – and always you have been most Precious – I've often thought that you are indeed an angel.

During these seventeen years we have had some special times and grown to share a very deep and everlasting love. You have brought many a tear to the old man's eye – but never one that didn't start in my heart. I am so very proud of you – your beauty, your personality, your caring and love for others.

This note is not very fancy, but then neither am I. I just felt that I must express to you my feelings – as you know, sometimes I can't find the right words to let my heart express what is really inside. Perhaps this silver bird can remind you always of the freedom you have, with outstretched wings, to do as you like and become your own person. May the silver remind you of the value of your own person and help you bring Peace to your soul. For no matter how far from me your silver wings may take you, no matter how pure and elegant you become, no matter what may happen in the future, you will always be my special Angel. I love you with all my heart and all my life. *Dad*

Ten years ago I would have never believed a day like today would come to pass – ten years ago there were a lot of dreams I didn't dream.

That was until I met this incredible life force called Lauri. Back in the fall of 1986, I was on a week-long tour interviewing at potential residency programs, including one located in a rural town in West Virginia. Heretofore, I knew next to nothing about West Virginia except that the family practice residency program there looked good on paper and seemed like the kind of place I was looking for. After a lengthy day of interviews and splashing through puddles under a bleak sky, I bundled up and was headed out the door when this woman met me on the door-step and introduced herself. We talked for a while and then it was off into the months of weighing my options and waiting for that all important envelope on match day. I compared pros and cons of programs based on objective findings. But in the end what tipped the scale was the experience I had the night before my interview. The moon was bright, and the closer I got, the stronger this invisible tug became – a silent beckoning.

Upon crossing the threshold of residency the following summer, our paths converged. Thus began a friendship that was destined to change my life forever. I eventually learned the significance of that chance meeting on that rainy day. The day Lauri fell in love.   JAL

Bravely I reached out, sharing myself thru written word.

I glanced about me today
and the horizon
seemed to have broadened...
the sun a bit warmer,
and the cool breeze
more gentle.
Shadows have faded
and there is new growth
in gardens once shielded
with walls.

I tore not   them down
and yet,   in their absence
there is a fullness
which calls not
for need of protection.   LRB

A special piece not signed due to fear,
but forever the writer's name
is sealed in my heart:

And then I looked in your eyes
and saw a love
that must come from the depths
of a heart which has known
many a pain wracked night,
and wept silently in the day;
which bears the scars of untold wounds
and the mends that only time
and God can fashion.

Those eyes caught mine
   and beckoned
      I enter a place
         where sadness and hope,
           despair and joy,
              longing and contentment mingle;

But most of all
   I felt gently surrounded
      by a warmth, a peace, a trust –
         that inexplicable something
         called love.

It stretched far beyond
   logic and words
      and fantasy and rules –
   for it comes from a Presence
      beyond and within you and me,

I count it a rare privilege,
   by no means deserved,
      but gratefully received,
   to reach across these boundaries
      that most often confine us –
         and meet those eyes.

They belong to a precious wounded healed.   JAL

The irony of my life has been:
   that which has brought my life its greatest meaning,
     has also brought the greatest pain.

Meaning and fulfillment for me
    comes through other people,
        in loving and giving

Being there when someone needs you,
    to share the joys and sorrows,
        big and small;

Bringing joy,
    a smile that comes from deep inside
        because they know how very much you care;

Having a relationship without walls or pretenses,
    only freedom and comfort
        with being yourself with each other;

Doing little special things   just because.

Joy is when the greatest moment of the day
    is seeing the sparkle of love in someone's gentle gaze.

I have no doubt that life's greatest meaning
    is found in loving,   pure simple love.

I've been there
    and there's nothing   to which it can compare.

Except,
    for the pain and mental anguish
        that burns deep inside,
            tearing you apart

when those same eyes reflect fear,
confusion, and rejection...
because you love.   LRB

Ah, Life is so inscrutable at times – like now, when I am deeply aware of how much you have come to affect me – you have left very noticeable traces on my heart. Your touch unleashes a resonance that ripples from outside in, and back again.

I would have never dreamed that I would fall in love with you. I am caught off guard – with a myriad of feelings washing through me – disbelief, excitement, guilt, longing, and joy.

Somehow, you've found the keys to unlock my doors – you've walked thru those walls – was there a window you caught a glimpse of me through?

Perhaps you have already discovered – there is no small portion of passion and love in this frame. It is very deep and very real and very enduring.

I sensed your reaching out. I reached back, and oh! what a spark. The fire that's there can be both destructive and purifying; tormenting and healing.

It is such a precious burden, this love that I find for you in my heart – for I would like to lavish you with the wealth of emotion that is there – but I fear the repercussions for you and those you already love.

I do not seek to undermine your commitments or challenge your loyalties – they are indeed very sacred, and deserve to be preserved at all costs.

But you must know: it is not for lack of love that we define our boundaries − you are and will always be very significant in my life − and that means more than words can ever say.

I love you,   *Jo*

The past decade has seen growth within, often in fits and starts sometimes barely discernible. There were times I nearly lost myself in the poignant struggle to be the person I thought I must be. But for the Grace of God, this did not come to pass. I began to respect my inner voice, to grant allowance for mistakes. To stop judging my emotions − particularly negative ones. To become honest with myself, to foster tolerance, to love the body mind and soul I have been entrusted with.   JAL

Change often requires change.

    Times come in life when one must cast off part of oneself
        in order to allow for new growth.

Only through death is life reborn.
    Spring has come again to brighten the world;
        bringing forth new beginnings, new joy and beauty.
A time of growth and renewal.
    Yet, Spring must always be preceded by Winter,
        and it by Autumn.
It is the way of the seasons,
        the way of the world.
    Each a series of gradual change;
        a cycle of life −
            precious and beautiful.

Spring has come.
     It is within me and surrounds me.
But first winter came.
     It was cold and bitter; numbness prevailed.
Then the snows began to melt;
     feelings gained life   and tears flowed.

No matter how cold or deeply hidden the ice of winter;
    once it rises to the surface,
      the sun warms it.
  The waters that thus flow bring the gift of life and renewal to
     all those awaiting spring.
Await we must,
     for the coming of spring is an exercise in faith.
  Believing in the beauty of a flower
     when it is but a seed.

Once here,
    spring is hope given meaning today.
    Spring has come,
     it is within me and surrounds me.
I am again whole.
    My world is again bright and wonderful.

I thank you.
    I thank you for believing in the seed planted long ago.
I thank you for the warmth of your love,
     that like the sun warmed my soul.
    Least not,
      I thank you for waiting.

         Spring has come.
       Hope is given new meaning today.   LRB

Jo A. Longenecker, MD, is the eldest of four children. She was raised in the Lancaster County heartland of Pennsylvania and spent her formative years in Virginia and Washington, DC, before finding her calling in West Virginia as a family practitioner. She pursues a daily balance of priorities and takes great pleasure in the cycle of the seasons.

Laurinda R. Beckstead, MD, was born in the shadows of the Wasatch mountain range in Utah and nurtured by the rich fields and woodlands of southeastern Pennsylvania. She now draws strength and wisdom from the ancient Appalachian mountains of West Virginia. Retired from her medical practice, Lauri continues to embrace the beauty and challenge of each new day on the Longstead Farm.

God will speak to and through whomever God will, without our permission. But for Christians whose primary allegiance is to Jesus of Nazareth, Jesus is the lens through whom we interpret all biblical content.

~ Titus Bender
Welcome to Dialogue Series, #1

~ *nineteen* ~

The Rest of Our Life Was but Three Years

Nadine R. Anderson with Janet Therese Markee
(Janet passed away on May 26, 2001)

On June 27, 1998, we had a joyous gathering of family and friends as Janet Therese Markee and I exchanged vows to love and cherish one another till death do us part. On May 30, 2001, we had another gathering, more somber, of family and friends as we gathered to celebrate Jan's life and lay her to rest. She fought very hard to live, but she finally ran out of the energy and ability to do so.

Looking back, I see that from our beginning Jan was narrowing her focus, restricting her attention to the central aspects of her life: family and long-time friends. She did not have the energy to make many new friends, so we spent her energy living within a small circle of family and friends.

During the three years and three months we lived together Jan was in the hospital twice a year – for heart problems, for respiratory problems, then for breast cancer, and finally for respiratory problems that came from a reoccurrence of the lung cancer that first appeared in 1996. She also suffered from many psychiatric problems, but she rarely let her many difficulties get her down. Recently her former husband of twenty-five years told me that she was given a one-year life expectancy prediction in 1996, so she had to fight very hard to live this long. When her beloved sister passed away of lung cancer at the end of December 2000, Jan's ability to continue to fight for life was compromised.

Jan and I became part of each other's lives rather late in her life. Jan came to a meeting I organized of Lehigh Valley Lesbians at the Unitarian Church in Bethlehem, Pennsylvania. She arrived and saw the LVL sign with an arrow pointing up the steps. She struggled slowly up the first short flight, to see another sign up – and another! She continued to struggle and finally made it to the third floor meeting room. That was when I began to learn how much disabled people are excluded by simple decisions we make with no thought, such as having the meeting on the third floor because the best meeting room was there. LVL moved down after that.

Jan supported what she believed in. That evening some folks from PA-GALA, the group working for rights for lesbians and gays, asked those present for a donation to support the upcoming voter guide. Jan gave a generous amount and said to list her as "Jan is back!" Yes, she was back from the fear of death and back into the community.

We were getting to know each other during the summer of 1997 – and it was as if a whirlwind with a bird on its shoulder had entered my life. Jan was always very intense and was interested in so many, many things. And she took her cockatiel, Honey, everywhere she went.

Music was a central passion for Jan. In high school and college she generally had her guitar with her and would play and sing at any excuse. With her mother and sister, she was a part of the Long Island Singers Society, and they sang in many concerts together. When I knew her, she always had music playing. This was okay; I grew up with constant music. Mom was as apt to be singing as talking to us. However, Jan took it a bit farther; she wanted music playing all night long. No more could I wake up to my music alarm and know if I heard no music, it was okay to go back to sleep. But I loved most of her music – birds and thunderstorms as well as everything ever recorded by such marvelous folk singers as Joan Baez.

Jan and I attended church together at Metropolitan Community Church of the Lehigh Valley. Though I was very involved in the life of my Lutheran congregation, I had been attending

MCC as a great way to be involved regularly in the lesbian and gay community. The bar scene was not for me, and the sports route of involvement in the community is rather limited.

I had gone through a typical adolescent rebellion against the religion that was a part of my daily life as I grew up, but the values of that Christian upbringing – supporting justice and the inherent worth of all people – stayed with me. During the early '80s, I got involved in the Equal Rights Amendment (ERA) campaign while living in Louisiana and became state chair of that campaign for the Louisiana National Organization for Women. I was organizing public meetings to convey information about and garner support for the ERA.

Since meetings were opened and closed with prayer, and I was not about to lead prayer in public when it was not a part of my private life, I began to seek out all the women in religious positions who would lead the prayers. One such effort brought me back to the church and to extensive reading of the Bible and of feminist theology.

At the same time, I was meeting a lot of lesbians through one of the organizations I was involved with and learning of their pain at society's rejection of them. I worked through both issues at the same time and came to realize that the only limits God has are those we impose. The God of my upbringing is all-inclusive, provides support for us when we have troubles, and loves all people just as we are created.

There were definitely limits on acceptable behavior, but those were conveyed more in examples of good behavior and through youth groups to support good behavior than with judgmental sermons. Sex was definitely one of the things that had to wait for adulthood and marriage, but I don't recall ever hearing about homosexuality in adolescence. Since it precluded traditional marriage, I would have known it was wrong.

A short time after the ERA campaign, I was reevaluating my life and trying to figure out why I had achieved all my major life goals except one. I had completed a Ph.D. and had a job that I loved, I had a great network of friends and was involved in many community activities, but I had never married and had the family I had expected. *Why was that?* I realized that the picture of a family in my head included me with children, but the spouse was always very vague or not in the picture. I also realized that there were many women with whom I was very close, but that there were very few men with whom I was close. Though I had dated men, I found those relationships a lot of work for very little return. Friendships with women also took effort, but that was easy effort and the friendships were very rewarding.

While I had been physically attracted to women, I simply interpreted it as strong friendship. But when I did respond to a male's attraction, the chemistry was weak and the relationship never developed into something I wanted for the rest of my life. On the other hand, I had many women friends that I hoped to know for my whole life. I do think God used the ERA campaign to bring me back to the organized church and validate my attraction to other women. Though my family still does not really approve of a lesbian or gay life, they have stayed true to the inclusive values of our understanding of Christianity and have always been loving and supportive of me.

Jan grew up in the Roman Catholic Church, but felt at odds with her church. She felt they rejected who she was, so she did not feel welcome there. She reported that for several months as a teen she had gone daily to Mass to pray for God to change her. Though she did not feel changed, she followed the prescribed route of marriage and having a child, but never felt that was her real self.

After twenty-five years, she was unable to continue to suppress her inner self and she left her husband. They remained friends and cooperated in raising their teenaged son, Kieran. A couple of years later, Jan was diagnosed with lung cancer and in late 1996 moved to Pennsylvania to be with her sister. As Jan put it, her sister brought her home to die. But Jan was still into living. She got her own apartment and set out to become acquainted with the community. Luckily for me, Jan walked up those three flights of stairs to attend the meeting of the LVL that evening in 1997.

As we grew closer that summer, life took on a sparkle and brighter hues. I had begun to be bored a lot of the time, but with Jan life was again fascinating. I discovered that she was an extremely intense woman. She loved all of nature and was passionate about birds. We would be driving along – I would be hearing the traffic, the radio, the sound of the engine, typical driving sounds – and Jan would say, "Listen!" I would think, "To what?" But inevitably, along came the birds she had heard. She never failed to pause to listen to the birds flying overhead before anyone else was aware of them and to exclaim joyfully over the birds that swept by.

Jan would also get very upset over what she saw as an injustice or something that was very unfair. She lived in the present, but sometimes her present reached back decades. She would intensely decry an injustice and, given the level of emotion, it seemed that the problem must have just happened. As I listened more closely, it would become obvious that she was exclaiming over something that went awry twenty years ago.

That was Jan – injustice, unfairness, and misfortune that came to her attention never failed to move her no matter how long ago it had occurred. When she could, she would right the wrong. For example, when she found out a friend who sang beautifully was losing his hearing, she became upset. If he could not hear, he could not sing, so she bought him hearing aids.

By December of 1997, we knew we were in love and started looking for a one-story ranch house to buy together. I would go check them out, then take Jan to see ones that I thought were possibilities – it is amazing how many levels there are in some ranch houses! I saw one that was very pretty, but I didn't think we would buy as it had a swimming pool, and Jan did not want that work. When Jan saw it, she was enchanted by the airiness and later by how well the owners had fixed up this forty-year-old house. We bought it!

Jan was always insistent that we do things now – she, the eternal pessimist, was never sure she would live out the year. I, the eternal optimist, knew she would live a long, long time, but usually went along with her requests if I could. And that explains why I ended up frantically packing and arranging to move at the end of February – the start of the busiest time of year for a school psychologist.

After moving into our house, we began to plan our Holy Union ceremony. Jan wanted it in April, but I insisted on the summer, and we planned it for June 27, 1998. Jan and I both had Christian values and felt that it was most appropriate to have our relationship blessed and legitimatized before God, our families, and our friends. Though I was on the council of my Lutheran congregation, I was not prepared to fight that battle there. Since we both belonged to the Metropolitan Community Church, we had our Holy Union there. However, we did have my Lutheran minister participate in the service.

Our families were supportive. Jan's sister was her attendant; my older sister played the piano as I had always assumed one of my sisters would do, and another of my sisters and Jan's father read the welcome-to-the-family statements we substituted for the give-this-woman-away statement. Our sisters sang solos and a duet.

Jan had to use the lift chair to get to and from the sanctuary on the second floor of the church, so we had the guests sing three hymns at the end to give us plenty of time to get down the stairs before they came down. It was a joyous day as we celebrated our love before our family and friends.

Our life together was mostly marvelous, never predictable, and always full of love. We were not able to take a honeymoon right after our Holy Union, but we did so in two parts that summer. In July we went over to Long Island where Jan showed me where she grew up, and in August we traveled up to Provincetown, Massachusetts.

Accessibility has clearly not hit that very picturesque little town on the seashore; even some of the hotels seemed surprised to be asked about accessibility and had steps to be negotiated. After calling several places, we found one picturesque old Victorian guesthouse, The Tucker Inn, which had a room on the ground floor, with only one extra-high step to negotiate to enter the house. We stayed there for four marvelous days. We explored Provincetown by car and with Jan in her wheelchair – you can get a wheelchair along some of the sidewalks there.

The first couple of years we were together, Jan was still driving on her own, and she would often call, saying something like, "Where am I? There are a lot of trees and a sign that says Bangor; how do I get home?" So we would talk until finally I would recognize something and either direct her home or go find her and guide her home. One time she ended up by a cornfield and ballpark at an intersection with Easton Road that I did not recognize, so I called the police – it was a different Easton Road. They told me where it was and how to get there; I went – but no Jan. I called home; Mom was visiting and answered the phone, but Jan had not arrived. With nothing else to do, I headed home – to find Jan sitting in the driveway in her new yellow bug. Seems an officer had come by and guided her out to someplace that she recognized. She barely beat me home.

Christmas of 1998, we went to Yuma, Arizona, to spend the holiday with my family. It was very good to have warmth in December! It was even better to have Jan with me as we visited my family and celebrated Christmas. Jan decided she didn't like drifting sand for Christmas any more than drifting snow. Most other holidays we spent with her sister's family in Pennsylvania.

Flying did not work out well for Jan. After we returned, she had increased respiratory problems, which she blamed on the poor air in the airplanes. Shortly after that, she needed oxygen constantly. She was already using a wheelchair for traveling any distance, such as in a shopping mall or at church.

The end of 1999, we wanted to go to the First Night millennium celebration in Bethlehem. They have music and other performances in a couple of dozen places, with bus transportation between them, and no alcohol. It was very cold, well below freezing, and Jan could not be out in that weather. We decided to get a suite in South Bethlehem, where we could watch all the millennium celebrations on TV and watch the local fireworks out the window.

It was an especially significant celebration for Jan, as she had been told by most of her physicians in 1996 that she would not see the new millennium. She outlasted several such predictions. I gave her a Wedgwood millennium clock that Christmas, which happened to be set for one minute after midnight when it arrived. She would not allow me to start it – she took the time on it as a trophy for beating those many predictions.

The last year or two, when Jan was not comfortable driving herself, we would go out for an hour or two after I got home from work. I liked it best when we just drove up to a high spot with a view or to a place by the river and chatted while we enjoyed the scene. Jan also liked to wander through a mall, looking for the many things she could not do without. She loved gadgets and CDs and could buy them faster than we could find a place for them.

Many an evening was spent together at home, listening to Jan's marvelous CD collection or watching TV or a video. Those were the best times, when we were together sharing time, listening to the birds, talking, enjoying being together. And Jan had a great capacity to enjoy life. She was so positive about enjoying the marvelous world God gave us and loved being with family and close friends.

Jan had long felt a conflict about wanting to reunite with her church yet feeling rejected by Roman Catholic theology and policy. In the beginning of May of 2001, a week after she came home from the hospital with the diagnosis of terminal lung cancer, she called her parish of the Roman Catholic Church. She spoke with the Monsignor, and he agreed to come see her. He anointed her with oil and said a blessing as well as prayers.

Two weeks later, after she was gone, I called to ask about last rites. The Monsignor said the blessing he had performed provided that. It had not occurred to me that she was asking for last rites, but thanks to the Monsignor, who came when she asked, Jan did feel somewhat reconciled with the Church that was so much a part of her.

The last Thursday evening in May, I had a work event to attend and had arranged for two friends, Judy and Louise, to stay with Jan. She announced to them, "I have a plan!" Off they went to get a Rita's Italian Ice. Since she was diabetic with her blood sugar barely under control, I wouldn't stop and get one for her as often as she wanted. As they were eating the ices, she said, "I have another plan!" Off they went to the mall where she bought my birthday gift. She was very tired after arriving home that evening and went to bed almost immediately.

She was up early to spend an hour with me as I prepared to go to work Friday morning. That evening she was very tired and went to bed early. She seemed to sleep okay and, as usual, slept in Saturday morning. But as the day passed, she did not wake up. She was still sleeping when I checked on her a bit before 5 p.m., but when I came back into the room just after five, she was not breathing. Judy and Louise came over in record time and helped me get through the immediate shock. We all agreed Jan looked more relaxed and peaceful than she had in a very long time.

All my communities gathered to provide support. Jan's and my family came from many parts of the country. Friends from work and from the local community and those who had cared for Jan at the end joined us at the service to bid Jan good-by. A combined choir from my Lutheran church and from MCC sang

"The Twenty-Third Psalm." A good friend sang "The Lord's Prayer," using the nonsexist language we preferred.

Jan's son Kieran was very important to her, and he visited frequently. She was pleased when he became engaged to a wonderful young woman. They came together to the service and Kieran recounted several stories of his childhood that showed the closeness of their extended family. He ended his tribute to his mother as follows:

> There is one more story that seems fitting. My mom had always had problems with her breathing. Even as a kid, she had asthma. When she and her younger sister, my Aunt Allison, would horseplay, eventually my mom would give up and play dead, laying as still as possible. My aunt would always get freaked out and run away crying. It was not until years later she went up to my mom and yelled at her for doing something so mean. My mom, more than puzzled, asked what had caused this to come up so many years later. My aunt answered, rather embarrassedly, that she had finally figured out that dead people don't wheeze.

> It brings me much sadness to say this, but I listened downstairs for a bit at my mother's side and there is no wheezing. This time it is for real. One thing is for certain though and that is I will love my mom forever... and yes, I do mean "forever."

Now I come home to an empty house – but it is never really empty, for it is still filled with Jan's spirit reflected in so many of her things that remind me of her indomitable spirit. As I sorted out the things we accumulated, I found one of her tee shirts that says, "Be sure the song you came to sing does not remain unsung." Jan lived by that idea as long as she could deal with the pain and her medical problems. As much as I miss her, she looked so peaceful after she was gone. When I am feeling lonely, I have but to open the door and listen to the birds outside, singing their hearts out, and know it is another song from Jan.

Jan left us Memorial Day weekend of 2001. When those of us who loved Jan celebrate Memorial Day in the future, we will take a moment to listen to the birds and think of her. The greatest gift Jan gave me was a reminder to slow down, listen to the birds, and enjoy the beauty of God's earth. She taught me to rearrange my priorities. When those of us who loved Jan see the birds flying overhead or hear them chirping in the back yard or hear music playing in the midst of the busyness of life, we will think of Jan and follow her lead. She would be saying, "Listen!" And we'll try to do what she did – to take the time – all the time – every day – to enjoy this world and all the wonderful things God created.

Nadine R. Anderson grew up in the far northwestern corner of California, but now lives in the Pennsylvania home she shared with Jan. Nadine received her B.A. from California State University at Hayward in 1966 and her Ph.D. in social psychology from the University of Washington in 1972. She taught at the university level for sixteen years, including three years with University of Maryland on U.S. military bases in Europe and four years at Bermuda College. Nadine gave up the scholarly life to become a clinical psychologist, earning a respecialization in Clinical and School Psychology at Widener University in Chester, Pennsylvania. She worked for three years in an inpatient child and adolescent psychiatric unit and has been a school psychologist since then. She has often been involved in community activism to make a better world.

Janet Therese Markee grew up on Long Island, New York, then spent twenty-five years in California near San Jose before returning east to Pennsylvania where she and Nadine met and shared life together until the end of Jan's life. She attended Farmingdale Agricultural College and Suffolk Community College on Long Island, then left school to be married. She later took paralegal studies at DeAnza College in Cupertino, California. She also took some courses there with her son when he was taking advanced placement courses as a high school student. Her medical conditions precluded holding a job after she was married. Music and birds always enriched her life.

Just before Christmas of 2001, Nadine, Jan's son Kieran and his fiancée Jen, and Jan's former husband Fred and his wife Cathy took Jan's ashes to the redwood groves that she had endowed in her lifetime in Big Basin, California. As Fred suggested, she is in a better place now.

~ twenty ~

Joined Together by the Grace of God

Earl D. Ball with Tim*

Reaching down into his pocket, he pulled up a handful of coins. I was standing next to the juke box that night when he deliberately dropped them onto the dance club floor. Coins rolled everywhere. Tim just had to get my attention somehow!

This was the fall of 1976 in a small western New Jersey town. I had just ended an unfulfilling relationship and was certainly not looking for a date. In fact, my friends had to coax me out of the parsonage and my self-imposed exile that evening. I was feeling hurt, vulnerable, and in no mood to dance. I needed time to grieve. I also needed time to reflect and pray that God would heal my brokenness and someday lead me into a truly loving relationship built on mutual respect. I needed time – and space.

Emotionally numb as I stood next to the juke box, I was oblivious to Tim's change hitting the floor, let alone my friends crawling around on their hands and knees to come to his aid. Despite my fog, I had noticed Tim out of the corner of my eye as he walked in the door earlier that evening. I even commented to my friends on his striking appearance – the proverbial tall, dark, and handsome man, who happened to also be my age at the time – twenty-nine. Unfortunately, this moment of acknowledgment was short-lived, as my fragile self-esteem led me to dismiss any possibility that I could meet someone as attractive as Tim.

---

* While my partner is out and open, his current position prohibits participation in any for-profit venture or lending his name to such. Hence, he has left the writing of this chapter solely to my discretion.

Later, I learned that Tim had first seen me months earlier in a club in Allentown, Pennsylvania. Watching from a short distance, he offered a prayer to his Creator that we might meet someday and that I would not turn out to be a *turkey*. I was not aware of his interest that particular evening, so we departed separately as strangers.

Fortunately, this time, Tim's friend Tom urged him to approach the juke box and initiate conversation. I quickly learned he was an architect and architectural artist – interests I also shared. We both loved New York City, enjoyed the simple pleasures of walking, dancing, conversation, historic preservation, old movies, and classical music. I found him to be a considerate, intelligent, and creative person with whom I felt immediately comfortable.

When I revealed that I was an ordained minister serving my first pastorate, Tim responded positively. He respected my calling even though he was disenchanted with organized religion at the time. Tim is a very spiritual person, with a deep reverence for life, nature, the arts, and music; we bonded right from the start. To this day, we believe God brought us together that night – the same loving God who created us gay and has blessed and sustained our relationship ever since. Tim and Earl – Earl and Tim. That's the way we believe it was meant to be – that was our Creator's plan for our lives.

I passed Tim's *not a turkey* test. We saw more and more of one another. It wasn't long before I showed up at his apartment door one day, loaded down with groceries. I filled his refrigerator, then cooked our first dinner. After dinner, at the dining table, we started to plan our future together.

On occasion, Tim would visit me in the parsonage a few miles north of Easton. At that time, I was concerned that his visits might arouse the suspicions of parishioners or neighbors. After all, the parsonage was located right in the center of a very small Pennsylvania town. Despite living in a fishbowl, I loved the pastorate and felt respected by my parishioners.

One day, however, an unfounded rumor started that I was having an affair – with a woman! How ironic, I thought. She was simply a friend with whom I shared cultural interests. Besides, I was very much in love with Tim at the time and our relationship was maturing. By revealing my orientation and my relationship with Tim, I could have quickly dispensed with that ridiculous rumor – as well as my pastorate. I felt hurt and angry, as did my woman friend. This certainly was not the type of rumor I would have expected! It all seemed so unfair to me and to her. She chose to discontinue our friendship. The rumor soon faded, but my frustration and hurt remained. I prayed to God for strength and healing.

Sometimes Tim and I would go to a club in New Hope, Pennsylvania, and dance the night away. Other times we would visit New York City, hold hands and stroll through Central Park, the Village, or Chelsea. We enjoyed being together, especially in a place where we could *be ourselves*. Such a simple and natural gesture – holding hands with the one you love. Yet, a gesture many would consider somehow threatening to society or traditional family stability. A gesture some would label *flaunting* unless used by a mixed-gender couple. A gesture which could result in verbal or even physical abuse in most places outside of New York City.

In a time when politicians are falling over one another in a mad rush to deny gay, lesbian, bisexual, and transgender persons rights others take for granted, holding hands with the one you love – especially if that person is of the same affectional orientation – is an important gesture. So far, thank God, doing so is not yet deemed illegal.

As a young gay pastor serving my first rural church, I soon realized I would need to continue living a closeted life if I were to remain in the pastorate. While the denomination into which I was ordained (United Church of Christ) had taken progressive stands at a national level for many years in support of gay and lesbian persons – as well as the ordination of openly gay clergy – in reality most local congregations were far from open and affirming of gay persons and relationships.

I soon felt torn between following my lifelong calling to pastor a congregation and the realization that to do so would mean sacrificing much of who I am and what I have to offer. It would mean staying in the darkness of the closet, allowing others to make false assumptions about me. It would mean expending much emotional and spiritual energy holding that closet door tightly shut for fear of discovery – pretending to be someone I am not – failing to be the whole person my loving God created me to be. Most of all, it would mean pretending to be single when I was very much part of a couple and it would mean denying the very existence of the one person to whom I felt closest – Tim.

I coped as best I could through prayer as well as Scripture. Two passages from Hebrews, in particular, offered me hope and strength: "Do not neglect to show hospitality to strangers, for thereby some have entertained angels unawares,"[1] and, "Jesus also suffered outside the gate in order to sanctify the people through his own blood."[2] This latter passage served to remind me that Jesus was crucified just outside of what was then the center of religious/political power (Jerusalem). He died "outside the gate" for those *on the outside* looking in – those banished to the margins of society. Jesus lived and died for persons such as Tim and me – those excluded from full, open, and honest participation within the centers of religious and secular power. He lived and died for all GLBT persons seeking equal (not special) rights and open participation in church and society.

The former passage from Hebrews reminded me that I was truly a *stranger* in the midst of my parishioners. They really did not know me fully – probably would rather not know the real

---

[1] Hebrews 13:2. Unless otherwise noted, all Scriptural references in this story are from the *RSV Bible*. New York: Thomas Nelson and Sons, N.T., 1946; O.T., 1952.
[2] Hebrews 13:12.

me. I often wondered how *hospitable* and truly *Christ-like* they would be had they known of my relationship with Tim.

Another passage of Scripture that took on new significance for me was the story of Sodom and Gomorrah,[3] a passage which is so often used to bash gay people. I came to understand that both Ezekiel[4] and Jesus[5] recognized the true sin of those places to be their refusal to warmly welcome strangers *from the outside* into their midst. Any possible sexual references in the story, depending upon how one interprets the word "to know," would refer to rape that, in ancient cultures, was a way of humiliating a vanquished enemy – a display of power and domination. As this account states, even Lot offered to expose his daughters to rape!

Certainly this is not what we today understand as the gay/lesbian way of being in which sexual expression arises from the natural attraction or affection of one person for the other. It seemed to me that true sodomites are those who, like the men of Sodom and like many people in our churches, seek to abuse and cast GLBT persons – along with the spiritual gifts they bring – from the church community. The result? Many of our churches are often left spiritually impoverished.

During this time in my first pastorate, I came to understand the degree to which the church historically has always conspired to foster dishonesty in relation to sexual orientation. Play the role, and you will be welcome. Be honest, be yourself, and you are out the door. I found I could no longer accept the "loving the sinner, hating the sin" theology. I could find nothing sinful about the loving relationship Tim and I shared and the many ways in which we expressed that love.

In hindsight, I believe I underestimated the personal sacrifices I had to make in order to follow my calling as a pastor. Perhaps I was in denial of the damage such self-deception

---

[3] Genesis 19:1-11

[4] Ezekiel 16:49-50

[5] Matthew 10:5-15

would do to my self-esteem, integrity, and spirit. I began to feel emotionally and spiritually stifled. I became disenchanted with organized religion, which had been responsible for fostering much of the hatred and misinformation directed against gay people. I came to believe one could be Christian yet not be Christ-like.

Living a closeted life proved more and more to be a difficult tightrope to walk – especially now that I was in a fulfilling relationship with Tim. I grew tired of lying, of pretending, of carefully editing Tim out of my life and conversation. I wanted to be free, as anyone else, to display photos of my *spouse* on my desk and talk openly about vacation plans and important life events we shared without making up fictional stories or feigning an affectional interest in the opposite sex.

I was part of a couple – a reality that was underscored for me each time I would perform a mixed-gender wedding. I knew what love and commitment were all about, yet I appeared *single* to others. I also knew that being gay is not just about sex, any more than being non-gay is just about sex. It was about who I am. It was about who Tim and I were and are as a couple in love.

Eventually, we realized the time had come for a change in our lives. I needed to live more openly and honestly as God had intended for me to live. I needed to live openly as part of a gay couple -- something I knew I could not do as a small town pastor. We both were tired of playing games and wanted to live together where we could be ourselves. New York City seemed to be the obvious place. This was early in 1977.

In New York, Tim worked for an architectural firm, while I found a position at the headquarters of the United Church of Christ. I also used that time to earn another master's degree in pastoral counseling. Those years in Greenwich Village and Chelsea are among our fondest memories. We learned, as most New Yorkers do, how to *toughen up* – to become more assertive and sort out what's important and what's not in life. We found our niche and enjoyed all that Manhattan had to offer. But, most of all, we found freedom in a place where we could live openly and be ourselves. In this sense, we found Manhattan to be a very spiritually energizing and welcoming oasis. We joined Judson Church on Washington Square – an open and affirming congregation, where we encountered the *good news* of God's unconditional love for all persons.

Living in Manhattan often means sacrificing one's personal space. For two persons interested in historic Victorian architecture, living together in tiny New York City apartments became too confining. While visiting our friend Tom in Easton, Pennsylvania, we learned of a house in the area that was for sale. Though it needed complete renovation, we could see its potential and history. We also found the asking price laughable by New York standards. So we bought that first house together, consigning ourselves to indentured servitude for many years. But it was a home – our home together – and we filled it with love and Mr. Kitty, our black cat. This was our *chosen* family.

Relationships with our families of origin have been less than warm and fuzzy. My coming out to my parents in the early 1970s was followed by years of total silence and shunning. While we have communicated more, and our relationship has improved slightly over the years, I believe my parents have never really accepted my orientation and my openness. Tim's family has been more accepting and supportive, though never to the degree we would hope after all these years. We have learned the importance of creating our own family of supportive friends – a *family of choice* – friends who accept us for who we are as individuals and as a couple.

We commuted from our work in Manhattan to our home in Easton for a while until that trek became unbearable. Leaving our apartment and positions in Manhattan in the mid 1980s was a very difficult decision. Yet, through all these transitions, we supported one another and always talked openly about our feelings, our goals, and our hopes for the future together. We had our dreams – still do.

As our relationship matured, so did our awareness of God's presence and love as the glue which held us together through good times as well as bad. We would often reflect upon situations in our lives apart and together where we sensed our Creator guiding us in certain directions. We learned the value of being *open to the moment* – of truly listening to the subtle and not-so-subtle ways in which God speaks to us and coaxes us in directions along life's journey that bring growth and learning – and sometimes pain.

Fortunately, employment searches in the Lehigh Valley of Pennsylvania provided Tim with an architectural position, and I assumed another pastorate. While I enjoyed serving a church again, I had to go back into the closet. I guess I thought it would be different somehow this time. Wrong! It didn't take long before a mean-spirited neighbor started another rumor – this time about my orientation. Fortunately, I was supported and pleasantly surprised by the leadership of the congregation that chose not to respond to such rumors. While this "don't tell" approach squelched the rumor, it also carried with it the unspoken message that I had better remain very tightly in the closet if I wanted to serve that pastorate.

Rather than leave the church altogether, I sensed it was time for me to explore other avenues of ministry to which I was feeling called by my Creator. Of all my pastoral responsibilities, I found visiting the ill or dying the most challenging and spiritually fulfilling.

Illness often causes one to question one's beliefs about the meaning of life, suffering, and death. Illness can also cause one to be more *real* and share more openly one's struggles, fears, and hopes, especially one-on-one in confidence with a *stranger* who will listen. I discovered a spiritual connectedness with many patients at the bedside as they shared their own struggles and concerns. I could certainly relate to their feelings of alienation, fear, loneliness, and helplessness.

At the bedside of patients, I also encountered God's presence in the midst of suffering. I experienced God's grace offering hope. At the bedside, I found *holy ground*. This is where I needed to be. After much prayer and discernment, I left my second pastorate and trained to become a chaplain. In 1992, I assumed the position I currently hold as director of chaplaincy in a hospital.

The death of Tim's twin sister Pat and the sudden death of our friend Tom were among our most painful moments together. Through those experiences, as well as my work as a hospital chaplain, we both have come to appreciate the fragility of human life and the value of truly living and loving fully "one day at a time." Our relationship and our love continued to deepen and grow.

After a few years, we sold our first house to buy another in the Lehigh Valley where we have been living for the last eighteen years. Our current home is also a *work in progress* as our relationship continues to be. Our *family* now consists of our three black cats – Inky, Blinky, and Fluffy. We often feel that these are our "good old days." Sometimes we feel like relics of a bygone era – having survived the '70s, '80s, and '90s while many of our dear friends succumbed to AIDS.

Though we share most interests in common, we also value and respect our slightly differing viewpoints on certain subjects. We consider trust and mutual respect essential to our relationship – a willingness to communicate, share our concerns and needs, and be open and honest with one another. I have always considered myself to be a rather quiet, introspective, independent person, who needs regular space and time alone. When I first met Tim, he appeared more verbal, extroverted, and sociable than I. Through our relationship, I have become more assertive and sociable, while Tim has come to value more private, quiet meditative time alone. We help balance one another and challenge one another as we grow together emotionally and spiritually.

We still find Manhattan to be an important source of cultural and spiritual inspiration, and currently we are members of the Metropolitan Community Church of New York[6] – a welcoming place where we are spiritually nourished and supported. For me, the MCC-NY is *church* as it was originally meant to be – a place of genuine hospitality, where all are welcome whatever their God-given sexual/affectional orientation or gender.

In the MCC-NY, the word *Christian* is not used as a badge of self-righteousness or power or judgment, and the Bible is not used as a weapon or worshipped as an idol, but understood as an inspired account of our Creator's grace. The MCC-NY is a place where we can bring our brokenness before the broken bread of communion and be made whole again. We have found our spiritual home – a church that reaches out to those marginalized in society – a church that welcomes those whom Jesus welcomed and for whom he died.

We have experienced countless *grace moments* during our relationship – times when we have encountered our Creator's presence in ways and through signs that have guided us through the peaks and valleys of our lives together. We have come to believe *there are no coincidences.* We have learned the value of truly being *awake* to our God's promptings and coaxings along life's journey. We have drawn inspiration from both Christianity and Buddhism, as well as the people who have come in and out of our lives these past twenty-five years.

Perhaps the most moving spiritual experience we shared together was our civil union on October 18, 2000, that took place in Vermont. We sensed God's presence with us every moment of the trip and ceremony. On our way up through New England, the colors of the leaves provided a beautiful welcome carpet. Pulling into the parking space of our hotel, I looked up and saw

---

[6] Affiliated with the Universal Fellowship of Metropolitan Community Churches.

a license plate with the word *Early*, my fond nickname when I was a child.

As we applied for the civil union license at the clerk's office, there was a picture of twins before us. We felt the presence of Tim's deceased twin sister. There was also a calendar with a picture of three black kittens, just like our *family* back home. We were homesick, but then were surprised to learn that the hotel had mistakenly booked us for only one night instead of two, so we were free to leave earlier. The entire experience was filled with so many *coincidences* and *cues* that assured us we were doing the right thing at the right moment in time.

We met the Rev. James J. Olson, pastor of the Greater Hartford United Church of Christ, Hartford, Vermont, in the lobby of the hotel. Together we drove to his beautiful Congregational church – one of over four hundred churches in the United Church of Christ which has voted to become "Open and Affirming" of GLBT persons. Standing before the pastor on that chilly evening in the dimly lit sanctuary, we pledged our vows. In all my years as a minister, I have never felt God's presence and blessing more intimately than I did in those moments. Tim and I joined hands as we exchanged rings with tears in our eyes. Twenty-four years and here we were, before our Creator, proclaiming our love and commitment to one another. It all felt so right!

The words of the Book of Ruth, which we had chosen, conveyed our feelings as we joined hands: "Entreat me not to leave you or to return from following you; for where you go I will go, and where you lodge I will lodge; your people shall be my people, and your Creator my Creator; where you die I will die, and there will I be buried. May the Lord do so to me and more also if even death parts me from you."[7]

After the service, Pastor Olson sat down at the old pipe organ and filled the sanctuary with a wedding march – just for us. As

---

[7] Ruth 1:16-17. Earl and Tim's paraphrase of the RSV Bible selection.

we walked out the door into that star-filled evening, all was silent except for a distant train whistle that reminded Tim of his grandfather, who was a conductor on the railroad when Tim was a child. A very familiar and comforting sound. In many ways, we felt that all our departed friends and loved ones were with us that evening.

On September 19, 2001, we celebrated our twenty-fifth year together, though those were bittersweet moments as we grieved, with so many others, the terrorist attack on New York City a week earlier. Ironically, Tim had been working on a series of paintings of the Twin Towers of the World Trade Center (WTC) for the past few years. They express the theme of *twinness* and his twin sister, who died in 1986. Her spirit was represented in the paintings as swirls of cloud, color, and light encircling the towers.

On September 3, we hung these paintings in our home. To celebrate, that weekend we sailed around New York harbor and watched the moon rise between the towers. The skyline never looked more dazzling as we raised our glasses in a moonlight toast to the final completion of Tim's exhibition. A week later the towers were gone. Viewing the paintings the day after this tragedy, the swirls of cloud, color, and light now came to depict – in a prophetic and eerie way – the shattering glass and smoke that engulfed the towers prior to their collapse.

While we grieve along with the rest of our nation the events of that tragic day, it only heightens our awareness of the inequity and additional injustices suffered by many LBGT survivors of those evil actions. "There are twenty-four women and men known to have lost same-sex partners in the attack. Several gay advocacy organizations believe there may be twice that number."[8] I believe our compassionate response as a nation must include all gay men and women who now find themselves without partners.

---

[8] Raab, Barbara. NBC News article, December 20, 2001.

This tragedy has raised many important questions for Tim and myself:

1. What if either of us were to have been a victim of the terrorist attacks? Would I be allowed to visit Tim in the hospital and make medical decisions for him? Most likely not, since we are not legally married or next of kin.

2. Would I be able to donate blood for him? No, since the Red Cross bans anyone from contributing blood who has had same-sex relations.

3. As his survivor, would I be entitled to receive any of the financial aid which the government and other agencies are making available to families and survivors of mixed-gender couples? Unfortunately, most states only allow for a spouse, parent, grandparent, sibling, adult child, or legal dependent of a deceased victim to receive survivor benefits. The exception, however, is New York State where Governor George Pataki signed an executive order granting surviving partners of gay victims of the WTC attacks equal benefits from the NY State Crime Victims Board. The Red Cross also chose to recognize same-sex partnerships in the distribution of survivor benefits.[9]

4. What about funeral arrangements? Would I be excluded? Tim and I lost one of our church friends in Tower One. She leaves behind her lesbian partner and son. We who are LGBT continue to see our grief *disenfranchised* by society and the church. Ours is often a loss that "is not socially sanctioned, openly acknowledged, or publicly shared."[10]

---

[9] *National NOW Times,* Spring of 2002, "Same-Sex Couples Face Post-September 11 Discrimination," by Rebecca Farmer, Press Secretary.

[10] Doka, K.L., ed. *Disenfranchised Grief: Recognizing Hidden Sorrow*. (Lexington, MA: Lexington Press, 1989)

5. What if I wanted to openly join the military and fight for my country? Clearly, I would be banned despite the temporary "Stop Loss" order which claims to end procedural discharges of homosexual personnel yet doesn't suspend the "Don't Ask, Don't Tell" policy that has actually caused a rise in discharges.

While persons such as Rev. Jerry Falwell and Rev. Pat Robertson have used the terrorist attacks to also attack gay persons (as having brought down God's wrath upon America), we have been encouraged that so many, including President Bush, have denounced such irresponsible pronouncements. Clearly, many Americans are coming to see the violence wrought by extreme religious fundamentalism. After all, the terrorist attacks were *faith-based initiatives.*

Americans have been introduced to many true heroes of September 11, including many gay and lesbian individuals and couples, such as openly gay Mark Bingham, who is thought to have helped fellow passengers confront terrorists in a plane over Pennsylvania; heroes such as David Charlebus, who was a pilot on one of the doomed airlines, and two men and their adopted toddler killed on one of the planes; and heroes such as the beloved New York City police chaplain, Rev. Mychal Judge, another victim, whose helmet was presented to Pope Paul II in St. Peter's Basilica. How ironic that this same pope continues to incite anti-gay violence by labeling gay and lesbian persons *intrinsically disordered* and a threat to the family.

Apart from these concerns brought on by national tragedy are the daily injustices of which Tim and I are aware in relation to inheritance issues, health insurance coverage, social security benefits, pensions, and all the other rights and privileges mixed-gender couples take for granted.

Regarding inheritance, for example, married spouses automatically inherit from one another even if there is no will. On the other hand, same-sex partners are not automatically entitled to the home or property of the other, and don't have the automatic right to administer their estate.

Consider the issue of health insurance. For married couples, one spouse's policy can also cover the other (uninsured) partner. For gay or lesbian couples where one partner is uninsured, there is the additional hardship of purchasing expensive health insurance coverage.

Also, after a lifetime of contributing to workers' compensation, social security, and pensions, neither Tim nor I would have those benefits available upon the illness, injury, or death of the other. Such legal and financial benefits provide a safety net married people take for granted, as they deal emotionally with the illness or death of a spouse. Imagine, if you can, heterosexual marriages suddenly stripped of all such rights, protections, and privileges!

I also find it frustrating that it is perfectly legal in most states to deny persons employment or public accommodations in restaurants, hotels, or housing, solely on the basis of real or perceived affectional orientation. I am surprised that many of our non-gay friends did not know that we could be thrown out of a job, restaurant, or apartment in many places simply because the owner doesn't like gay people, and we would have no legal recourse to redress such action. It is perfectly legal to discriminate in such situations.

I find it disheartening that many are still victims of hate crimes every day, and our politicians have yet to pass national Hate Crimes legislation. We recall the time when Tim was confronted in Allentown by a group of young men wielding baseball bats as they approached his car. Thank God, he managed to escape unharmed.

I am aware of the times we are *shunned* by family and friends who don't approve of our relationship. I have come to realize that convicted felons and murderers in prison have many more rights than we have – especially the right to marry.

Yet, in the midst of all this, we remain hopeful and committed to caring for one another – being responsible for one another in an often hostile and insecure society. We draw strength from our Creator who loves and respects us for who we are as individuals and as a couple. We love our country – *our* country – and pray for peace.

As a couple in a long-term relationship, I write this chapter in the hope that it might somehow challenge the misconceptions, ignorance, and prejudice many still hold about the stability and viability of a same-gender relationship. The reality is that "nearly half of all marriages break-up"[11] despite the "1,049 rights, protections, and responsibilities society provides to support such marriages."[12] "Aside from ... Nevada, no region of the United States has a higher divorce rate than the Bible Belt ... [in the] Southern states."[13]

It would seem, if so many persons have had so many failed marriages, Tim and I should have the opportunity to have at least one successful one also supported by those same rights and privileges. Jesus did not address the subject of *homosexuality*. He did, however, speak about divorce, affirming the importance of lasting relationships built on love and mutual respect.

It would seem that the growing number of same-gender couples living in the United States without societal support, in itself, speaks volumes about the stability, longevity, and commitment of so many same-gender relationships and what some consider *non-traditional* family structures.

Tim and I hear stories of young people today who are victims of constant verbal or physical abuse in school, in society, and in the churches. The role of homophobia in such acts, as well as its relation to the high rate of teen suicide among gay

---

[11] "Bible Belt Leads U.S. in Divorces," National Center for Policy Analysis, http://www.NCPA.org.

[12] U.S. General Accounting Office of the Federal Government.

[13] "Bible Belt Leads U.S. in Divorces," National Center for Policy Analysis.

boys and lesbian girls (one out of three suicides[14]) is often ignored.

While the events of September 11 have focused national attention on a new enemy, GLBT individuals still remain the last American minority toward whom prejudice, discrimination, and violence are still considered allowable, fashionable, and encouraged by many in society and the church. Many still quote selected biblical passages, taken literally and out of their historical and cultural context, to condemn gay and lesbian persons. They conveniently fail to recognize that the Bible is replete with *non-traditional* familial arrangements.

How unfortunate that same-gender committed relationships are somehow considered a threat to mixed-gender marriage. How unfortunate that many still consider one's sexual orientation to be a *choice* or a *lifestyle*. I never *chose* to be gay any more than I believe anyone can *choose* to be heterosexual. I believe one's affectional sexual orientation is a gift from birth – a gift – not a sin, sickness, biological error, or unnatural occurrence. While a careful reading of reputable scientific research and biblical interpretation can do much to dispel misinformation and stereotyping, getting to know GLBT individuals in the pew and in the world on a personal basis can do much more to replace prejudice and ignorance with love and compassion.

As we continue to share our hopes and our dreams for the future together, we also pray for the day when our society may *catch up* to the growing number of enlightened European cultures that are beginning to recognize the value of supporting same-gender relationships and family structures. Until that day comes, we believe it is important for LGBT individuals and couples to live as openly and honestly as possible in every aspect of their daily lives. This includes simply holding hands in

---

[14] In a study of gay male and lesbian youth suicide, the U.S. Department of Health and Human Services found lesbian and gay youth are two to six times more likely to attempt suicide than other youth and account for up to thirty percent of all completed suicides.

public or proudly displaying a partner's photo on one's office desk. It means moving beyond fear and intimidation. It means courageously claiming the same (not special) rights mixed-gender couples take for granted.

Though Tim deliberately dropped his pocket change on the floor back in 1976, that gesture failed to get my attention. What did get my attention was the intervention of a loving Creator who, we believe, brought us together that night. This is the same God who has blessed and sustained our relationship for a quarter of a century – an open and welcoming God who will continue to challenge our churches to likewise love and welcome, as did Christ himself, all marginalized persons in our midst.

Rev. Earl D. Ball, M. Div., S.T.M., is an ordained minister in the United Church of Christ currently serving as the director of pastoral care/chaplaincy in a Pennsylvania hospital. His partner **Tim** is an architect in the Lehigh Valley of Pennsylvania.

None of us ever possesses Truth. The best we can do is to be aware of this, and to try to discern Truth, and live as God has given us grace. Our worst enemies are always those who believe they own Truth.

~ Don Broyles

~ twenty-one ~

Undefined Border?

Roy Dahl and Paul Hawkins Jr.

*The border between Canada and the United States of America is at forty-nine degrees north latitude for much of its length. It has been called the world's longest undefended border. This designation seems ironic for Paul and Roy, who have experienced it as **well-defended**. They are citizens of different countries who have tried to live together for the past ten years. They have discovered that without legal recognition of their relationship, the process can be complex and tiresome.*

The date was September 21, 1996, and together we drove through the woods of southwestern Michigan with an address and directions in our hands. We had not yet been to the country home of friends from Oak Park Mennonite Church, a congregation of folks we had come to know and love during our years in Chicago. They had kindly offered to host us for this celebration, and we looked forward to arriving at their home near the small community of Buchanan.

At several crossroads we hesitated, straining to check signs and landmarks and feeling unsure as to whether we should turn at this corner or go to the next. We made some choices and moved forward with the information and the feelings that we had. It was fitting that the journey through those woods felt like a metaphor for our lives together. In our relationship on that particular day there were expressions of agreement, anticipation, anger, hope, frustration, misgivings, confusion, and excitement. But most importantly, we were on the trip together and we were convinced of our love for each other.

Invitations had gone out weeks before. It occurred to us several days earlier that we should allow for some flexibility regarding the starting time. Friends were coming from several neighboring midwestern states, and Indiana's non-conformity regarding daylight savings time creates some interesting time-change dynamics throughout the course of a year.

We first met each other five years and eight days earlier. Roy had moved from Calgary, Alberta, to Elkhart, Indiana, to begin studies at Associated Mennonite Biblical Seminary (AMBS). Paul was living and working in Elkhart after having spent four years studying theology in that seminary. We met through friends who learned to know each other within the BMC (Brethren/Mennonite Council for Lesbian and Gay Concerns).

Our relationship developed quickly after an initial meeting on a warm September evening when we went out for coffee and ended up talking for hours. During the next several months, we related our personal histories to each other. Life experiences that we shared up to that point in time included our childhood years, our family dynamics, our high school years, and our coming out experiences – to ourselves, to our families, and to our friends. We also spent time talking about our hopes and dreams. In the weeks and months following, it became clear that we wanted to share our lives with each other.

We spent our first Christmas together at the home of Roy's parents in Alberta. It was Paul's first time meeting Roy's family and the congregation of Calgary Inter-Mennonite Church where Roy had been a member for the previous decade. One of Paul's most memorable moments of that first Canadian Christmas was when Roy's aunt asked him to carve the turkey at a Boxing Day[1] family gathering.

---

[1] Traditionally, Boxing Day was observed in Canada and England on December 26 as a day to give gifts to the poor and those who have provided service throughout the year. Originally, priests opened the *poor boxes* on that day and gave the contents to the poor. For many modern Canadians, it has become just an additional holiday following Christmas Day with no special meaning or celebration.

After that first Christmas, Roy moved from his dormitory room on the seminary campus into the house that Paul was renting in Elkhart. It felt as though we were taking the first tangible steps on a journey as a couple. We were starting to build dreams of what our future might hold. We both knew that our spiritual convictions were, in part, the reason for our lives coming together. Our spiritual lives and our search for how to begin a journey together in the Mennonite Church led us on a difficult path.

Just as Paul had learned that graduating from AMBS with a Master of Divinity degree would never become a reality, Roy learned the same in 1992. Roy, however, was determined that he would complete what he had come to the United States to do and continued his studies at McCormick Theological Seminary in Chicago, beginning in the fall of 1993. Over that previous summer, we had moved from Elkhart to South Bend so we could continue to live together. Paul commuted to his work in Elkhart while Roy traveled to and from Chicago.

It was during that time of painful transition – saying goodbye to some previous goals and making new ones – that Lloyd and Mary Jo Miller came into our lives. We met the Millers at a local Mennonite congregation, and they immediately welcomed us into their household. We had both felt the love and support of our own families of origin – individually and as a couple – but the Hawkins family was hundreds of miles to the east and the Dahl family thousands of miles to the west of the midwestern United States. The Millers became adopted parents to us. Their home was a place of refuge and relaxation where we truly felt welcomed as sons.

When Paul took a position with a company in the South Bend area, the seminary in Chicago offered Roy part-time employment. That opportunity required more than the one or two days a week that he had previously been spending there. The work also came to include overseeing a recently purchased seminary guest house that provided Roy living accommodations at no cost. It was now Paul's turn to commute to and from Chicago on the weekends. At this time, they gave up their South Bend apartment, and Lloyd and Mary Jo invited Paul to share their home.

It was during our years in Chicago that we connected with Oak Park Mennonite Church. They welcomed us in their congregational life and encouraged us to share the spiritual gifts that God had given us. Up to this point in our lives together, our associations with congregations in the Elkhart and South Bend areas had ended in disillusionment and pain.

Roy graduated from McCormick Theological Seminary in 1995. Paul's work was progressing well and held a lot of promise for the future. However, graduation presented a completely new set of challenges for us. Roy could only remain in the United States of America on a student visa if he enrolled in another educational program, so he began investigating the possibilities of Clinical Pastoral Education (CPE).

We often acknowledged the providence of God as we witnessed doors of opportunity open continually before us. The company that employed Paul offered him a transfer to the Fort Wayne area where Roy had learned of CPE programs at two different hospitals. One of the programs accepted Roy as a resident, and, after several years of commuting and living together part-time, we were able to move to Fort Wayne to study, work, and live together. It was in those first few months that we finalized our commitment ceremony plans. It seemed odd to call it a commitment ceremony since our commitment had already been in place for five years. Therefore, we named it a "celebration of continued commitment."

The day was somewhat overcast and misty. The possibility of rain hung in the air. All the guests assembled outside on the large porch that spanned the width of the house. Roy's closest friend from McCormick Theological Seminary delivered the message to the assembled group. She and Roy had graduated together the previous year. Our pastor from Oak Park Mennonite

Church led the assembled group in a litany of commitment and support. The congregational chairperson, in whose home we gathered, articulated a blessing for the couple. Our adopted dad led the group in singing hymns. We exchanged vows with each other. Roy read the promises he had written to Paul while Paul recited his from memory, including his feelings of the moment. Paul still keeps that little piece of paper on which Roy had written his thoughts.

At the close of the ceremony, there was a spontaneous "circle dance" around the outside of the house to the beat of the "Proclaimers" singing,

> But I would walk five hundred miles
> And I would walk five hundred more
> Just to be the man who walks a thousand miles
> To fall down at your door....

The celebration continued. Guests gratefully consumed a mountain of fresh strawberries and a cake carefully transported from Chicago. The sky relinquished its misty overcast and opened up in time for a sunset to shine through the deep woods. The atmosphere was one of relaxation, joyfulness, and strength of community, even though some in attendance were meeting others for the first time. The young son of a couple who attended would recall the day in years following, as he reminded his parents of "that birthday party in the woods for those two men."

In many ways, our life stories define themselves in opposites. Paul is the oldest of four children – Roy is the youngest of four. Paul was born and raised in the New England states and Roy's upbringing took place on the prairies of western Canada. Paul's religious tradition was in the Roman Catholic Church – Roy's was in the General Conference Mennonite Church. Paul served in military service while Roy's religious upbringing made military service a very unlikely career choice. Paul's forebears had lived in North America for generations. Roy's parents had been born in eastern Europe during the years following the Russian revolution. His grandparents lived in Mennonite settlements that eventually became part of the former Soviet Union, and they emigrated to Canada in the early 1920s. Paul's family moved often as they followed the dictates of the textile industry in which Paul's father was employed. Roy's family was rooted in the family farm east of the town of Didsbury, an hour's drive north of the city of Calgary in the province of Alberta.

Roy had never been in a committed relationship. At the age of eighteen, Paul married a woman he dated while in high school. Eleven years into their relationship, Paul came to understand himself as a gay man while attending seminary. With the support of his wife, he came out to his family, his church, and his community. Although they separated at this point in their marriage, they chose not to pursue a divorce for another two years. They remain friends to this day, and Paul's former wife continues to relate to his family as her own.

We share some common interests. We share an appreciation of music and have both studied in that field. We also enjoy participating in theatre. Both of us grew up in the church, took seriously our spiritual pilgrimages, and each felt a calling to prepare for ministry. We both came to understand in our twenties that we were affectionally attracted to those of our own gender. We also recognize in our journeys the need and appreciation for community. Coming out to ourselves, our families, our friends, and our church has provided a complex mixture of affirmation, blessing, surprise, struggle, and pain.

The journey continues. Now we try to find ways to be together during the time of waiting. Paul is working on the application documents necessary to immigrate to Canada. We look forward to a time of creating roots in the same home, same city, and the same church community. We feel strengthened by our love for each other and by the love of the communities that have affirmed us. We feel the love and support of our parents and siblings, extended families, and friends. We have found homes in inclusive church communities like Oak Park Mennonite Church and Calgary Inter-Mennonite Church. We do feel blessed and cared for, but grieve for the places and times when we were not accepted for who we are. Many uncertainties and unknowns exist at this time. Nevertheless, there is also a real sense of hope that comes from a decade of God's Spirit leading us into new and meaningful experiences.

Paul Hawkins is the firstborn of his parents, Paul and Janet Hawkins. He spent his childhood in Rhode Island with his younger brothers, Ronald, Jeremy, and Bruce. Bruce died several years ago, after living many years with AIDS. Following his marriage to Marguerite, Paul pursued his musical interests at the New England Conservatory of Music. Later he served four years in the U.S. army. The last three years of his military career were in Germany, where he remained another two years to work as a civilian. In those years, his interest in spirituality and the church was reawakened, and he began a search for new ways to express his faith. When he and his wife moved to Phoenix, Arizona, so Paul could begin theological training, they encountered a Mennonite church community and became part of that fellowship. Later, they moved from Arizona to Indiana in order for Paul to enter seminary life. During those years, Paul became increasingly aware of his identity as a gay man, and they began the process of ending their marriage.

Roy Dahl grew up near the small town of Didsbury in the province of Alberta, Canada. His family's life centered around the family farm and the local Mennonite church community. Roy is the youngest child in a family that includes his parents, Jacob and Elsie; his sisters, Carrie and Connie; and his brother Dennis. Following his years of schooling in Didsbury, he studied at Bethany Bible Institute in the neighboring province of Saskatchewan. Later he attended the University of Calgary in Alberta, where he worked in the field of office administration and became a member of Calgary Inter-Mennonite Church. During those years, he also pursued an interest in drama that he had begun years before. He was able to supplement his regular work by acting in local theatrical productions. In his early twenties, Roy became aware of his sexual orientation and began to cautiously share this knowledge with those he loved and trusted. In his early thirties, he began a process of discernment around career issues that led him to the Mennonite seminary in Elkhart, Indiana.

During the writing of this story, Roy moved to Ontario, Canada, where he works in a pastoral care position at a hospital in the city of Hamilton. While Paul pursues the possibility of emigrating to Canada, he continues to work as a fund-raising consultant for various arts organizations throughout the Midwest and continues to live in Fort Wayne, Indiana.

I believe that the church needs gay and lesbian members, both those in committed relationships and those who are celibate, to show us who they are as believers in God and followers of Jesus. We need to understand better the people we now understand very little. We need to move from a position of fear and judgment to one of trust in God's ability to preserve the church. Though our fears are real, we dare not allow them to dictate our actions, especially our actions toward fellow human beings, lest we be guilty of condemning that which God has redeemed.

~ Sandy Fribley,
Welcome to Dialogue Series, #1

~ twenty-two ~

Unexpected Parenthood

Dan Swartz with Philip Venticinque

I remember a childhood experience that probably precipitated my first feelings that I was different from other people in my family and acquaintances. I was around four years old. My entire family was enjoying a swim party with friends at an indoor pool.

There was a rule that anyone who wanted to swim had to shower in the nude first. I observed that some of the other kids and their fathers were simply showering in their swimsuits. Rules have always been of utmost importance to my father. I did not want to take my clothes off in front of everyone. Consequently, my father was angry with me and said that if I wasn't going to shower, I could not swim. So I sat pouting on the bleachers while the others had fun swimming.

Why did my father want to make me do such a thing? I was terrified of being seen by others without my clothes on. I believe this moment was a precursor of thoughts, feelings, and emotions concerning sexuality that would surface later.

My father grew up in a strict, fundamentalist, Christian home in the Mennonite faith. It was assumed that boys played sports and hung out with the men folk at church outings or family reunions. I abhorred sports of any kind and felt inferior to the other people we associated with. Early on, I dubbed myself a sissy and resigned myself to living in the shadows, where I needed to constantly make up excuses for why I did not want to play ball with my cousins. I felt separate, alone, inferior, and different.

When I was ten and a half years old, an event happened that forever changed my life. My fourteen-year-old brother committed suicide in our home one afternoon. From then on, there were two parts of my life – before and after – simply that.

I was always inhibited when it came to dating and sexual matters. I never dated any girl regularly. If I did once or twice, it felt weird to bring her home to meet my family. Yet, at the same time, I developed close relationships with females at a very early age. During most of my growing-up years, I rarely hung out with boys. Oh, there were a few seasons when I had a male friend to pal around with; but at school and at church, it was girls I preferred to be with.

My first sexual encounter – also my first homosexual encounter – was with a man who was hanging out at a store. I was about sixteen. I remember so clearly wanting to be with a man and not knowing how to go about doing it. I asked him if he needed a ride and then made my move. It did not go well, and the end result was that I got scabies! It was during the summer, so my mom assumed I became infected with it at camp. So much for *dating*!

From then on, I struggled with my *impure thoughts* as most teens probably do. However, I imagined mine were so much worse than other teens' thoughts. I was sure to go straight to hell if I did not stop. Time after time I spent on my knees with God, trying to make sense of it all. *How could God make me this way? Why? Why couldn't he just take this part of me away? I prayed enough, I read the Bible enough, and I truly believed and served God. Why then? Why me?*

When I was seventeen years old, my family changed churches and began attending the Church of the Nazarene. The people in this church believed in entire sanctification. I was unfamiliar with that term. I was saved and thought that was sufficient. However, in this new church setting, I became filled with the Holy Spirit and thought that was the end of my nightmare.

A frequent prayer of mine, in one form or another, was: "Dear God, I will do anything to be rid of these desires. Give me cancer; strike me down so that I may know your grace. Please take this out of me." I cannot believe now that I actually prayed to be struck by cancer or some other life threatening illness.

It did not work!

I decided to attend Olivet Nazarene University, sixty miles south of Chicago. What an experience! I will never forget the friends and experiences I had while there. I finished my bachelor's degree in three years. (The strong work ethic my father instilled in me served a purpose after all!)

It was in that cocoon of learning and Christianity that I actually began to come to terms with some hard issues: my brother's suicide, my father's role in my life, and my homosexuality. I began counseling with a wonderful school professor and psychologist. I will never forget her and the help that she gave me. Even though I don't know if she would agree with the way I live my life now, she helped me through one of the most difficult, dark, and traumatic times of my life. I will always be grateful to her.

During my college years, I made trips to Chicago with another *special* friend from school. He was gay and knew just where to go. I had no idea about bars or clubs, but he did. I will never forget walking into my first gay bar. I was astonished! I remember turning to my friend and remarking, "Do you mean that all these guys are like me – they like men, too?" How naïve I was!

When I returned home after securing my degree, it became clear to me that I had an internal conflict. It was a given from my upbringing that I could not have fellowship with Christ and be gay. Yet, I also knew from my recent experiences that I could not deny what I was feeling. So it seemed logical to move to Chicago – to get away from all that reminded me that what I was doing was wrong.

I had a brief involvement with a wonderful young woman in Detroit that continued for a short while after I moved to Chicago. When I broke it off, I told her we would just be friends. Some years later, she and I discussed the situation, and I discovered she had figured out that I must be gay.

I still did not have peace with my parents or my family. This bothered me greatly. Every time I went home to visit, I felt like I was living a lie. I felt dirty inside. Everyone wanted to know if I was dating anyone and plied me with all the usual questions. I became very adept at coming up with clever lines in return: "Too busy." "Chicago girls are too fast for me." "Haven't found the right one yet – still looking." (This one was closer to the truth than anyone could know!)

The month of May, 1988, is very important to me. That was when Philip came into my life. I was very intrigued by him. He was so open about his sexual orientation that it was a non-issue to him. Being on the other end of the spectrum, I drew from his strength in this area. He was everything that I was not: carefree, creative, good looking, out, and had a huge circle of friends. Philip was unaccustomed to a lover who rarely drank, worked hard, and was in bed early. In spite of our diverse backgrounds, we were attracted to each other and began dating. Over the next year and a half, we grew closer and became a couple. People referred to us now as "Philip and Dan." That was a nice feeling to me.

However, I was still not out to my family. Once when we were both visiting our families in Michigan, we agreed that I should meet Philip in the airport at Detroit, and we would fly home together. I knew that he would meet my mom and sister since they were there to send me off. I was very afraid that they would instantly know he was gay, and my secret would be revealed. This bothered me so much that I asked him before we left home if he would take his earring off before meeting my mom and my sister. We had a huge fight over this as he was firm in his conviction that he did not bow to anyone and that this was my issue to deal with, not his. He was absolutely right, and I could not believe that I was asking him to change something about himself to meet my emotional fears at the time.

Just prior to his arrival at the airport, I *prepped* my family by telling them that I might run into a friend of mine who is also going back to Chicago. "He is kind of wild," I said, hoping that this would explain the earring and clothing. When Philip arrived, I introduced him to my mom and sister, and, lo and behold, he had removed his earring! I was so touched by that. I will never forget it as long as I live. That he would do something like that for me, when I had no right to ask him, was truly meaningful.

Soon after that experience, I decided to come out to my family. The pain of hiding this part of my life – making up stories at family gatherings – was too much of a burden for me to bear any longer. I wanted to be done with living a lie around my family. I went home to Michigan to tell them my story.

After hesitating all weekend, I finally got the courage on Sunday, just before heading out to the airport again. My mom cried, and both my parents said that they had suspected that I was gay. However, they were firm in their belief that this was not what God intended for me.

My father did most of the talking and was very loving in his way. He told me that it was wrong to act out on my feelings. He made it very clear that he viewed homosexuality like alcoholism. His admonition was, "You will always live with the temptation, but should never act on it. God will help you through it." We didn't talk much more about it after that. In our family, my father's word was meant to be final.

When I came home to Philip and Chicago, I felt drained, yet relieved! My secret was out of the bag, and I did not need to pretend any longer. No longer did I need to cover up who I really was. However, it was still hard to come to terms with being gay, much less being with someone on a long-term basis. Before Philip came into my life, I could date whomever I wanted to without owning my homosexuality. At some subconscious level, I was still "playing a game" or "going through a phase." In my mind, perhaps I felt that God would understand since I was not *really* making any *final* choices.

After Philip and I had been together for two years, I decided to take a promotion and transfer with my job to San Francisco. I decided that I was going to go on my own. I could not deal with the work that it took to keep a relationship going. *After all, wasn't this just a gay thing – not a real relationship? Gay people didn't really make commitments to each other like straight couples, did they?*

Philip was devastated to think that our relationship meant so little to me that I could pick right up and move without a thought of how he would feel about my leaving. After much soul searching, I began to realize that this was not *playtime*. I was involved with someone who loved me very much, and I knew I loved him in return. I could not deny that any longer. After we talked it out together, we decided that Philip would move to California with me.

We did not last long in the *gay mecca* of the United States and moved back to the Detroit area where we both grew up. After we made the move, we received some startling news. Philip's unmarried sister was expecting a child! And to make matters more complicated, she was going to jail for crimes she had committed (nonviolent in nature). Six months later she was released, but she had no place to go, so she came to live with us two weeks prior to her due date.

When Philip's sister came home from the hospital, a beautiful little creature came with her – a bundle of joy – Alixandra! *How could I deserve such a gift? Was this right? Here I was, taking care of a new life, and yet I was gay! God must surely be displeased now. But how could God frown on this tiny creature? She was so pure.* The joy of helping to care for such a precious, helpless gift overcame my fears.

Philip and I were both out of work at the time, so we were "stay-at-home uncles" and loved every minute of it. We were so proud of Alixandra, showing her off to anyone we could. She was absolutely adorable – Uncle Philip made sure of that! Every bit of clothing and hair ribbon was the best it could be.

It is amazing how one event can so completely change your life! We never dreamed that we would be in a position to be *parents*. Adoption did not seem feasible or likely to be approved. We ended up like many parents, not necessarily planning to start a family, but then it happens!

Philip's Italian family was and continues to be very supportive. When Alix was about a year and a half old, her mother got into trouble again, and we asked her to move out. Only this time we made it clear she was not going to take Alix with her. The baby stayed with us. We could not and would not risk Alix growing up moving from place to place without the security of a stable environment. She deserved more than that, and we were there to ensure that she received it.

Being gay with a child affords interesting experiences. Sometimes we receive the strangest looks. Two men in a shopping mall with a stroller, gushing over a toy or an outfit, soon attract attention. Since I didn't have Philip or Alix's coloring, everyone assumed she belonged to Philip – that he was her daddy. He was quick to point out that we were her uncles, and that we were raising her ourselves. Now if that didn't raise eyebrows! "Where was her mother, where was her father?" folks would ask.

I suppose I was more uncomfortable at times with these situations than Philip was. I did not like needing to explain who was responsible for her to the day care or preschool personnel or to suffer the harsh looks when the two of us showed up together to register her for a class or to have her photo taken. Sometimes people can be so cruel!

One of the most interesting events happened when it was time to enroll Alix in first grade. Since Philip's family is Roman Catholic, and she was baptized as a Catholic, we decided a good Catholic school would be the right place for our Alix. Although it would be expensive, nothing was too good for her. She did not have a mom or dad in the traditional sense, so she would have whatever else it would take to give her every advantage possible.

When it came time to fill out the application, I stumbled over the part where you were to list parents' names. There was no other definition available. How was I to write in two male names and send this to a Catholic school for consideration of admission? I decided to cross out parents and write uncles instead. Alix was accepted and did very well in her first weeks.

When the time came for our first open house for parents new to the school, we wondered, *How would people react? What would they say? Who should we tell them we are? What if they found out we were not really her parents? Would they refuse to let her continue in the school?* All of these thoughts ran through my mind, perhaps more out of my fears than any basis of fact.

When the time came for the open house, we entered the school and began visiting from room to room. In the computer lab, I found myself alone with the principal of the school. With great fear and trepidation, I introduced myself to him. "I don't imagine you know who I am, but I am Alixandra's Uncle Dan." At this point he looked at me and very dryly replied, "Oh, yes, I remember the application." It was at the same time both alarming and yet hysterical. Every fear I had about filling out that application came true; it did send a red flag to them. Yet we were still there with no apparent issues!

While Philip's family continues to be a source of love, affection, and strength, most of my family has not been supportive. Both my parents are living, and I have two siblings. My brother and his family accept Philip, Alix, and me completely. However, my parents and my sister and her family do not.

Being true to his Mennonite upbringing, my father is firm in his position that we are living a life of sin. They are polite when we meet (which isn't often), but when cards are sent for holidays, they are addressed only to me. When gifts are sent at Christmas, they are sent to my name alone. This really hurts!

I have been a parent for over nine years and they know nothing about that part of me. They know nothing about how Philip and I care for Alix, nurse her wounds, comfort her when she is unhappy, help her with her homework, and attend her sports games and dance recitals. They know all about my other nieces and my nephew and have been active in their upbringing, but my child knows nothing of my parents or my sister. According to them, acknowledging us would be like "condoning our lifestyle," and this they cannot do. I am thankful to God that my brother and his family, although living miles away, open their hearts and minds to us without reservation. I realize that, in many ways, pain has been my teacher.

Our family is blessed in that I have a good job and Philip's schedule allows him to drop Alix off and pick her up from school, dance, soccer, and other activities. We are what you would otherwise call a very typical family with very typical lives, stresses, concerns, and joys.

Alix is nine years old now and continues to be the light of our lives. We hope and pray that she will grow up not judging others, but accepting and loving those around her for who they are – children of God.

Dan Swartz grew up in Union Lake, Michigan, the third child in a family of four. In 1983, he received his B.A. degree in psychology from Olivet Nazarene University. He has held a variety of managerial positions at various companies and is currently the director of command center operations with SITEL Corporation, Detroit, Michigan, a leading customer and relationship management outsourcer.

Philip Venticinque grew up in St. Clair Shores, Michigan, the third child in a family of five. After holding several jobs in the service industry, he finally settled on his life's calling as a residential interior designer with clients across the U.S.

Dan and Philip reside in Detroit, Michigan, with the light of their lives, Alixandra, who is "nine going on twenty!"

Sin is by no means a uniform concept in the biblical record. Jesus represented an exponential leap forward in the process of deleting from previous lists of sins certain forbidden practices, foods, clothing, and places. As happened then, many people today are reluctant to follow Jesus' lead in this process.

~ John Stoner,
Welcome to Dialogue Series, #3

~ *twenty-three* ~

Missing Links

Michael J. De Rosa and Randy L. Dax

Often in the course of our lives there are certain realities that we don't understand, refuse to accept, or in our self-defense, keep out of sight and hidden away. These actions invariably may prevent us from attaining the many true loves that God has intended for us.

Michael:

In 1956, I was born in Brooklyn, New York, into the Catholic faith. I am the oldest of four children. My two younger brothers and my sister are straight. They are all married and have been blessed with several beautiful children. My grandmother or Nanny, as we lovingly call her, was mostly responsible for raising me. She is a living saint, who taught me manners and respect for myself and others. She made sure I went to church every Sunday and said my prayers every night. We were poor by most standards, but I didn't know it. Nanny always said, "The Lord provides," and we didn't want for anything.

When I was six years old, my mother married my stepfather, and I was taken away from the happiest childhood a young boy could ever wish for. He was a difficult man, and he knew I was gay the first time he saw me. He called me cruel names and was nasty most of the time. I paid no attention to him since I didn't know what the names meant. My mom said very little in my defense. I feel certain she also knew I was gay and could not resist the truth. I was a late bloomer and had no clue about my sexual identity. I can't say that I felt any different from the other boys. I played sports and had an occasional interest in girls.

I was seventeen when I became aware of the bohemian and outwardly gay cultures that were very visible in Greenwich Village. The '70s were a very exciting time, and the Village was alive with diversity. I spent most of my time on Christopher Street, where the people were very friendly and uninhibited. I admired them and their ability to express themselves freely. I was at ease with myself and felt comfortable being there. The more I went to the Village, the more I was compelled to return as often as I could; but I didn't want to give my stepfather the satisfaction of being right, so I didn't associate myself with what was happening around me. Instead, I followed the conventional way and did what was expected of me. When I turned nineteen, I met a nice girl and got married. We were very much in love, but I was still being drawn to the Village and the excitement of it all.

Then it happened! Two years later I met a guy. It was not by chance – I wanted it to happen, and it changed my life. My stepfather was right. I could not ignore the truth any longer. After all, he made it clear in my growing up years that I was gay. Now I knew that I really was gay and did not feel that I could ignore it any longer.

My wife took the news rather hard and *outed* me to everyone I knew. In a few months we were divorced. I was more fortunate than most in this respect. I didn't have to bear the trauma of coming out to everyone. My wife had already taken care of that, hoping in some way to hurt me. To my good fortune, there were no repercussions. My family still loved me, and all of my friends stood by me. Even my stepfather mellowed a bit, although he never admitted to me that he accepted my diverse sexuality.

I settled into my new relationship, and a few years later my partner and I left New York to live in a quiet country town in northwest New Jersey, where we enjoyed a peaceful life. Over the next twenty-three years, we made friends – some were gay, but many were straight married couples. On the surface it was ideal, but we were slowly drifting apart. Soon we were living separate lives. But I needed to be loved, and I feared my life would be lonely and uneventful. I silently prayed with an uncertain heart, wondering if God was listening to my feeble prayers.

I have always loved music. As a teenager, I learned to play the bass guitar. During the '90s, I got together with a few friends who had started a band. It was apparent that none of us had a good enough voice to be the lead vocalist, but before we had a chance to place a want ad, the Lord sent Glenn to us.

Glenn and I became instant friends. We kept no secrets and made no judgments against each other. One day he asked me if I would like to go to church with him and his wife. During the years following my coming out as a gay man, I did not attend church except for weddings and funerals. I declined Glenn's invitation with the excuse that I didn't belong and would feel uncomfortable. Intuitively, Glenn knew what I was trying to say. He smiled, put his arm around me, and said, "Jesus loves you no matter who or what you are." He continued to tell me that God knew me before I was born and knew what I was destined to become and what I would do with my life. He added that God has a plan for all of us and there is work to be done.

Not knowing the Spirit of God at that time, I had no clue what he meant by this. I snickered and asked, "What kind of work does God have for me? I already have a job."

He insisted we all had gifts and the Lord had a purpose for each of us. He said it would be good for me to go to church, and I would be a better person for it. All I had to do was to open my heart, know Jesus, have faith, and believe in the power of prayer. Glenn is a very good friend and is very persistent. Not only does he have a strong voice to participate in a band; he also has a strong voice for Jesus.

The following Sunday I went with Glenn and his wife to their small Methodist church in the country. Reverend Kojobo was a soft-spoken man from Africa, and his English was difficult to understand. But, as I sat in the pew, I felt as if he were speaking only to me. I heard every word he said clear as a bell. *Was it a coincidence that he repeated many of the very same things Glenn had said to me previously that week?* I doubt Glenn clued the pastor in about me beforehand. If he did, I am truly grateful.

I left church that day a different person. I realized I had kept myself from God, and there was no reason for it. I returned many times. Rev. Kojobo always made me feel welcome. I believe he knew how difficult it was to be different, especially since some members of the congregation openly complained about his English and their inability to understand him. I told him his English was perfect because the Lord was talking through him – and I understood him. Many times before the service began, he would come to where I sat to tell me how happy he was to see me. For two years, both Glenn and the pastor nourished my spirit. Then Rev. Kojobo's term expired, and he returned to his home village in Kenya to start a church there. After he left, I felt that I could not stay without his support. Sadly, I slowly began to drift away.

In February of 1998, my feeble prayers to be loved were answered in more ways than one. The Lord crossed my path with Randy's path and blessed us with a sense of inner peace and contentment.

Randy:

I was born in 1955 in Nazareth, Pennsylvania, where I lived my entire life. I am one of four children. My family is Catholic, but we were not particularly religious. For as long as I can remember, I never quite fit in or felt comfortable doing the same things other guys my age were doing. The jokes, snickers, and innuendo by some of my family and classmates during my youth racked my emotions to their very core. *What was wrong with me? Why didn't I feel the things I was being labeled to be?* I tried so hard to be invisible to everyone just for the sake of finding some inner peace. At one time, the thought of taking my life seemed the only way out. One lame attempt rendered a more level head.

Puberty began to reveal the feelings that I wanted to deny. *Could this be true? God, why me?* Being raised Catholic all my life and living in a small town where everyone knew everyone else's business did not exactly prepare me for a coming-out party. There were no gay role models for me to follow. The attitudes of the society in which I lived only confirmed my need to hide. I knew these deep, dark, unholy feelings must be kept a secret forever. I was certain that all I needed was a wife and a family.

Then, in my junior year of high school, I met a girl I liked and respected, and three years later, at the age of twenty, I was married. We were very happy and much in love. I thought I finally had put all those doubts and feelings to rest and was certain I was on the right path in life, but somehow I still felt unfulfilled and at odds within myself. About eight years into our marriage, I actually began to explore my gay feelings, confirming what I had for so long denied to myself. However, my guilt and my respect for my wife sent me back into my own guilt-ridden closet. I just could not accept at that point that I was gay.

My wife and I had unsuccessfully tried to conceive for thirteen years. It was a terrible strain on both of us. *Was God punishing me – or telling me something?* I remember now how strongly I felt that dilemma. Our final attempt to conceive with medical assistance produced no results. So we decided to give up. Suddenly, one month later, we were expecting! What a profound impact that moment had on my faith. After all those years of trying, God had proved that we could conceive, but only on God's terms – not ours.

"Please, God," I prayed, "don't give me a son." How could I be a good father and role model to a son when I was so unsure of my own manhood? God heard me and gave us a beautiful daughter. Three years later, another daughter arrived. Once again my gender request was answered. The fear of my inability to be a good father was quickly erased by unbelievable love for my children. It's amazing how profound and life altering the experience of parenting is.

I became more involved in church, and we enrolled the girls in Catholic school. I was active on the church council and many other church and school activities. However, in our twenty-four years of marriage, my gay feelings were becoming increasingly more difficult to suppress. All the role-playing in the world could not make me something I was not. I accepted then that I was gay and now know without a doubt that I always was gay and had been born this way. It is not a learned behavior; it is a God-given trait just as all other traits and characteristics are.

Then one fateful day I met Michael, the man I would fall in love with. On our first date we talked for hours, exchanging our stories and realizing we had so many parallels that it was hard to believe we were two different people. It was easy to talk about our feelings, and the love we were beginning to feel for each other was inescapable. I knew, however, I could not lead a dual life. That would not be fair to me or to my wife or to my children. I respected my wife too much to do that.

Gradually, I introduced Michael to my family as a *friend*. Ultimately, signs of *us* became evident, and my wife began to suspect the relationship for what it was. The most traumatic time of my life ensued. I was suddenly forced to choose which life I was going to follow. I had done what others expected of me for so long that the thought of making a decision of this magnitude seemed selfish. Judgment day had arrived – for once in my life I had to be true to myself – and I chose Michael.

We were each other's missing link, and we knew our destiny was to be together. We had wanted this kind of love all our lives, and we had finally found it. We moved in together and began our new life. We knew the hardest part was yet to come –

dealing with my very homophobic wife. She has tried very hard to alienate and discourage my daughters from being involved in our *lifestyle*. She even went so far as to convince them, through lies and generalizations, that their father had AIDS.

There has also been the unfortunate loss of my relationship with some family members and people who I thought were my friends. I loved these people very much. How sad it is that they feel that my sexuality should change their opinion of me when it has absolutely nothing to do with my relationship with them. I'm still the same person I have always been and the person they have always known. They have no concept of the torment that plagued me most of my life. That hurt and anger have now been replaced with inner peace. I accept the hand that has been dealt me regarding these so-called family and friends and know that it is their loss. How quickly they abandoned me when I needed them the most! Their actions speak more of their character than of mine.

Now my daughters remain our most important consideration, and we can't allow anyone to destroy that relationship. Although it is very discouraging at times, we have vowed to fight the fight. With perseverance and patience, we know we must be the ones who will be responsible to teach the girls about tolerance, kindness, and respect. We are convinced that with faith and love we can break down the barriers of ignorance and instill in them the message of love for all people that Jesus has taught us to live by.

Along the way it became evident that we could not do it alone. God was always present in both of our lives; but now, as openly gay Christians, we were feeling somewhat dissected from traditional organized religion. We talked with each other about our need to belong to a church and wondered with great doubt if we would ever find one that would be friendly to us as a couple. Once again the Lord heard our concerns and, by divine intervention, moved us to attend the First Night celebration on New Year's Eve of 1999 in Bethlehem, Pennsylvania.

A friend of ours, who is a member of the Lehigh Valley Gay Men's Chorus, was performing with the chorus at one of the churches in town. To our surprise, it was a church that welcomes GLBT people, even GLBT couples! This was our Christmas miracle. We were looking for a place to worship Christ, and we were led to this church in a town named after his birthplace one week after celebrating his birth. Shortly thereafter we attended our first worship service at the Metropolitan Community Church of the Lehigh Valley (MCCLV), where we were very warmly welcomed. This new fellowship of gay and lesbian Christians is another missing link the Lord has revealed to us. Now we are able to worship as ourselves, without shame, in a faith community that is woven together by God's love and by people whose lives and experiences are similar to our own.

In the summer of 2001, we took Lauren, who was then thirteen, and Lindsey, who was ten, to the COLAGE[1] Family Week gathering in Provincetown, Massachusetts. It was very inspiring and a revelation for all of us! There were all kinds of families with children of all ages attending the event. Many of the gay and lesbian families were new parents with infant babies. We were surprised at the lengths to which many of these brave people went in order to have a family. Nothing was taken for granted.

It was evident we were all at the COLAGE gathering for the very same reason – *Love*! – love for one another and support for the family unit through camaraderie with others like ourselves.

This third missing link[2] helped us to see that families are held together by love, whether they are in the traditional family role of father, mother, and children, or in the less familiar role of families headed by single mothers, single fathers, two moms, or two dads. It's a shame that the majority of gay people actually believe they can never have a family when so many have proven that it is possible.

[1] Children Of Lesbians And Gays Everywhere.
[2] (1) Each other, (2) a welcoming church, (3) GLBT family group.

It was an emotional week for all of us. We learned a lot and met many wonderful people. The girls had mixed feelings about their first real *outing*, but were able to handle it quite well. It was a shock for them to see so many same sex couples in one place, especially since our daughters live in a town where gay couples are not welcome and do not live openly.

We have taken the girls along to various gatherings, concerts, and other gay-related events. Sometimes we take them to a church service at MCCLV, and the congregation always welcomes them with open arms. The difference at our MCC church is that everyone is welcome. This is very contrary to most mainstream churches where the congregations seem to be hand-picked.

It's only human to want to be free to live our lives and to be happy and fulfilled. Many people spend their years looking for someone or something to bring meaning to their lives. But they are thwarted in their search by strong social barriers or specific qualifications that limit them and leave them unaware that what they have been looking for has already been found or has always been there.

We are thankful that we have been given the sight to see the realities of our lives. The links that were missing for so many years have enabled us to craft a chain of faith and love that provides us with the stamina to face the truth and live it. They endow us with a stronger love and commitment for each other, with the willingness to do God's work and to share our gifts with our friends, our family, and those who come into our lives.

Michael J. De Rosa and **Randy L. Dax** work together in a retail furniture business which compromises any substantial time that could be spent with their daughters. In the near future, they intend to move from New Jersey to Pennsylvania, where they will live only a short distance away from where the girls reside with their mother. This will enable them to make better use of visits, extended sleepovers, and vacations and to have more involvement in the lives of these two precious family members. By the grace of God, they also hope to someday become involved in foster parenting. They are planning a commitment ceremony, and both of them intend to grow old and gray together.

~ twenty-four ~

Me + Him = Us

Ralph Hackett and Jean Rabian

Me - Ralph's Story

I was born and raised in Philadelphia, Pennsylvania, and attended public schools. My family included my mother, father, one brother (who is two years older than I), and myself. We lived in a row house in southwest Philly, a blue-collar, predominantly Catholic neighborhood. We were Presbyterians, and I liked going to church and Sunday school.

My family did not have a strong religious background; however, I joined our church when I was eleven years old. My mother was a homemaker until my parents separated when I was about ten years old. My father (ex-Marine and Air Force) worked for the state and federal governments in the National Guard. He remarried when I was twelve, but my brother and I continued to live with our mother.

I had a happy childhood and liked school, being blessed with many friends in the neighborhood and a few at school. I spent most of my time with the Catholic boys in my neighborhood.

I never liked sports and was not good at any of them. I greatly lacked coordination, skill, and interest in all sports. I loved going to the local park, riding my bike, and climbing trees and also enjoyed being alone. Early in my growing-up years, I felt I was different from the other boys since I didn't like all the same things they liked, but I enjoyed being with them.

After my parents were separated, I often went to church alone and prayed that God would keep us together as a family. My mother had a drinking problem that was part of her marriage problems. I felt ashamed and alone when church members would ask why my parents were not in church, so I started to go to church less often. I was tired of making excuses for my parents' absence and did not know how to ask for help. My church family didn't see that I needed help, either.

Between the ages of nine and twelve, several things happened in my life that troubled me. A car hit our pet dog, and he had to be put to sleep; I was heartbroken. My grandfather died of cancer. My best friend from Cub Scouts was dying of cancer. I remember coming home from his house after each visit and crying myself to sleep as I prayed to God to make my friend better. God did not answer my prayers in the way I wanted.

One of my playmates was electrocuted while climbing on top of a boxcar at the railroad tracks. We often played on the tops of the boxcars even though our parents warned us to stay away from them. Again I asked God, "Why?" As a child, I guess I expected God to answer my prayers and help me with all my problems. I thought that God had let me down and did not care or love me.

At the age of twelve, I had my first crush on a boy in my sixth grade class. I was entering puberty, and my hormones were flowing. I knew it was a crush and that I liked boys; I had no interest or similar feelings for girls. I don't think I knew the words "homosexual" or "faggot"; however, I had heard the word "queer." I thought my feelings for boys were wrong, but I didn't know how to change or stop them. I asked God to help me to like girls instead, and that did not change either.

As a teenager in high school, I had a small group of friends – both boys and girls. I liked to dance, so I went to many of the dances on Friday nights that were sponsored by the Catholic school. I certainly did not want anyone to know my secret. By now I had stopped going to church altogether.

At the age of sixteen, I had my first sexual encounter with a boy from my school. For him I think it was just kind of *experimenting*, but for me it was not. I thought it was wrong, but I liked it. I also dated a few girls, hoping that I would start to like them. But the more I dated girls, the less I liked the experience. It was then that I decided I must be gay, but I didn't know what to do about it.

After graduating from high school, I spent one year on active duty in the Air Force and six years in the Air Force Reserves. During my years in the Reserves, I was hired as a mail boy for a large, blue chip aerospace company in Philadelphia. In order to broaden my job possibilities, I went to night school for twelve years, and the company paid for most of my college education.

I became a computer programmer for a company that built software for the federal government. I worked for that company for more than thirty-seven years. I had a security clearance; therefore, I could not come out at work. If I had, I would have lost my security clearance, and it would have caused me to lose my employment.

In 1964, when I was twenty-two years old, I went to *P'town* (Provincetown, Massachusetts) for a week's vacation with two friends. I told my mother I was going to Boston. P'town has a large gay community, and we stayed in a gay guest house. It was a wonderful week for me, as it literally introduced me to the gay world and others who were like me. I continued to be in the closet, but now felt that it was all right to be gay.

At age twenty-nine, I found my first special friend and fell in love. I thought I was going to spend the rest of my life with him. Two years later, we were planning to buy a house together when he decided he wanted to move to Atlanta, Georgia, for a new job. I was devastated and heartbroken when he left.

The following year my mother became ill and was diagnosed with terminal cancer. That was a rough road to travel, but I'm glad that I was able to be there for her. She lived to see me graduate from college the following year.

For many years I had not been to church. I still prayed to God, but at times I said to myself, "Why bother?"

I fervently wanted someone special in my life, but was beginning to think it was not going to happen. One night at a party, I met another fellow, and we dated for about a year. Finally we went our separate ways, but are still very good friends today.

At age thirty-five, I felt very alone. On a Saturday night in February of 1978, I went to a gay bar just to get out and have a good time. I had given up looking for that someone special. Little did I know that on that night my whole life was about to change.

In that gay bar, I met *him* – Jean – the future love of my life!

Him - Jean's Story

I grew up in a small village next to a lake in western New York State. Our family consisted of my strong-willed mother, my sixth-grade educated father, two sisters (one older and one younger), and myself. We lived in a blue-collar neighborhood, and both my parents had to work to support our family. My mother often worked at night; therefore, she was not home many evenings. My grandmother often "kept an eye on us". We didn't have much, but that didn't bother me. What did bother me was the lack of affection I received as a child. I don't ever recall my parents saying, "I love you!"

Growing up in a small town rather than in a city was great. I loved the atmosphere of our little village with the twenty-two-mile lake to enjoy. In the summer, we sat on inner tubes and floated around the lake. In winter, the frozen lake provided the surface we needed for ice skating.

Two blocks away was an amusement park with more than a dozen rides, and a short distance down the road was a wooded area where my friends and I built secret forts. I could walk, play, or ride my bicycle in safety. Many of my relatives lived in the village; it was comforting to have them nearby.

I knew in my preteen years that I was attracted to other boys. I also knew those feelings were not considered *normal* according to the hellfire and damnation preaching I heard coming from the pulpit of the Salvation Army where we attended church. Our normal church attendance on a Sunday included Sunday school and early worship service in the morning, youth Bible study in the afternoon, followed by an open-air service on the street corner, and finally, an evening worship service.

I remember on several occasions hearing from the pulpit that people who had homosexual thoughts or experiences would be condemned to hell if they did not confess, repent, and let God come into their lives. I was deathly afraid, but I could not publicly admit to being gay. Much as I wanted these feelings to go away, they did not. Somehow I was able to keep them hidden deep inside of me.

When I was a child, a relative sexually abused me. Even though I tried to resist the advances, I was unable to stop them. I was warned not to tell anyone or I would be blamed and be in *big trouble* with my mother. This bothered me so badly that there were times when I had thoughts of suicide and wished I were dead. These abuses finally stopped, but I was never able to forgive this person, and I often wished he were dead.

To complicate my growing-up years even more, there was an occasion when the leader of a church in another city tried to make a sexual advance on me while I was at a youth gathering. After stopping him, I was later touched by another prominent male member of that church. I thought, *How could this be happening when it was exactly opposite to what the church was preaching?* I was confused, frightened, and distressed; I did not want to go to church ever again.

My teenage years were very difficult and painful as I began to feel like I didn't fit in with the other neighborhood kids. While I liked to watch sports, I was never athletically inclined when it came to playing them. I was always afraid my friends would find out my deep, dark secret and, if they did, there would be "hell to pay." While I could not rid myself of those feelings, I did manage to keep from acting upon them.

In college in the late 1950s, I met a lovely lady, whom I would later marry. I sincerely thought that if I would get married, my attraction toward other males would go away.

My wife and I attended a Methodist church and started a family. We later moved from New York State to Delaware, where I accepted the position of underwriting manager for a large international life insurance company. We joined a Presbyterian church, where I became active in church life and was elected a deacon.

Marriage, four wonderful children, and being actively involved in a church did not help. *It* just would not go away! I was living a lie, feeling guilty, and was very unhappy. I felt like a hypocrite and just didn't know what to do. As our relationship began to deteriorate, I again had thoughts of suicide. Anything would be better than to continue to live such an unhappy, closeted life.

In 1974, I met someone with whom I could share my deeply personal thoughts. This person finally helped me to realize that in order to have a meaningful and happy life, I would have to divorce my wife and be true to who I really was.

After my separation from my wife in 1974 and divorce in 1975, I had almost no involvement in religious life. I was convinced that there was no place in the church for me – a thirty-five-year-old sexually abused, gay male, who had been married for almost fifteen years, fathered four children, was divorced, and now was out of the closet. My faith was completely broken. I was beginning to think that maybe I would never meet anyone with whom I could have unconditional love and share the rest of my life. I thought God didn't love me and maybe no one else would either.

My first homosexual relationship began in 1974 and lasted less than a year due to his extremely jealous personality. Shortly thereafter, I met someone with whom I had a longer partnership; but we lived many miles apart, and this relationship ended in late 1977. I had a few "one night stands" and was beginning to think that maybe a long-term relationship was not going to happen for me.

And then – I met Ralph – the love of my life!

Us - Our Story

On a cold February 12 in 1978, our eyes made contact in a Philadelphia gay bar. There was an immediate strong attraction. After playing "cat and mouse" for much of the evening, we finally conjured up enough nerve to start a conversation. We spent the evening and the next day together and realized this was not going to be another "one night stand." Having each been without a "significant other" for several months, we were both lonely and had a void longing to be filled. Each of us wanted someone special to share life with.

We began dating – sometimes spending weekends at Ralph's apartment in Philadelphia and other times at Jean's apartment in Wilmington, Delaware. We soon discovered that we had many common interests. We both loved going to the theater, listening to music, dancing at Philadelphia discos, dining out at fine restaurants, walking in the sun on sandy beaches, traveling, and spending quality time together.

It didn't take long before we were a *couple*. We decided not to move in together because of the distance between our places of employment and Ralph's concerns regarding his security clearance. Some of our friends said it would not last, but we have certainly proved them to be wrong.

Eight years later in 1986, we purchased a home in Newtown Square, Pennsylvania, and moved in. We live in a middle-class residential area with wonderful neighbors, who don't seem to be bothered by two middle-aged men living together.

Over the years we visited several area churches, but failed to find one where we felt comfortable. We heard about a gay and lesbian church that had started nearby and attended for a short time. We stopped worshipping at that church because of infighting by some members, and we didn't particularly want to become part of a gay church. What we wanted was a church where we, a gay couple, could worship along with gay and straight members and be totally welcomed and accepted. We wanted to be an integral part of the community of faith.

In 1994, we heard about a church in Wayne, Pennsylvania, (less than ten miles from our home) that welcomed persons of all sexual orientations. The church was a Baptist church; it was difficult for us to believe it could be so liberal. We said we would visit this church, but kept putting it off until December of 1995. On December 24, we attended Christmas Eve services at Central Baptist Church (CBC).

That evening the congregation consisted of a number of elderly persons and many young couples with little children. It was a nice service, but we didn't feel particularly comfortable. We decided we should come back again on a Sunday morning to "give it another try."

For one reason or another, we did not return to Central Baptist Church until Christmas Eve of 1996. This time we were greeted by young and old and made to feel very welcome and comfortable. We don't know why it felt so different on our second visit, but it definitely did. We believe the church was still going through its spiritual growth in becoming a truly welcoming and affirming congregation when we first visited there.

What makes CBC so special is that everyone is welcome, and no one tries to change anyone's sexual orientation. You can be yourself! CBC is a caring body of believers that strives to be a sensitive and safe place for all. We started attending CBC on a regular basis. In 1997, we made the decision to formally join this community of faith.

In 1998, we decided to take early retirement from our places of employment after many years of service. To celebrate our retirements and also our twentieth anniversary as life partners, we hosted a party at our home attended by forty-five of our close gay and straight friends, family, and several members of our church. It was a wonderful time of celebration. There was an especially meaningful moment when, as we bowed our heads for grace and held each other's hands, one of our pastors included a blessing on our long-time partnership.

The next summer, as a gift to each other, we went on an Alaskan cruise-tour. On the ship we met a husband and wife who, realizing we were a gay couple, asked, "Who does the cooking?" We spent a lot of time with this couple and continue to remain in touch.

We feel blessed because most of our family members have come to accept us for who we are. Our sexual orientation and our partnership in life as a gay couple does not make any difference. We are truly loved by these people who are dear to us.

As we look back over the years, we recall some of those moments in our lives when we felt broken and hopeless. We now realize that it was our lack of faith that caused our feeling of despair – not God abandoning us. Little by little, our faith is being restored as we allow ourselves to open our hearts and minds and nurture our souls through our active involvement in our loving and caring church community.

We feel very blessed that the faith that had been missing from our lives for an extremely long time has returned. As we continue on our life's journey as long-time gay partners, we also continue on our faith journey at Central Baptist Church. Knowing that we are *all* children of God and that God loves us unconditionally has changed our lives forever.

Ralph Hackett, age sixty, was born and raised in Philadelphia, Pennsylvania. He has a degree in Electrical Engineering from Spring Garden College. He retired in 1998 after more than thirty-seven years of service as a senior computer programmer/analyst for a large aerospace-defense contractor.

Jean Rabian, age sixty-one, was raised in the small village of Celoron at the foot of Chautauqua Lake in western New York State. He graduated from

Bryant and Stratton Business Institute in Buffalo, New York, with a degree in Secretarial Science. In 1998, he retired after more than thirty years as underwriting manager for a large international life insurance company.

Ralph and Jean have been life partners for more than twenty-four years and live in Newtown Square, Pennsylvania. They enjoy family, friends, reading, theater, traveling, water gardening, and spending time at their shore house in Rehoboth Beach, Delaware. They continue to enjoy their active involvement as members of Central Baptist Church in Wayne, Pennsylvania, a welcoming and affirming community of faith.

When I began my journey, I felt sorry for homosexual people. I then found I enjoyed their company. Then I saw God in them and knew God loved them because of who they were. That day I knew I would be impelled and empowered to speak out on behalf of my brothers and sisters.

~ Peggy Campolo,
"The Holy Presence of Acceptance"

Christians & Homosexuality: Dancing Toward the Light
Special issue of *The Other Side*

~ *twenty-five* ~

The Love That Would Not Be Denied

Randy McCain and Gary Eddy

Randy's Story:

When I was five years old, I lived with my parents and my two older sisters in a rural Arkansas town and attended a small Pentecostal church. Before the church service would start, the members would gather around the altar for a period of prayer. I remember very clearly one such night.

My mother always took me with her to the altar and asked me to kneel beside her, and I remember hearing Mama pray. She really got down to business with God in those times of prayer. This specific night, as she had her arm around me, she prayed, "God make Little Randy your servant."

I knew she was praying for me. In my childish mind, I could see myself holding a great big silver tray filled with scrumptious pastries and luscious fruit. I was standing in front of this huge ornamental door that went from the ceiling to the floor. The doors magically opened, and I walked in sheepishly. I saw before me a decorative throne and sitting on that throne was my childish interpretation of what God must look like. As I remember, he resembled Santa Claus quite a bit – a kind, elderly gentleman with a long, white beard and eyes that twinkled. I approached the throne and offered my tray up to him. That was my concept of being God's servant.

I believe God heard my mom's prayer, because all my life I have had a strong desire to draw as close to God as I could. When other boys wanted to play outside, I wanted to be in with the grown-ups who were having a Bible study. I loved Sunday school and children's church (a service held for children while the adults were in the Sunday morning service). In the summers I lived for vacation Bible school. I began singing solos in church at the age of six, and I would often get up before the church and give a testimony of my love for Jesus throughout all my preteen years.

Every evangelist who held a revival service at our church would tell my mom and dad, "This boy has a special calling on his life. He is going to be used of God in a very mighty way." This thrilled me every time I heard it. When someone would ask me what I wanted to be when I grew up, I would square my skinny, little shoulders, stand on my tiptoes, and proclaim, "Someday I am going to be a minister of the gospel."

All my life I studied the Bible and pored over Scriptures to learn more and more about my Savior and Lord. Sometimes I was asked to sing at other churches. In my teen years, we moved to a larger city in Arkansas, and I became very interested in Christian drama.

When I graduated from high school, I let it be known that for graduation gifts I needed money to buy a sound system so I could travel the following summer, singing and preaching as a youth evangelist. I traveled throughout that entire summer.

In the fall of 1974, it was time to leave my home for college. However, I was totally unprepared for the separation from friends, family, and all that was familiar. My older sister Linda had attended Evangel College in Springfield, Missouri. I decided that was where I would go to study for the ministry. When I got there, I was one of the few southern kids, and the guys from up north loved to make fun of my southern accent. I thought, *What accent? You are the ones with the accent!* In many ways I felt alienated and alone.

Even before my thirteenth birthday, I began to notice that I was different from the other guys in my church and at my school. I found myself developing crushes on my male friends instead of being interested in girls. I actually began experimenting sexually with other guys. I had heard very little about homosexuality. It was only mentioned in hushed tones, and those speaking seemed to be appalled at that kind of behavior.

Then I discovered a handbook for Christian teens. It spoke of homosexuality as the sin for which God destroyed Sodom. The article stated loud and clear that homosexuality was an abomination to God and that God hated it.

When I was about sixteen, my parents gave me a book on sexuality. It also spoke of homosexuality as a perversion and stated that those who were homosexual were basically mentally ill. This frightened me. I knew that I was very much attracted to other boys. *Did that make me a homosexual? If it meant that I was a homosexual, how did God view me?*

I immediately felt the condemnation that I had read about in the teen book. *God must really be angry with me*, I thought. *Here he has called me to the ministry, and I have promised God that I will strive to be all he wants me to be – and now I am flirting with something that could totally disqualify me from reaching my dreams.*

I had no understanding of sexual orientation. I thought that I was the one who chose to have these thoughts and attractions. I immediately saw myself as dirty and despicable. I would promise myself over and over again not to allow myself to have those thoughts ever again, and I begged God to forgive me for the experimentation and the fantasies.

Yet the harder I tried to say no, the stronger these attractions became. I read one statement in the book my parents had given me that gave a little ray of hope. The book stated that boys go through a time during puberty where they experiment with other young boys sexually and are not really attracted to girls, but that this is normal, and they grow out of this stage.

I hoped against hope that I would reach that magical age where I, too, would grow out of my attraction for boys. Then I noticed that my friends didn't want to *mess around* anymore and started dating girls, but my attraction for boys still did not change. My small ray of hope was extinguished.

By the time I got to Evangel College, I was still fighting this raging battle inside of me, yet I thought that I would just throw myself totally into my Bible studies and somehow push away my sexual feelings for other men.

I met a friend at Evangel from an eastern state. He and I really hit it off. He had a roommate named Gary Eddy from South Dakota. I would go to my friend's room, and when he wasn't there, I would talk to Gary.

Gary was a good listener. I told him about my homesickness, my self-doubts, and my disillusionment with the college. He was an art major and asked me to sit for him so he could sketch me for class. We became very close friends, but I never got up the courage to tell him about the battle that was fiercely raging inside of me. Little did I know that he, too, was struggling with the same issues.

At the end of my first semester, I was in a deep depression. I decided not to come back after Christmas vacation. I told Gary about my decision to quit college, and we exchanged addresses. Then I went home and tried to travel more as an evangelist, but my heart just wasn't in it.

Gary and I stayed in touch by way of letters. One day I received a letter from him that spoke of his attraction to me. He wrote that after we would finish our visits, and I would leave his room at college, he would have to go for long walks because he was so attracted to me. On these walks he spoke of having fantasies where he and I were shipwrecked on a deserted island. We were naked and unashamed, and we lived and loved each other. No one was there to judge us or bother us in any way.

I was shocked. I did not know that he, too, had feelings for guys. I felt an exciting tingle when I read his account of the beach and the waves and the sexual love – but at the same time, I was horrified. Had I somehow given off signals to him that I had homosexual feelings? I thought I had them hidden. I felt like I had been busted!

I sat down to answer his letter. "How dare you have these kind of feelings for me?" I wrote. "Don't you know that this is an abomination to God? Please do not think of me in this way. I want to remain your friend, but that is all it can be – friendship."

He waited for two weeks to write back. In his letter he told me that he had first been very angry at me, but after he cooled down, he realized the reason why I wrote as I did. He was also raised in an Assemblies of God home, and he knew the company line on this subject. He apologized and said he would try in the future to only think of me in a pure way as a friend and nothing more.

Later I made a trip back to Springfield and visited the college campus. Gary and I spent an afternoon together, and he apologized again for his letter. He wrote to me after I returned home:

> Randy, I am so happy that you still love me. I should not have doubted it. Please forgive me for writing that bad letter. I'm really sorry. But putting all sorrow behind, I am happy to be writing to you again.
>
> I'm super happy you came for a visit and that we were able to set our relationship right and clear the air of the misunderstanding between us. It hurts me to know that I hurt you by my letter, and I'm sorry.
>
> I love you very much, Randy. You're a beautiful guy. Thanks for loving me. Take care of yourself. God bless you.
>
> With all my love,
> Your buddy, friend, and pal, Gary

In the fall of the next year, I decided to go to Southwestern Assemblies of God Bible College in Waxahachie, Texas. It had more of a southern feel, so I was less homesick there. Gary and I remained in touch by way of letter, but then, as friendships often go, we somehow lost touch with each other.

In 1980, I finally could not ignore my sexual orientation any longer. I was very angry at the church, because I urgently needed to confide in someone about my inner struggle, and yet I knew what would happen if I were to mention my attraction to other guys. I knew that I would be ostracized by my closest friends.

Finally I decided that I had to go and find *my own kind,* so I searched and found gay friends. I also got involved in theater and met gay people through contact with other actors. It was so refreshing to be around people who were not judgmental toward gays – people who accepted me for *me.* At the same time I felt very alone, because I thought that I had to choose between being gay or being Christian.

Consequently, I left the church and ran from God. I felt that living as a gay person put me at war with God, so I tried not to think of Jesus or the church or the ministry I had walked away from. The gay people I met decided they would introduce me to the gay scene. To them, being gay meant going to the bars, drinking, smoking, dancing, and having sex – lots of it. There were no gay Christian role models, and there were no books that gave any guidelines to gay young people. I got caught up in the entire gay scene of the early '80s.

One day I came across an old address book and saw Gary Eddy's mother's address in South Dakota. I thought I really should try to get in touch with Gary and let him know I was now out of the closet. I needed to apologize for that mean, judgmental letter I had written to him back in 1976. I worded the letter in such a way that if his mother opened and read it, she would not have a clue, but if Gary read it, he would understand the *code.*

"Gary," I wrote, "something *very interesting* has happened in my life, and I think you would be *very interested* to know about it." I sent the letter off, but never got a reply. I sent that same letter two or three more times over the next three years, but received no reply.

Then in 1985, I came across the address again. In the meantime, I had met and fallen in love with a man who was very mentally abusive to me. We had been together for two years, and I had lost most of my friends because of his jealous and demanding personality. Yet I was so codependent that I could not see how sick he was or how unhealthy I was to stay with him.

When I found the South Dakota address again, I decided to try one last time to write to Gary via his mother's home. I decided if I got no response this time, I would throw away the address, because his mom had either moved or died. This time I got a response. Gary wrote and told me a fascinating story about how he had decided that it was wrong to be gay, so he decided that he would change. He married a girlfriend, and they tried for five years to make the marriage work, but he finally came to the realization that he was still gay and could not change. He and his wife divorced, and he moved home with his mom. His wife stayed in the house they had lived in together. The day he moved in with his mom, my letter arrived! He said he was anxious to hear what my big news was all about, but that he thought he knew.

I wrote and told him that I had finally come out as a gay man and was living in a relationship with another fellow. Gary decided to come visit us. When he got to Arkansas, I realized right away that there was still an attraction between us, but I wanted to be a faithful spouse. Gary saw how badly my partner was treating me and told me that I was far too good a person to put up with the abuse I was suffering.

I found myself more and more being drawn to this kind and gentle man. Gary spent five or six days with us. By the time he left, I found the courage to tell my partner I was leaving him. It was not easy, but I did leave. Gary wrote and told me he wanted to move to Arkansas and spend his life with me. He told me he loved me and felt he really had all along.

At first I told him yes, but then I began to think about the sacrifice I was asking him to make to sell his house and quit his job. What if he moved to Arkansas, and I was still not over my breakup and could not relate to him? I called Gary and told him not to make the move.

Gary was devastated. He felt he had been rejected by me twice, yet he still reached out to me. He said I could always count on him to be there for me. He also told me I could call him collect any time I needed him day or night. I took him up on that. Some months Gary had to decide whether to pay his rent or his phone bill!

I ended up going back to my partner again, and endured one more year of hell before I finally came to my senses. In 1986, at the end of that final year of abuse, I decided that if being gay was this painful and there was any possible way out, I wanted to find it. I left my partner and went back to the Assemblies of God church. I contacted an ex-gay ministry. I was determined that if there was any way for me to not be gay, I was going to find it.

I prayed, I pleaded with God – yet I was still the same gay person that I had always been. Gary also decided to try the ex-gay route. At one point I even thought of getting engaged to a young woman. I remember calling Gary to tell him the news. He said, "Randy, I feel so jealous of her."

I reminded him that we were not to think of ourselves as gay anymore. "I know," Gary replied, "but I always have the thought in the back of my mind that someday we will be together. If you get married I will have to say goodbye to my dream." I decided to break the relationship with the young woman. I told her that she deserved to be loved by a man who could appreciate her feminine charms. I felt frustrated and at my wits' end.

In 1991, I was hired as music minister for the Cumberland Presbyterian Church, a position that eventually led to the position of assistant to the pastor. The church was only three months old. It was a mission work. I loved the opportunity to minister again.

During the previous five years, I had volunteered to work in hospitals as a caregiver and minister to those with AIDS. I had watched many of my friends die and had preached at some of their funerals.

I had also worked in the drama department of my home church, writing and directing plays. One of my scripts was a one-person play of the life of St. Paul. I traveled to several states performing this play.

It was exciting to be on a church staff again. I was up front with the young pastor about my sexuality. I told him that I had struggled with this for years and still had not seen a real change in my orientation, but I was not acting on these feelings. He seemed to be very nonjudgmental and offered to listen if I ever needed to talk more with him about my struggle. He didn't see it as a roadblock to my ministry at the church.

I loved being part of a brand new church. The pastor had just finished classes in seminary on new church development and he drilled into me the new thoughts on how to grow an effective ministry. I loved the people in the church, and they seemed to really accept me. I often shared with Gary by phone and letter how much I loved the church.

The church had an outreach to those who felt that they had not found a place in the traditional churches. This nonjudgmental atmosphere in worship allowed me to explore my feelings about my sexuality in a less threatening place. I also wrote to Gary that I was studying the Bible more carefully on the subject of homosexuality, and I was beginning to think that God never said anything against loving, committed relationships between people of the same gender. The only time I could find that the Bible spoke about same-gender sex was always referring to a lust-filled act of selfish sexual gratification at the expense of another person.

I was slowly beginning to feel that our Creator made us the way we are, and that God does not have a problem with gay people forming loving, committed relationships that are Christ-centered. I received a very sweet letter back from Gary. He wrote, "Randy, if you decide that it is okay to have a significant other, I want to be the first applicant!"

WOW! What made him love me so much after all these years? I had always thought of Gary as a very persnickety person. I was basically what you call a slob when it came to cleaning house. Gary, on the other hand, had always kept a perfectly clean room at college. His bed was so flawlessly made that you could bounce a ball on it. He always looked like he just walked out of a band box. *We could never live together,* I thought. *We would drive each other crazy.*

In February of 1992, Gary's mother died. Gary had been her caregiver, and now he was free to move. We decided that he would come for a visit in May, and we would explore the possibilities of a relationship.

The first week of his visit we went camping. I loved it, but he hated it! Gary found camping to be dirty and unorganized, in spite of the compromises I had made for him. I found a camping site with electricity and brought along a television and VCR with lots of movies, but he still did not enjoy it. I was starting to think this was just not going to work.

The second part of his visit we spent in a beautiful, quaint mountainous town called Eureka Springs. We both fell in love with its charm and beauty. We found a nice motel room that pleased Gary. Eureka Springs is known for its elaborate outdoor Passion Play. The story of Christ's life, death, and resurrection is played out in a beautiful amphitheater with special lighting and sound effects. We went to see it together.

I had seen it before, but it was Gary's first time. As we sat there watching the crucifixion, I felt tears streaming down my cheeks. I found myself worshipping my Savior, while at the same time, I was sitting next to a man I was beginning to fall in love with. For the first time in my life, I was experiencing both at the same time – my sexuality and my spirituality together – not fragmented. When the play was over, Gary dropped a bombshell. "I want to move to Arkansas and spend the rest of my life loving you," he said.

I froze. What would this mean to my ministry? I was just now getting reestablished and was respected in the ministry. If I made a commitment to live with a man, and people found out we were a couple, I could be fired.

I found myself wanting the vacation to end. I couldn't wait to get Gary back on that plane. However, as soon as he was gone, I began to miss him. One day I sat down and looked realistically at the possibility of having a relationship with Gary. Here was a man that I had known for eighteen years. He had proven to be a trusted friend. I knew him to be honest and caring – a man of integrity.

We were attracted to each other. We both came from the same faith background and understood our long struggle to ac-cept ourselves as gay Christian men. He loved Jesus just as much as I did. All at once it was clear to me – *Randy, where are you going to find all these qualities in another person?* There were just too many building blocks for success for me not to ac-cept his offer.

I called Gary and told him, "Yes, I will accept your pro-posal." He was thrilled – and so was I. But now we had to wait for five more months, because he had to train a new person at work to replace him. Those were the longest five months of my life! Many phone calls, many cards, and many love letters later – the day finally came. He walked in the door of our apart-ment for the first time. He was wearing a flannel shirt and blue jeans, and he had just bought gas for his car, so he smelled like gasoline.

I had been longing for this day for five months. I reached out and grabbed him and held him, and he held me. I could not let him go. We shuffled over to the couch and, still holding each other, sat down together. It had taken us eighteen years to come to this place but, believe me, it was worth the wait!

Gary fit right in at the church. The pastor and his family appreciated his willingness to serve in the church. He took on the task of teaching a young adult Sunday school class. All the folks in the church started thinking of us as Randy and Gary. If they invited one of us over for dinner, they would ask the other one as well. Even though we still had not come out to the majority of the church, I know at some level they must have known. The pastor told me he thought I made a good choice in Gary.

I now know that it is possible for two people of the same gender to love each other and live together successfully, because I see the reality of it every day. Gary and I have a loving Christ-centered relationship and home. We had a beautiful covenant wedding ceremony in 1993. We wrote our own vows and read them to each other for the first time in the ceremony. Gary read poems he had written to me, and I sang a love song to him. We had communion together and committed our lives to each other and to God in front of two ministers and twenty-five dear friends. There were flowers and music and laughter and tears. Many who were there made mention of the fact that they felt the presence of God's Holy Spirit very strongly. The pastor of the church I was working for was present at the ceremony, although he refused to take an active role in it. Afterwards he told us that it was one of the most beautiful weddings he had ever attended.

There were many heartaches and happy times ahead. I was eventually fired from my position in the church because of my relationship with Gary. We journeyed on to start a new church in our home called Open Door Community Church. We met there for five years before moving into a building that God has provided for us in a very miraculous way – but that is another story!

The pain we went through when I was fired from my job at Cumberland Presbyterian Church was tremendous, but it only sealed our relationship to each other. Gary has proven to be the perfect pastor's spouse. He has never felt jealous of my work or felt put out having people in our home every week. He brings me breakfast in bed every morning. We have been together ten years, and our love grows stronger and stronger.

When Gary and I first got together, my parents would not let us both come to their house for Thanksgiving and Christmas. I sent them a loving letter telling them that I loved them, but Gary was my spouse and until he was invited to come with me I would not be able to spend the holidays with them.

There were two years of sad holiday seasons, but in 1994 the invitation came for both of us to come home to be with the family. My father told me that he was beginning to understand that I did not choose to be gay. He said that he loved me and he was my father and I was his son. He said that no matter what anyone said or did nothing would ever change that fact.

My parents even started remembering Gary at Christmas and on his birthday. It was a miracle! My dad went to be with the Lord in September of 2000. Gary was such a support for me through the whole ordeal. People were able to see us supporting one another as a loving gay Christian couple.

We did not have gay Christian role models when we were growing up. Today we desire to be role models for young gays and lesbians, so that they will know that they can be both gay and Christian.

For me, the questions have been answered. Yes, I am gay. No, I did not choose to be gay. My sexual orientation is a gift from God. God asks us all – gay and non-gay alike – to deal responsibly with our sexuality.

I gave my sexuality to Jesus thinking he would keep it, but he gave it back to me. He transformed it into something beautiful just as he does with everything I give to him. If someone were to come up with a pill tomorrow to change a person's sexual orientation, I would not take it. I could not be happier or more fulfilled than I am today.

If I die tomorrow, I will have known what it feels like to love and be loved. I love Gary Eddy, and I am so grateful to him for not giving up on me. He kept believing in us through the years – kept loving me – kept forgiving me. Thank you Gary. I love you with all my heart and always will.

As I close this story of how God brought us together, I want to share one of the poems Gary wrote to me:

In the dark of loneliness,
Poems have cried out silently
With pages of rhyme and pain
So deep that only God can feel.

This poetry was grasping for love,
So God came down to show us
(By living love in Jesus)
Just what love is.

But some of us (then and now)
After reading the heaven-sent poem,
Cannot grasp, as easily as do others,
The meaning of that love.

So God again sent someone to me –
A living poem –
To teach me, an oft-sightless seer,
The truth of his love.

And so here you are –
A poet of love within the poem of life.
God grant me many, many years
To read this sweet sonnet.

Gary's Reflections:

After reading Randy's account of how we met and eventually got together, I am in awe that we have actually lived this life of subtle miracles. Although I did not have the revelation, as some do upon meeting their spouses, that they were going to marry them, I did know that I was very attracted to Randy and that he had a strong touch of God on his life.

As time went by, it seemed our relationship was going to be one of contrasts: the joy of meeting him and dreaming of a life with him – only to be crushed by the stinging rejection of his letter (although I knew exactly where he was coming from); the joy and elation to read of his acceptance of himself as gay and thinking maybe now we can be together – and the slap of reality to learn that he was already in a relationship; the excitement and relief that he was leaving that abusive relationship – then to learn he was going back to his ex-partner to try one more time; and the joy and relief once again to learn that he had left his ex-partner for good – only to have my feelings dashed by learning he was going back to the church.

I lost him twice to his ex-partner and once to God! But really, God was only keeping him safe for me, and, once both of us saw the truth, God put two finally whole people together and created a greater whole.

Whatever the reason may be that God chose me to be the one for Randy, I am in awe of the privilege, am amazed at the journey, and am excited about the future.

Rev. Randy McCain and **Gary Eddy** live in Sherwood, Arkansas, where Randy continues to pastor the Open Door Community Church that he founded in January of 1996. He also has been involved with Christian drama and music for over twenty-five years and has traveled with his one-man productions of "The Life of St. Paul" and "The Life of Christ." Gary enjoys serving the church as the pastor's spouse and also has a housecleaning business. He is an accomplished poet and artist. Gary and Randy enjoy movies together as well as eating out with friends and family.

~ *twenty-six* ~

Faith Matters

Eva O'Diam with Mary Elinor Miller Kelly

In 1996, I was invited back to my twenty-fifth high school reunion. Each of us received a form to fill out as input for a class directory. It began by asking my name and the name of my *significant other*. Growing up in a small, conservative town in Ohio, this wording surprised me. I sat with it for several days and, finally, I couldn't resist! I wrote, "Mary Kelly." Next, it asked, "Where did you meet?" I wrote, "We met at church." Nothing interesting about that. (Oh, that's right, we *are* two women – I guess that might be a little different!)

We did meet in church – an important element of our relationship. We both attended the Metropolitan Community Church (MCC) of Baltimore. Mary was, and continues to be, an active member of that church. I attended regularly while I was searching for where I was to serve in ministry. At the time, my ministry was to recruit volunteers to visit in federal and military prisons. We both joined in worship, with Mary taking leadership roles, and in the various fellowship and study activities that were offered.

The first time we ever spent time – just the two of us – we rode together to go for dessert with friends after a function at the church. It was winter, and I drove. Mary, noticing my hands were cold, offered me her gloves. She delights in telling people that *I* put a hole in her glove! Over the next couple of years, we continued to notice each other in church.

Mary had been married for twenty-five years. In the course of that marriage, she gave birth to three wonderful sons. Her marriage ended when she came to terms with her sexual orientation. Growing up with three brothers, who were not married, and in a culture where women were expected to get married, she had done what the culture and her family anticipated she would do.

At age thirty-three, she entered into a depression. Working in therapy on issues of self esteem, family, and lack of both spiritual and physical fulfillment, suicide seemed a more acceptable alternative than divorce. Being lesbian was still relegated to the corners of her consciousness. Neither alternative fit the values she had learned from her church and family, but the door had been opened to seek for herself. She decided to honor her marriage to a wonderful man – but one she had grown to love more as her brother than as a husband.

Mary struggled with her journey over several years, and she returned to college to complete her education. She continued to raise her family, to be a wife, to start a career, and to dream of a different life. During that time, she came face to face with her love for a woman and found divorce a hard but necessary reality. This allowed both her and her husband to heal and to become integrated persons, adjusting their life journeys.

As Mary shared her transition with her brothers – all gay men – they were supportive, but had fears that they would somehow lose their relationship with their sister. Her brothers seemed to share a myth that most lesbians hated men, and, maybe in some sense, Mary had also seemed to legitimize them by being the one sibling who they thought was straight. Their strong sense of family, her mother's acceptance, and her sons' acceptance of their uncles and their mom have made it possible for the strong ties to continue.

After nine years, when her first lesbian relationship – a very closeted one – was dissolving, her eyes wandered as she entered into gay life in more open ways. She found herself in love again but not ready to commit. Entering therapy one more time, she went on hold while she assessed herself, her desires, and needs. Making friends of lovers sufficed until I came along, and our relationship grew in love despite more than a decade difference in our ages.

While pastoring a Church of the Brethren congregation in Long Beach, California, I had reason to study scripture and come to my own conclusions about whether one could be gay or lesbian and Christian. The Universal Fellowship of Metropolitan Community Churches (UFMCC) had asked for membership to the Southern California Ecumenical Council. I represented the Church of the Brethren on the council. Mainline churches said they would leave the council if we allowed UFMCC membership.

I looked at the group of people making the request and asked, *"Who are you?"* I found they were a Christian church that had a primary ministry to gay, lesbian, bisexual, and transgender people – not to change them, but to accept themselves and to be people of faith. As a member of the council, I needed to decide what I believed. My study led me to believe that scripture teaches that one *can* be gay, lesbian, bisexual, transgender, and Christian!

Having settled that matter for myself, I went on to pastor at the Dundalk Church of the Brethren in Maryland, where several lesbians were an active part of the congregation. I counseled them as I would any other members of the church. I helped them with their relationships as I would any others. All the while, I had never dealt with my own sexual orientation.

The family of my origin never talked about sexuality. The church never talked about sexuality. In seminary, a couple of staff personnel had raised questions about my sexuality, and I had vehemently denied any thoughts that I might be lesbian. However, my close friends were women. I always felt uncomfortable when I dated men. Nothing in the church or my family or the culture or my upbringing allowed me to consider anything other than the fact that I was heterosexual; I simply had not found the right man. So I kept searching.

One friendship I shared, in particular, met my needs for intimacy, so I found no compelling reason to search for these answers – until the day she told me she was getting married. Then I entered my own depression. I no longer had the one outlet for intimacy I had counted on. If she could get married, should I? Several times, I had asked if our relationship was more than friendship – we had said, "No." But the struggle within me cried out with another answer.

Friends in a clergy support group saw my depression and suggested I go for therapy. They helped me find a good therapist. I entered therapy saying, "A friend of mine just got married...Yes, it was a woman...you want me to talk about my sexuality?...not yet."

After six months of therapy, God used a series of events to show me the answer. I had a powerful dream that spoke to me of a major realization in my life that would result in my leaving the position of pastor at Dundalk Church of the Brethren.

I participated in a seven-day silent retreat at a Catholic retreat center where I experienced a wall coming down in my life. That week, I knew I was going to discover a part of myself that I had kept hidden – though I still did not know what that was.

I helped organize a church camp reunion in southern Ohio, where God used a friend to confront me: "Eva, you're a dyke."

Finally, God used a Catholic priest who posed the question, "Where has God spoken most deeply to you?" And I knew it was in my intimate relationships with women – all through my life – and with the answer to that question, I knew without a question or doubt that I was lesbian. I went to find the pastor of MCC Baltimore to help me on my journey.

I resigned as pastor of the Dundalk Church of the Brethren and took up a ministry with Prisoner Visitation and Support, a nationwide, alternative ministry of visitation. I recruited visitors across the United States for one-on-one visitation. My resignation was never because I thought the Dundalk church would not stand with me. For a fact, they supported my journey into MCC both officially and unofficially.

I resigned because I needed personal space to know myself as a lesbian. I felt as though I had lived a lie for almost thirty years. My pastoral ministry springs from who I am as a person. I needed to relearn who that person was. In the next two and a half years, I was in two relationships. The first helped me come out and share the news with my family and friends and learn to know a new community. The second helped me to realize what I really needed in a relationship was a shared faith, community involvement, and someone with strong ties to supportive family and friends.

It was March of 1991, when my second partner and I decided mutually to go our separate ways. Our priorities were different. I loved the church; she had been battered by the church of her family and had no desire to be involved. I valued a relationship with a partner; she valued her family, and they had said I could not come to family functions.

My therapist, coaching me, asked, "Well, what will you do differently the next time you look for a relationship?" I replied that I would move more slowly. I would date. "Who?" There were two women I named – Mary was one of them.

Unknown to me, Mary was probably first attracted to me back when I put a hole in her gloves. But each of us still had some journey to complete before that possibility would be realized. In the meantime, we remained acquaintances in MCC Baltimore, learning about each other from a distance.

In March of 1991, I was asked to preach at MCC Baltimore. My former partner and I decided that I should publicly share our decision to go separate ways. We wanted friends to know they did not need to take sides. We were both sure of our paths. After the service, several of us went out for lunch. Following lunch, I asked if anyone would want to come and play backgammon with me. Mary replied that she would love to learn the game, and it was her only Sunday off until April 15. (Mary is a senior tax advisor.) I drove her to my house and we played and talked the rest of the day. I had begun dating.

Another woman and I attended a concert of the New Wave Singers, a gay and lesbian chorus, in which Mary sang. I realized how much I enjoyed watching Mary sing. Her eyes danced. Her face and her entire body expressed the music, and she obviously enjoyed sharing that with others!

The next day at church, May 5, 1991, as we were putting hymnals away and folding up chairs following worship, Mary approached me and said, "You're not getting away from me today!" (Mary had noticed me at the concert the previous evening and tried to speak with me, but I left immediately after the performance.) I was scheduled to leave for California the next day for work. My afternoon was to be spent in doing laundry and packing. I told Mary that she was welcome to come over for the afternoon, and I would fix supper if she liked. She accepted. The rest is history....

What attracted Mary to me? The first quality she mentions is a *service orientation*. Part of this is the church, but it is more. It is something we share in being of service to others – to family, to friends, and to the stranger. And it is a quality that absolutely comes from faith. She would also point to my love of music, our complementing of each other's qualities, and her experience that I am easy to be with.

What attracted me to Mary? From the first time I saw her sing, I loved her *smiling eyes*. Her spiritual journey carries importance in her life. Love for family and friends, appreciation for all of God's creation, a listening heart and ear, and her recognition that every person needs to grow and change, are all qualities that attracted me to her. We have also come to recognize over time that I notice silver hair and Mary tends to notice blondes.

We began slowly. As we met, I was continuing to come to terms with an addiction to co-dependency in my own life.

Mary was committed to developing a healthy relationship. This was demonstrated as we began our own relationship in many ways. From the very beginning, we were committed to have time together and time alone. Mary helped me to begin to name my own needs and take ownership of them. (In prior relationships, I had sought to please the person I was with, disregarding my own needs.)

One day when I was house-sitting for friends, Mary came over to spend the night. I had been working on an application for a job. I met her at the door and gave her a hug and a kiss. I told her that I was working on an application for a job, so she sat down to play the piano. I stood behind her and played with her hair, attempting to distract her when I really needed to complete the application.

She turned to me and asked, "Do you need something?" Whether I had ever been asked that question before, I don't know. But it felt like the first time! *What did I need? I wasn't sure.* But in my work on my addiction, I knew that for a healthy relationship to develop, I needed to be aware of and be able to state my own needs.

I replied, "I need a hug." Mary kept me honest when she replied, "I already gave you one." I said, "I need another one." Being true to healthy boundaries in our relationship, she asked, "Then will you go back to your work and allow me to play the piano?" From that moment, I have thanked God for bringing someone into my life who would expect me to live within healthy boundaries and who asked the same for herself.

Our relationship grew over time. I moved from the house I had rented with my former partner and rented a room in the city. Mary owned a home in the city. Mary helped me move. In the fall of that year, I resigned from my work with Prisoner Visitation and Support and prepared to train for chaplaincy. I was accepted to two residency programs for Clinical Pastoral Education, but within a week the funding was lost in *both* programs.

I found myself unemployed, not sure how to continue in ministry and in a new relationship. The easiest thing in the world would be for Mary to invite me to move in with her, but it would have been the worst decision we could have made for our relationship. We intentionally decided that we would continue to have our own residences as we allowed our relationship to develop.

In the next two months, God continued to point me in the direction of my ministry. At the end of October, I began to realize how Mary and I complemented each other as we sat together at a District Conference. The district committee of the Mid-Atlantic District of UFMCC asked me to serve as interim pastor of Metropolitan Community Church of the Spirit (MCC of the Spirit) in Harrisburg, Pennsylvania. I was to meet members of the congregation after the final worship of the conference. During worship, I wrote questions that I would ask of the group. I passed the questions to Mary and she refined them! We have been working like that ever since. Sometimes I talk and she refines. Sometimes Mary talks and I refine.

I was called as pastor of MCC of the Spirit and, six months later, became the permanent pastor of that congregation where I continue to serve today. Where has that journey taken Mary and me over these many years? For ten years, we have driven between two cities, Harrisburg and Baltimore. Some people believe we are crazy. Others think we escape dealing with our relationship. We don't believe either of those to be true. Though the distance has been one of the greatest challenges of our relationship, it has also molded and shaped a relationship based in trust, respect, intentionality, and a deep bond of love.

We trust in our commitment to one another. A few years into our relationship, Mary had the opportunity to travel out West with a close friend. It was a dream they shared long before I was in the picture. They wanted to see the Grand Canyon and sightsee in the West with little schedule or agenda, but as the spirit led them. I encouraged her to go.

Friends at the church thought I was crazy. How could I *let* her go with another woman? How did I know whether I could trust her? My response was, "How could I not trust her?" We trust each other every week when I work in Harrisburg and she works in Baltimore. A relationship must be founded in trust. We do not *allow* each other to do a thing, but enable each other to fulfill both our individual and shared dreams in trust and love. We are each responsible for our own lives.

We respect the decisions we each need to make. Both of us have already had relationships in our lives where decisions were made based primarily on what the partner needed. Mary's ex-husband served as executive director of YMCAs, and they moved frequently as the job demanded. She did not need another relationship where she moved on the basis of her partner's job. We told the church that Mary would move to Harrisburg when and if that move was right for both of us. Mary has respected my need to sometimes work when I am supposed to have time off and to respond to the emergencies that come up. My church has respected our decision even though they would like to see more of us together.

We intentionally call when we cannot be together. It has been important to take the time to listen to each other even when we are tired. When I arrive in Baltimore late, because of work I needed to complete, I still try to take time to listen to whatever Mary needs to share. When she gets frustrated because of my work taking longer than either of us thinks it should, she puts the frustration aside to listen to my frustration.

A deep bond of love has developed over time and continues to grow. It is that bond drawing us to experience yet deeper intimacy (and financial considerations) that is now urging us to look for a house to buy together in Harrisburg. This same bond of love led me to immediately drop everything and go to Baltimore when I received a phone call from Mary that she was hospitalized for what turned out to be appendicitis.

The love we share calls us to know and appreciate each other's families. When my ordination was removed by the Mid-Atlantic District of the Church of the Brethren, it was our love that took Mary to that meeting with me and her love that held me as I wept following the decision.

Our challenges continue. There is a difference of fifteen years in our ages. Mary is ready to retire. I will not be able to retire for a number of years. Mary may travel more than I because of this difference. Yet we would like to share places together. The distance between two churches and two homes frustrates us. We look for houses in Harrisburg but know how much we love the one we own in Baltimore. Even when we find one that is right for us and make the move – challenges in and of themselves – we will need to continue to draw healthy boundaries between my work (which can seem never-ending at times) and our personal time.

Mary's leadership in MCC Baltimore has been and continues to be significant. Where will that leadership be known in a church where her spouse is pastor? In a time when we both can let the frustrations of ministry more easily roll off our back because we can *escape* to another city, where and how will we find our escapes when we live in one city full-time?

Regardless of the challenges, we each have a strong sense that God has led and is continuing to lead us – both individually and together. Faith matters. Family matters. Friends matter. Service matters.

Eva O'Diam and **Mary Elinor Miller Kelly** (Nell to her family) have been together for ten years. Mary has three supportive sons – all married to wonderful women – and six grandchildren. She was born and raised in the area of Summit, New Jersey. Eva was born and raised in Pleasant Hill, Ohio, where much of her family still resides. She enjoys having grandchildren in the family.

They love the outdoors, hiking, and canoeing or kayaking, especially in southern Vermont at a cabin owned by Mary and her brothers, named "The Clearing." It is a favorite place for their dog Sweetie, an English springer spaniel, as well. They also love music, reading, and travel.

Together
in Love

~ Part Two ~

Other Stories and More

Is not this the fast that I choose:
to loose the bonds of injustice,
to undo the thongs of the yoke,
to let the oppressed go free,
and to break every yoke?

Is it not to share your bread
with the hungry,
and bring the homeless poor
into your house;
when you see the naked, to cover
them, and not to hide yourself
from your own kin?

Isaiah 58:6-8a

~ ~ ~

[God] has told you, O Mortal,
what is good;
and what does the Lord
require of you
but to do justice, and to love
kindness,
and to walk humbly with
your God?

Micah 6:8

~ twenty-seven ~

Changing Rainbows

Renee Chernik*

The night of September 1, 1999, stands alone in my memory as an evening of exceptionally harsh, life-changing events. Until then, we lived a life that I imagined to be a comfortable, settled, married one with two kids and a dog. Our marriage of twenty-four years had been a mostly happy one. We had two wonderful daughters in college and an aging cocker spaniel, whom we loved in spite of the puddles he left behind whenever excited. Our home in the country had amazing views of the Blue Mountains. The skies seemed so close you could touch them.

When the girls were small, we would run around the yard searching for rainbows after a good thunderstorm. They were spectacular to see as the skies cleared. I continued the tradition even after the girls became "too cool" to run around with me.

Everyone liked my husband, Mark. My family accepted him with open arms. Our courtship was a short one; we married quickly. He seemed easygoing and comfortable to be with. However, physical touch and affection were hard to come by. I can remember wondering about the lack of intimacy, but I convinced myself this would work itself out as we went along. I hoped that the best of our union was yet to come.

I didn't pay attention to my inner red flags. Mark's occasional dark moods seemed to signal there were some dark corners in his mind and life that I did not understand. Early on, our marriage began to falter and was in need of some counseling.

---

* All names in this story have been changed.

Then we learned that I was pregnant. The pregnancy seemed to change everything for the better.

When our first daughter was born, it looked as if we were on our way to being a real family, and the birth of our second daughter added to that sense of security. Our attention was focused on learning to raise our children and keeping up with all of their activities and our jobs. Life was busy and good. Mark was an affectionate and proud parent. He was a good father. I still wonder how a man could be so affectionate to his children, yet not be able to share affection with me. His lack of affection was about the only thing we ever argued about.

I thought we were a good team. We did all of the things families do when they raise children. We recorded everything in pictures – school, church, Scouts, dance lessons, 4-H, family gatherings, on and on. We survived our girls' teens together. Mark and I were fortunate to always have good jobs, and we worked hard to be able to afford one good vacation each year. We always headed for the beach or Disney World. The multitudes of photos, home movies, and memories are now the only evidence we have of what looked like a traditional family.

We were both of Catholic background. Our daughters Karen and Tina both attended parochial school until eighth grade, and then they transferred to our local public high school. Our church attendance became more sporadic as the girls grew older. Some of it was laziness, some of it was because I was tired of being the only cheerleader to go. My faith in the Catholic church was faltering. I didn't feel connected enough to find solace in it or seek advice for what was happening to our family. The fact was, I didn't even understand what was happening. We were faltering in our marriage once again. Through everything, I still maintained a strong inner faith.

I trained myself to believe that holding hands was enough of a sign of affection. I was grateful for whatever crumbs of attention strayed my way. I say trained, because now I realize that Mark exerted a certain amount of control in our household and our relationship that affected me in ways I was not even aware of at the time. Intimacy was blocked into a controlled certain time of the week. Mark said that the everyday chores around the house were his signs of affection to me.

There were some serious concerns over the years besides the ongoing missing gestures of intimacy. Most pronounced was the confusing rage that surfaced in him whenever I broached the subject of intimacy. The rage would show itself again when he seemed to feel like he was losing control over our maturing daughters. It became borderline frightening.

Karen and Tina were confused about his behavior also. They brought their friends home less and less. I tried on many occasions to be the buffer in the family for the mounting tensions. This seemed to drive us even further apart. Mark's control over me was failing, and he resented that I did not agree with him on everything. After trying everything under the sun to help him work through whatever was bothering him, Mark's depression of two years was still a mystery and becoming more severe.

In the beginning of the depression, I felt we could fight it together. We tried the seasonal affective disorder (SAD) theory to no avail. He at long last agreed to have a physical, after much encouragement from me. This led him to hypothyroid therapy. I hoped that things would improve. I longed for the easygoing, quick-to-smile person whom I married. In his place was a grim person with little to say and diminishing interest in any emotional or physical intimacy. The statement on his face can best be described as one of turmoil. A darkness seemed to be engulfing him. I started to feel uneasy. I was unfamiliar with this person I shared a home with.

One day I found him sitting in a family room chair, rocking himself, staring, and detached. He wasn't even sitting in a rocking chair! Until this moment I didn't realize how severely depressed he was. *But why?* I knew he suffered sexual abuse as a child from a sibling and a parent. I thought this must be what was coming back to haunt him now. This must be the reason he was almost choking on the rage I could feel growing within him. We tried individual, couple, and whole family therapy. But he still had his bouts with sadness that were exhausting my empathy. I tried to stay understanding and concerned.

On a Saturday morning in March of 1999, over breakfast at one of our favorite diners, Mark informed me that when he found out what it was he needed to do with his life, our marriage might not work any longer. I asked him if there was another woman, and he denied it. He refused to give any other explanation. I started making lists of what I would have to do to survive if I were a single woman again.

He had been tormented with neck pain for a few months and then had a heart attack. I thought that perhaps these major physical concerns were not allowing him to feel better emotionally, even if he tried to. Surely the reason for his sadness must be because he didn't feel well physically. We learned all about low-fat cooking and eating. Now I rationalized that the medications he was prescribed, following his heart attack, were the reason for minimal interest in me. The more I tried to make it work, the further apart we grew.

His appearance started changing after the heart attack. He got slimmer, got a buzz haircut, and started expressing an interest in wearing a new men's cologne. Mark rarely wore men's fragrances before. He mentioned getting one of his ears pierced for a diamond stud.

Mark started taking walks in a parkway that was a half hour ride away from our home. He had never been an exercise enthusiast before, but it was the walking alone that was the clincher. Mark never did anything alone! He even admitted to me that before we were married he would buy two hoagies to avoid looking like he was alone.

One day, our youngest daughter asked me, "Why is Dad on the computer day and night?" Her question surprisingly sent a flood of relief through me. My daughter was noticing his behavior too. In a sense, it gave me validation for some of my concerns. Tina always told it like it was. She never sensationalized. Nor would she make mention of something if it were not a reality. It was amazing to me that I could not even recognize reality anymore. I had rationalized myself into a dream world – wishing so much for what did not exist.

I forced myself to stay quiet when he changed his computer screen over to a computer solitaire game every time I came into the room. One night, after I made four trips (three of them deliberate) through the room, his repetitive and secretive computer behavior became intolerably painful to me. When I confronted him, Mark told me that he was unhappy with our marriage and was seeking advice from cyber acquaintances. My husband of twenty-four years was seeking advice about our marriage from virtual strangers!

I visualized great satisfaction in throwing the computer out the nearby window. I went to bed crying that night again. I knew the end of our marriage was growing near, but I still could not understand why. My own self-esteem tumbled deeper and deeper into the ground. I felt responsible for not being able to keep my husband happy.

One day, while visiting Mark's brother at their beach home, I walked the beach alone for what seemed an eternity. I sat down on some pilings, stared at the ocean, and sobbed. The beauty of my surroundings in nature could not distract me from my sorrow and my deep dread for my family's future. Somehow, in the solitude of God's glorious ocean, I was finally able to let my emotions pour out. I prayed in earnest that God would make known to me the mysteries that needed to be exposed in order to preserve what was left of my very soul and sanity. I prayed for the end of this misery that was choking our family and driving our children away. The sadness had gone on too long.

Several times, while using our home computer, I stumbled upon gay sites that seemed to have been accessed by someone. A light began to come on in my head. I asked Mark if he was gay. His indignation and reluctance to answer my question did not convince me that I was wrong. I was getting closer to discovering his secret. He blamed the sites on the kids and said that sometimes things like that just came up at will on computer sites.

Looking back, I feel he knew it was just a matter of time. He wanted me to find out what his secret was. I now understand that he desperately wanted to move on, and his move would not include me. Mark tried to get me to say that I was the one who was unhappy in the marriage. It would have certainly made it easier for him to move on if he could call himself the rejected one.

On September 1, 1999, I sat down at our home computer to make a banner for our daughter's send-off to college. A gay site had not been deleted, and there before my eyes was a conversation typed by my husband to another man. It revealed that Mark was looking for someone to spend the rest of his life with.

When I confronted him that night, he finally admitted that he had been engaging in unprotected bisexual behavior that extended from abuse during his childhood and teen years (eventually as a willing participant) and throughout his adult years. He admitted unprotected encounters with other men in adult bookstores during our entire marriage and even during our engagement – whenever things would *slow down* – whenever he wasn't busy with the children. More horrific, he had participated in these encounters even when I was conceiving our children. Now I understood what his night rides, as he called them, were. The word "unprotected" sent a feeling of dread into me. What if our girls and I had been infected with a sexually transmitted disease (STD) or worse – HIV or Hepatitis C – because of his irresponsibility!

Mark disclosed that he was in love with a man from another state whom he met in a gay area of a local parkway. He actually asked my advice about what he should do. Should he move out and live with this man? Should he stay in Pennsylvania? He wanted both the bisexual life and our marriage. I think he actually thought there was a possibility that I would agree to this! His lies of two and a half decades unfolded one by one in front of me. He said it wasn't marital infidelity because there was no *other woman.*

He disclosed more than I could bear to hear, but I didn't stop him from spilling the details out to me. (I found out later some of them were still lies.) I needed to hear them to believe this was happening. I needed the anger that knowledge would fuel me with for the job of starting over by myself again. Knowledge gave me strength and faith in the long run to continue moving forward.

I felt a profound sense of grief. That night the man I thought was my husband died before my eyes. I felt fear. To know how skillful he had been in concealing the double life he described made me fear how emotionally ill he must be. I didn't know what he was capable of doing. I was fearful also because I knew I had to find a way to continue existing alone, if I was going to be able to exist at all. The feeling of despair, panic, and a sudden overwhelming loneliness was almost physically painful.

A deep sadness for my children overcame me. I knew their family was about to crumble before them. Our youngest daughter Tina was upstairs at the time Mark admitted to me that he was bisexual. I managed to quiet the rage within me, because I was determined that an out-of-control scene would not mark her memory.

I wanted to understand what was happening, but could not. Then, suddenly, it became clear to me that, at the very least, we would now divorce, sell the house, and Mark would no longer be allowed to have any say in my life. He had robbed me of the choice to make informed decisions about the most important elements in my life. As soon as was humanly possible, I was going to remove his ability to have control over any of my future decisions.

Our daughters were going back to college at the end of the week. I insisted that they would never believe anything but the truth, so he told them the truth the next day. He feared that they would not love him anymore. They told him they still loved him, but asked how he could have deceived us in this way. He had no answer. He seemed depressed, remorseful, and guilt-ridden.

He was compliant with many of my requests for moving on and separating the details of our lives. I was fortunate in this way. Many straight spouses find themselves in vicious divorce battles. Now that I knew he was an extremely competent actor, I pushed forward with my need to separate from him as soon as possible. I felt that I would suffocate if I didn't keep trying to free myself from his control. He was resistant to the changes I was exacting at times and was getting agitated over the control I was now exerting.

Most of the time though, Mark seemed relieved – calmer. He was more at peace with himself than I had ever seen him. Strangely enough, relief was also one of the emotions I experienced that first night. I now understood the huge void in our marriage. The answer was simple and devastating – deception! That night we toiled over the truth – for how long, I don't know. We went to bed in different rooms for the first time in our marriage. I felt isolated from the rest of the world. I was too numb and exhausted by his disclosure to even respond in anger.

Life changed for all of us. We rapidly sold the house, separated, and divorced. An excerpt from a journal I started during the first two weeks after Mark's disclosure describes some of the panic and anguish I felt:

9/16/99 – Well, here I am. Alone. It's around 7:30 P.M.. Almost dark. Hurricane Floyd is all around. Power is out. Karen's ceiling is leaking again. The basement is taking on water. My car is making a God-awful clunking noise. Trying to write this by candlelight. My other-half gone. Crying again.

Mark packed up and went away for a three-day weekend. God knows where and with whom. I'm trying to pack twenty-four years of life and ready the house for sale. Making a list of the money to transfer. My new lists sound like they are all about lawyers and shrinks. No more vacation or Disney savings. No more Mark and Renee or family vacations. No more Mark and Renee.

I'm so angry, but I still care that he is OK. Crying. How could he do this to me? – all these years. How could he knowingly commit adultery over and over in a way that could have endangered my life and our children's lives? His very own? How could he maintain keeping these secrets from the world? How could he betray me, our marriage, our family? How could he make it all seem so dirty?

I'm so alone. I've shared my pain with some, but they have their own lives to worry about. Mine has been shredded. It's dark now. The wind howling. My stomach hurts. Still no power. No supper. The roads are all closed. Flash floods. I'm exhausted but sleep is elusive.

Opened some mail. Opened my new "single person" checks. I'm moving too fast with all of this. It's only been two weeks. I feel so old and worn out. Wish I had my youth and innocence back. Wish I had been smarter, stronger, more self-preserving.

What am I thankful for? My children, my memories of our lives together as a family. How proud I was to be Mrs. Renee Westland. I was proud so many times. Our children made me realize how intensely you can love someone. My children make me confident that almost twenty-four years of marriage were not wasted. What is this doing to them? How do they feel? The family they thought they had is gone. Will they cope? I pray that they will. This is so freaky, alone, dark, candlelight, storm whipping. Very surreal. Very someone else's life or the stuff of a sad novel. There won't be a rainbow after this storm.

Mark was peaceful and happier. He was healing and openly living his new life before me, as I packed up and prepared our family home for sale, searched for a new place to live, and tried to keep my job stability. He seemed to be running full speed ahead into his new life with an unquenchable thirst for it. I was spiraling downward into a depression. My rainbows were gone. Ironically, he now seemed to own the rainbows that are a symbol of the gay life.

I was determined to show my daughters that one does not have to accept all that is thrown their way in life – that we could change a potentially harmful destiny being imposed on us by someone interested primarily in his own self-gratification – that we could survive this change. There were times that I honestly did not know if I could make it through the clouds.

I spent many nights and days crying – many days and nights depressed. The only thing that held me up was my faith that a higher power than any of us was guiding me and would show me what to do with the rest of my life. I hoped that eventually I would even be able to find enough forgiveness to prevent being consumed by bitterness and lack of trust and that I would be able to preserve what was left of my health. I didn't want to lose my wonder about the little miracles in life, and I wanted to preserve a certain degree of naiveté about it, too. I had always given new experiences and people the benefit of the doubt. I wanted to keep my cup more than half-full with optimism. I didn't know if I would ever experience love and passion again. Would I even recognize and trust it if I saw it?

The physical toll in stress and prolonged lack of sleep was wreaking its havoc. Initially my weight spiraled downward, then drastically upward with stress eating. Much of my hair fell out. For the first time in my life I ended up at the doctor's office seeking assistance for a depression that was deepening.

I tried to find the strength and resources to move on. Thank God, I found many angels along the way. Kind people seemed to be around every corner. I prayed more than I had ever prayed in my life. I found support groups. I went for therapy. I tried to figure out what was real about my marriage to this stranger. The only thing I knew for certain was that my daughters were real, and I was thankful for them. My family and Mark's family were unbelievably supportive to me. I thanked God for answering my plea for the truth.

Our daughters seem to have made the journey with minimal distress. The most telling statement our older daughter made to me was, "Mom, if you and Dad seem to be okay, so are we." I wondered what memories were real and meaningful to them. Would they be able to use anything they had witnessed of our relationship as a normal role model for their lives? How would all of these experiences color the special events of their lives – their weddings, baby showers, holidays?

When we rob those around us of truth, we take away their right and privilege to choose fulfillment of their own dreams. Life is precious. Therefore, I equate controlled and skillful deception with abuse.

Now, several years later, I have found my rainbows again. I rediscovered myself and have learned much. I have so much to be thankful for. I have found happiness in helping others and trying every day to give happiness back to the people in my life. I find self-therapy in supporting other straight spouses in their times of greatest need. New opportunities are always around us. Once we are given the gift of truth, there is no limit to what can be accomplished.

My rainbows have brightened even more. I have been fortunate in finding friendship, then love, truth, peace, and passion in the embrace of another man. This wonderful man has found his strength and life-path again, after his own failed marriage of thirty years when his former spouse realized and admitted the truth about her sexuality. The many years of therapy, confusion, and sadness they endured while trying to sort out their marriage has given us a strong common bond to share in our newfound relationship. Through Mark's truth, I have found happiness. I have come to believe that all of the events in life are learning experiences.

I hope that my story will help someone avoid the path of deception. I also pray that I can give hope to straight spouses reading this story who may be presently immobilized by their spouse's admissions. Whichever side of the coin you are on, seek help. Many people spend years trying to figure out how to go on. Many don't find their angels and attempt suicide – some succeed. Live your life with honesty and pride. Allow those around you to do the same, regardless of the choices they make. We are all different colors in the rainbow of life whether it be race, nationality, sexual orientation, or one of a kaleidoscope of other truths. Let the clouds part. Find the beauty of being true to yourself and the world around you. Life is a gift. Unwrap it with care.

Renee Chernik grew up in a small town in eastern Pennsylvania. She has been working as a nurse since 1973. Mark and Renee's divorce was final in the spring of 2000. Karen graduated from college with a degree in Recreation and Leisure Therapy Management and is working as a therapist at a rehabilitation center. Tina will graduate this spring (2002) with a degree in Elementary Education. Renee and her fiancé were joyfully joined in marriage on March 1, 2002 (read his story in the following chapter). Each of their four children by their previous marriages gave presentations in the ceremony. Everyone is working hard to adjust to the constantly changing faces of their family and their lives.

~ twenty-eight ~

A Miracle

Glen Chernik*

Life is good again. Renee and I have been engaged for a year now and will soon be married. The journey that basically began fifteen months ago - even though we first met under rather unusual circumstances over two years ago - has been nothing short of a miracle. A miracle in which God has been creating a beautiful relationship. Let me go back in time.

Two winters ago, Renee and I first met at a Straight Spouse support group meeting in Philadelphia. After long marriages, both of our spouses had revealed to us that they were gay. As each of us searched for support, we discovered this group of spouses who met regularly to help each other through the painful experience of having their worlds turned upside down.

Although neither of us was ready at that point to begin a new relationship, going to the meetings signified our willingness to begin moving forward. In order to do that, we needed to reflect upon what had transpired over the years in order to begin to see the bigger picture.

Support groups, such as Straight Spouse, are invaluable because they allow you to process, process, and process; and that is what we did. At the same time, I benefited from hearing the stories of other people with similar experiences. I quickly learned that I was not alone. I found out that other people have also been bewildered and have, at times, found themselves sitting and staring straight ahead within a whirlwind of emotions, remembrances, thoughts, and perplexity.

---

* All names in this story have been changed.

In my case, thirty years of marriage officially ended in 2001. In actuality, the marriage had lost its passion years ago. We had been in counseling for the final five years of the marriage – three years prior to my former wife Louise's disclosure and two more years following the disclosure. In the three predisclosure years, we had worked mainly on trying to improve our communication skills.

Although our communication was in need of improvement, and I will admit that I wasn't always the best communicator, I did feel at times that I was on the "hot seat." In other words, I was often feeling that it was my fault that we were having problems. Our sexual intimacy had stopped even before we had begun counseling, and we were basically just trying to get along. At times we had very difficult periods of arguing and accusations.

On one particular occasion, after a bitter argument, Louise left for a while. I worried tremendously that she would have a car accident. Fortunately she came home safely, and things calmed down. Perhaps the counseling would get us back on track to a full and complete marriage again. It seemed that communication was a good place to start. In addition to meeting jointly with the therapist, we met individually with him to work on our own personal growth issues.

It was in these individual sessions that Louise came to the realization that there was a deeper issue than communication at stake. She realized, and admitted to herself, that she was attracted to females. After some time of pondering this, she was able to bring it out in the open with me during one of our joint sessions. It was very difficult and painful for her to disclose this truth to me. Although she didn't verbalize the thought, she realized that our marriage was doomed.

It was with deep anguish and tears that Louise shared this information with me in the presence of the therapist. I pitied her and consoled her. Divorce wasn't a reality in my thinking. After all, isn't marriage forever? So I did what was natural: I hugged her and said we would work things out.

I must admit that a burden was lifted off of my shoulders. All of a sudden it was clear to me why things were the way they were in our marriage. No wonder the marriage wasn't complete. The problems we were having weren't just because of me. Suddenly things changed. Now we had a name for it. Now we could talk about it. Perhaps we could make the marriage work. How? I didn't know.

Over the following two years we continued counseling and even branched out to include some support group work on our own. Early on in the post-disclosure period, we attended a weekend retreat for couples who were in the same predicament. Couples were at this retreat from across the United States. One couple was from Israel!

It was good to meet other people who were struggling to keep their marriage together. However, we also came away from that experience bewildered and perplexed. All of the other couples present there had been dealing with extra-marital relationships. It was evident that this created much tension in their lives. The disillusionment became more apparent to me the more we got to know the other couples and particularly as I learned to know the straight spouses better in our separate meeting time. Even though extra-marital activity was not a part of our history, my former wife and I were beginning to see the handwriting on the wall for us.

Louise did not secretively go behind my back and forge a new relationship. Instead, she figured out who she was, admitted it to herself, then disclosed it to me. I could feel her pain in the disclosure. I could also feel her pain as we revealed to our kids that Mom is gay.

Our daughter took the news extremely hard. She immediately pronounced that we would split up in time. She was right. However, it wasn't evident to me then – to my wife, yes. She realized it would only be a matter of time until our relationship as husband and wife would end.

Our son had a feeling that we would be telling him what we did. He could sense it in his mother's gradual change over the years. Perhaps my daughter did too, but I am not sure. Even though I tried to be upbeat and say that things would work out, little did I realize that things wouldn't work out for the best *until* we would end our marriage.

As I mentioned before, I began attending the Straight Spouse meetings. Interestingly, my former wife passed the information on to me! She attended a Quaker organization for lesbian persons and derived support from it, and she wanted me also to have the support I needed. Not long after she told me about the support group, I went to my first Straight Spouse meeting.

I felt somewhat different from many of the other participants in the group. They told of bitter experiences of deception, and I knew they had a right to feel bitter. However, I did not share their bitterness. Louise had not cheated on me, and I was still working under the illusion that everything would work out all right.

After just one meeting with the support group, I took a leave of absence for a long period of time. I guess I buried my head in the sand and immersed myself in canoe and kayak building. Over time, however, I began to realize that things were not right for me. It took time for me to feel this. Louise reminded me often that I needed to think of myself – that things could be so much better for me if I did. I was looking at what I would lose by divorcing.

Two days stand out in particular during that period. One was an overwhelming sense of grief as I drove on the turnpike to a work-related seminar, and the other was one day while driving up the alley toward home after work. The tears flowed. Memories of our marriage, family, playing with the kids – and more – flooded my mind. I felt such an indescribable loss as it finally hit me that divorce was inevitable. I was recognizing how much I had and how hard it was to let it all go.

As the months passed, my grief must have been noticeable. My daughter and Louise both began to suggest that I should start getting out and meeting people. Oh, I had been a part of an important little personal support group that one of the pastors at our church helped to set up for me – and it was a good vehicle to express my feelings. I am thankful for the support and friendship that my two friends and the pastor offered during that period of monthly meetings over the course of a year.

However, things were changing. My daughter was beginning to understand that her mother and I could not just keep going through the motions of married life. By this time, Louise had met a female friend, and their relationship was accelerating. I was in limbo and beginning to feel lonely.

I remember one evening when my daughter accompanied me to Home Depot to pick something up for the house. While in the store, I couldn't help but notice, as I had on previous occasions in public places, that couples were walking around making decisions and sharing life together. It hit me that I no longer had that experience. It also felt as if I would never have it again. I even found myself resenting these couples!

When I got to the car, my daughter could read the distress on my face. She asked me what was wrong. I opened up to her and shared how I was feeling. She said, "Dad, you have to get out and meet women. They aren't going to come to you!" This struck home. I had heard the same admonition, over the months preceding this interaction with my daughter, from my therapist, as well as a friend, but I guess the timing wasn't right for action then. Now, here was my own daughter – with a special strength that can only come from God's grace – telling me to get out there and get on with life! I took her advice because it now felt right. I began attending Straight Spouse meetings again, and gradually I began to gain confidence in socializing once more.

Then another miracle happened! Renee sent out information about a social group that she found both fun and supportive. She shared that the group is a good way to socialize as well as to do helpful activities such as working on Habitat for Humanity projects. Both of these thoughts appealed to me, so I gave her a call. We went to a few functions and wound up getting to know each other and appreciated each other's company. Eventually we fell in love, and our new life together took root.

In retrospect, I have pondered whether my previous marriage was a waste of time, and I have come to the conclusion that it was not. We evolved over the thirty years from a passionate couple, who looked very typical, through our various family stages to a relationship that was not unlike that of a brother and sister. We were friends and still are, but some key ingredients that are difficult to describe were missing.

Yes, the physical touch, the warm embraces, and the laughing and crying together are important ingredients, but it is more than those individually. It is a depth of feeling that we receive when all the ingredients are present. It is difficult to dissect a marriage into various components since they all work together. All of the ingredients are present in the relationship that I now share with Renee.

Louise and I have two wonderful children. I can't imagine life without them, even though they are grown up now and on their own. Was the marriage a waste of time? No. Oh, it would have been good to have met Renee a long time ago. But that wasn't God's plan for us. We can't change what has happened, and it doesn't do any good to overanalyze the past. Our past lives have led us to this present point. It is time for a new beginning. Praise God.

On March 1, 2002, **Glen** and **Renee** (read her story in Chapter 27) celebrated their marriage in the presence of family and friends. Glen is a long-time elementary school teacher, who enjoys the hobby of making canoes and kayaks.

~ *twenty-nine* ~

A Boy at Ten and Then at Twenty

Helen Rawson Early

A Boy at Ten:

Waiting for the School Bus

We catch each other glancing at the clock;
He should be home by now.
Not worried, but anticipating.
Today we're both home,
We'll have some time with him today.

Time – earnestly we seek it, prize it,
But at day's end it's slipped our grasp.
Oh, the work's been done,
Well, mostly done, we've gotten by;
But what of joy?
Where was time to just enjoy the boy?

Boy, man-child
Soon to be no longer child
What was it we did together yesterday?

There was the game he found deep in his closet,
And with glee brought out.
"Look! I found it! Come and play."
I saw only Missing Pieces,
And at the end of my discoursing,
On Neatness and Responsibility,
No time remained to play.

Then I drove him for his lesson.
What was it he was describing?
I remember only chiding
"We'll be late again today."

Home again and TV claimed him,
And then the homework,
Does it really take so long?
Or is it just his way of escaping,
His excuse to close his door?
School has more of him than we do,
And knows him better, too.
They see him on the playground –
"Interacting with his peers"
They call it now.
They see his false bravado
On coming up to bat,
The flash of mad frustration,
When answers aren't down pat.

The bus has passed, he's coming down the lane.
There's someone with him –
"Mother, I brought Jenny home,
She wants to see the bird house that I built."

He tilts his head and gives a tentative, expectant smile.
I've seen that look before,
Been seeing it ever since, as two year old,
I found him at the cookie jar.

It says "I know we planned this morning,
You and Dad and I,
To bike out to Miller's field. I've my new kite to fly.
But you know I'd rather play with kids."

He knows we won't gainsay him,
I only hope that future Jennys will seem as fine.
I think of future waitings,
Perhaps soon there'll be no coming home at all.
Will Fort Lauderdale still be in with the college crowd?

Boy, man-child, child of our love,
May the world deal gently with you,
And so with us.

And Now at Twenty:

We have not lost him
There's still a coming home at times.
But there are no more Jennys
His partner's Daniel now.
He seems as fine as Jenny did,
That day so long ago.

We had no thought in those days
That this was where his future lay,
This, how it was ordained to be.

Now he's said the words
And we know the whole of him.
He trusted us, and we've grown closer still.

We've grown fiercely protective
Of this new family that is part of ours.
Our love surrounds the two of them.
May the world still deal gently with them
And with all of you.

Helen Rawson Early, MD, is a retired pediatrician who practiced for thirty-five years in Lansdale, Pennsylvania. She and her husband, Martin Luther Early, who died in 1991, are the parents of two children, Elaine and John. The Earlys were active in PFLAG.[1] Helen continues to be involved as treasurer of Lehigh Valley PFLAG and is helpline chairman for Philadelphia PFLAG. The helpline number is 215-572-1833.

Martin believed that he had never known anyone who was homosexual, and hardly knew what questions to ask his son. However, John remembers fondly a first PFLAG meeting when he and his father were in the same small group. As the sharing came around to his father, he said simply, "My son is gay and I love him very much."

John and his partner have owned a home together for ten years. Both are *out* at work and active in the gay and wider community. John drives his race car with EMRA, the Eastern Motor Racing Association. He and his mother have spoken at schools and at church and business groups about homosexuality and how it affects the family and community.

---

[1] Parents, Families, and Friends of Lesbians and Gays. The organization now includes Bisexuals and Transgenders.

> Whenever you find you are on the side of the majority, it is time to pause and reflect.
>
> ~ Mark Twain

~ *thirty* ~

One Pilgrim's Story

Rick Alan Alderfer

I have often told new acquaintances I grew up in Norman Rockwell's America. Life amidst the gently rolling farmlands of southeastern Pennsylvania afforded an almost perfect childhood. It was the kind of small-town community where everyone knew everyone else, where neighbors helped neighbors plow snow and till gardens (generously sharing the bounty, of course), and no one ever thought of keeping their doors locked. A place where every major life event – birth, death, illness, and more – required a personal visit as well as a casserole (or at the very least, home-baked goods).

I remember summers filled with working in the vegetable garden, helping to bale hay, and camping trips. I happily recall countless hours spent playing board games, riding bikes, and climbing trees. There were always dogs, cats, and other animals around to care for and play with. Eagerly anticipated summertime treats included fresh-picked strawberries, corn on the cob, garden mint tea, and homemade ice cream. Winters found us sledding, ice skating, and shoveling snow.

I also recall our family sitting in the same church pew every Sunday surrounded by almost exactly the same families. And Sunday afternoons were always spent visiting one or both sets of grandparents, where we would inevitably encounter an ever-changing mix of aunts, uncles, cousins, and other church folk. I also have wonderful memories of many, many picnics, summertime reunions, and holiday dinners, always being surrounded by a large, loving, extended family.

The first realization that I was somehow different than most other kids came early in grade school. I am not sure that I can explain it clearly even now, but somehow I sensed deep down inside I was not just like the rest of my classmates. I did not feel the same things they did or react in exactly the same ways.

I remember not understanding why the boys teased the girls — at least half of my closest friends were girls. I also recall having very little interest in the rough-and-tumble games that most of the boys my age seemed to delight in. I was far happier getting lost in creative and artistic activities such as music, books, or arts and crafts projects. I do not remember anyone else ever noticing these things or being concerned about them, but I realized very clearly I just did not quite fit in.

Junior high school brought even more intense feelings of isolation and of not being like everyone else. I remember about the time most of my classmates were starting to look for their first boy- and girlfriends that somehow I did not understand what all of the interest and excitement was about. Quite obviously, I was missing something that every other teenager found completely natural. I also recall becoming aware that it was the handsome guys that caught my eye instead of the pretty girls. I had absolutely no idea what any of this meant — certainly not that it was sexual in any way — but I knew instinctively this was a secret that I must keep to myself. And so I did.

My early high school years were filled with much confusion. I remember very often feeling isolated, lonely, and different. So many times and in so many ways I felt like I was all alone and peculiar, not like everyone else. Health and family life classes made it clearer than ever that all of the wild emotions rolling around inside me were simply not the norm. I also realized that while I had a clinical understanding of sex and sexuality, I could not even begin to comprehend the feelings, drives, and desires that went along with them.

It was a harmless conversation around the lunch table in the Christopher Dock Mennonite High School cafeteria the fall of my junior year that would forever change my place in the world. It was simply a casual conversation among friends, but for me it would be life-changing. We were talking about two of our classmates – a perfect match, we all believed – who had just broken up as a couple. Prevailing sentiment was that one of the two thought that things were moving a little too quickly and needed to call things to a halt. Sitting there surrounded by oblivious classmates, I questioned all that possibility entailed.

For the very first time, I tried to grasp the concept of sexual intimacy. The more I thought about it, the more I realized it was a lost cause. At best, I simply could not comprehend it, had no desire for it, and was completely uncomfortable with even the thought of it. Even worse, I must admit to feeling the whole idea of the mechanics of sexuality were more than a little disconcerting – horrifyingly not what was expected of any *normal* adolescent male. I remember being stunned – and completely terrified – by the thoughts and feelings that raced through my mind that afternoon. Going through my afternoon classes in somewhat of a daze, I desperately tried to figure out exactly what this unsettling realization revealed about me.

What was the direct opposite of *normal*? So horrible that no one even dared to talk about it? Such an abomination the Church barely mentioned its existence? For the very first time in my life, I suspected I might be a homosexual. That thought hit me with almost the force of a physical blow. *And what was worse, I did not even know how I could know for sure.*

For the remainder of my high school years – and even several years beyond – I anxiously searched for the answer: *Could I really be gay?* I did not even know any homosexuals – had never met one. *How could it be remotely possible?* I read every book, magazine and newspaper article, and pamphlet I could find on the subject of homosexuality. None seemed to be of much help. I read of activists and demonstrators, supporters and accusers, rights and oppression, even morality and degenerates.

None of these things, however, were much help in explaining what I was feeling or why.

One of the major turning points in my life came on a Sunday afternoon the autumn before I turned twenty-one. I had learned through a television newscast that a local film festival was showing a controversial art-house film about two lifelong teen-age friends, each of whom grew up painfully hiding the secret that he was gay and in love with the other.

I remember driving into the city that beautiful September day with a mixture of both anticipation and anxiety, unsure of what to expect. I recall watching the story unfold on the screen until the pivotal scene where one of the boys breaks down and con-fesses his feelings for the other. Instead of the physical beating he anticipates, what follows is a warm embrace followed by a tender kiss as the second young man admits his feelings as well.

I vividly recall waves of emotion washing over me that sent tears coursing down my face. In that one instant, so many things became crystal clear to me. Suddenly I knew, without any shadow of a doubt, exactly who and what I was. I under-stood why I had felt so isolated – so different – all those years. In that one moment, I finally understood desire and passion and sexuality like I could not have even imagined before. All at once, so many things made sense; I finally understood why I had not felt all those things that others had found so completely natural – I was undeniably a gay man.

I do not remember the rest of the movie, but I recall it did not have a happy ending. I also remember aimlessly driving around the city for hours afterwards, a million thoughts racing through my mind, before finally driving home. During those long hours, I did something that I would spend countless nights and years doing; I prayed to God to change me – to make me normal – to make me right.

Those next few years were filled with petitions to God, beg-ging, pleading, even bargaining with my Creator to change me.

I answered every invitation and altar call that was given and prayed the sinner's prayer more times than I could count. I was involved in Bible studies, fellowship groups, and healing services and even requested the laying on of hands in order to be *delivered* from such an evil. I claimed every Scripture I had ever learned in order to be changed into God's image – certainly Jesus could not have meant for me to be something I had been taught was an abomination in God's sight?

But deliverance did not come. No matter how much I tried to change, begged God to change me, pretended I was changed, or simply refused to think about it, it became very clear – nothing changed at all. I – a lifelong, born, raised, and baptized Mennonite – remained a homosexual!

The ensuing couple of years were the most painful of my life. I questioned again and again why the God I professed to love, honor, and serve seemed to continue to turn away from me. I could not imagine what I had done that had been so awful that even the Lord of grace and mercy decided I was beyond help - unworthy of divine love and care. There were many, many long sleepless nights filled with agony during which I pleaded with God to take my life. Regardless of what was to come, it could not match the despair and pain I was living with on a daily basis. I tried to continue studying the Scriptures, but failed to see how the good news or promises of the Gospel could apply to someone as despicable and depraved as I felt I must be in the eyes of the Lord.

My darkest point came following the final night of a Christian music festival. I had been anticipating it for some time, spending several weeks in intense Bible study and prayer, hoping the Lord was going to use this special service to finally turn my life around and make me whole. I could feel an excitement in the air as the final speaker began winding up for the invitation. I listened intently to the speaker's testimony, put my whole heart and soul into the songs of worship, and at the invitation, practically ran down the aisle to the altar.

As I knelt there, I waited for my new life in Christ to begin – waited for a transformation – waited to finally know deliverance. I waited to no avail! As the final chorus of "God Is So Good" was being sung, the tears flowing down my face were not the tears of joy like those around me. Mine were the bitter tears of realizing that once again God had not heard the deepest cries of my heart.

After the service, I sat alone in my car in the dark for a very long time trying to decide what to do next. I knew that things had to change in my life. I could not go on for even one more day filled with the deep despair and self-hatred for who – and what – I was. I was at a breaking point; something had to give. I did not have the courage to take my own life, and as much as I tried with every fiber of my being, I could not change the feelings deep inside me.

There, in the quiet, dark of night, I took what I saw as my only – albeit almost unthinkable – course of action: I abandoned my Creator. In one final, desperate prayer, I explained to God that I was willing to be changed any time and any place, according to God's plan for me. Until then, I was through torturing myself, trying to do the impossible. I stopped praying all but the most benign of prayers. I gave up on Bible studies and even daily devotions.

I never stopped attending church services, but I no longer believed the sermons were meant for me, and the great hymns of faith – once so comforting and inspiring – now simply rang hollow and empty. For several years, I simply existed in this spiritually and emotionally devoid state of mind. I was certainly not happier or any more comfortable with my sexuality, but I did manage to let go of a lot of the self-hatred and anger I had been carrying around for so long. I stopped despising myself for things I had no control over or punishing myself for things I could not change. And then, one afternoon – completely by surprise – I found hope. Actually, hope found me!

While browsing through a bookstore, I happened across two books that would begin to rekindle my faith in God. In *A Place at the Table*, Episcopalian Bruce Bawer argues for a seat at the proverbial table – of both the Church and the world in general – for gays and lesbians. The second book, *On Being Gay*, by Brian McNaught, shares the story of his coming to terms with being both a faithful, practicing Catholic and a gay man.

While I could not agree with everything either author shared, these two books were my first exposure to persons of faith who were also homosexuals. They awakened a sense of hope within me I had not felt for many years. Perhaps I did not have to choose between the God of my childhood and the absolute, unchangeable fact that I was gay.

Several weeks later, I found the book that would forever change – perhaps even save – my life. *From Wounded Hearts*, by Roberta Showalter Kreider, shares the faith stories of many gay and lesbian Christians. Even more than that, the book shares the pilgrimages of a number of Mennonites, several of whom I discovered I knew personally. I could identify with these stories of struggle and reconciliation completely.

For the first time, I read stories of others who shared my experiences almost exactly. Some of them grew up within just a few miles from where I did. These intensely personal faith stories brought something of a revelation to me: *Maybe God had not abandoned me after all. What if God had not given up on me as I had given up my faith in God? Could it be that I was too busy listening to the world's – and even my own – condemnation to even hear of my Savior's love, mercy, and forgiveness? Perhaps God did create me in God's own image and loves me unconditionally – homosexuality and all?*

With a renewed sense of hope and purpose, I read all the books I could find regarding faith, homosexuality, and the Church. I started praying again, earnestly asking the Lord to show me the truth, free from the biases of society or religion. I resumed carefully studying the Scriptures, now going so far as to compare original Greek, Hebrew, and Aramaic texts with many of our various modern translations. Many of the texts that had been used dogmatically and absolutely over the years to condemn homosexuality as an abomination read very differently in other languages and other translations. Side-by-side comparisons found such diverse interpretations and shades of meaning that universal condemnation using any particular text became almost an impossibility.

There are so few condemning texts in the context of the entire Scriptures as a whole, and now many of those became ambiguous at best. That is so, even without taking into consideration the contexts in which those Scriptures were written or to whom and for what reason they were written. All in all, I found far less absolute condemnation than I would have ever dared dream possible.

These past few years, as I have been digging deeper into the holy Scriptures and strengthening my personal relationship with my Lord and Savior, Jesus Christ, I have been able to come to terms with my sexual orientation. While it has certainly not been easy, and while mysteries and questions still remain, I have been able to make peace with the fact that I am both a Christian and a homosexual.

I do not have all the answers, nor have I found an absolute, affirming Scripture text that eases all of my doubts and fears. I do, however, have the wonderful hope that I am a fellow pilgrim, striving with all of my heart to be a committed and faithful servant of the Lord. I have found much comfort in the words of the Apostle Paul, as stated in the last part of verse 12 in I Corinthians 13: "Now all that I know is hazy and blurred, but then I will see everything clearly, just as clearly as God sees into my heart right now." (*Living Bible*)

Rick Alan Alderfer is a ninth generation Mennonite of Swiss-German heritage. He grew up and resides in the historical Pennsylvania Dutch country farmlands of southeastern Pennsylvania near Harleysville. Most of his working life has been spent in the food business, including eighteen years as the owner of a catering company. For seven years, he was director of food services for Christopher Dock Mennonite High School in Lansdale, Pennsylvania, where he had graduated with the class of 1982. He is currently working as a special events coordinator and is also involved in a variety of writing and publishing projects.

An avid reader, he also enjoys singing and listening to Southern Gospel Music, teaching and taking cooking classes, and traveling. Exploring new cities is of special interest to him. Rick also enjoys Fraktur, the old Pennsylvania German art of Illumination. He can be reached by e-mail at menno.too@juno.com.

I have faced my fear with the spiritual discipline of trusting in the grace of God. I also trust more deeply than ever in the power of resurrection that calls us to stand up out of death and to choose life. Life cannot be shut up in the grave (or the closet) unless we allow it to remain there. Neither death, nor its first cousin, fear, need to have the last word.

~ Melanie Morrison, "A Crisis of Pronouns"

Christians & Homosexuality: Dancing Toward the Light
Special issue of *The Other Side*

~ *thirty-one* ~

A Lament

Ruth Linscheid

How long, O God, must these, our gay brothers and lesbian sisters,
   suffer?
How long must they endure the slings and arrows of hate and
   derision?

How long, O God, will the church disown and dismember them?
How long will the church judge them by their sexual orientation and
   not their faithfulness?

How long, O God, will family and friends need to hide and be
   fearful?
How long till parents can say, "My child is gay and that's okay"?

How long, O God, till society respects them?
How long till equality and fairness come to them?

How long, O God, till our eyes are opened and justice rolls
   over us?
How long till we speak words of love and compassion?

How long, O God, till we see diversity as a gift from you?
How long till we love your children as you do?

> O God, let a resurrection come upon us.
> Let Christ's spirit of love enfold us and grow in us.
> Let Christ's healing hand touch our fevered emotions.
> Let Christ's compassion and comfort dwell in us –
>   driving away fear and hate.
> Let Christ's forgiveness in us cleanse the wounds
>   that we have caused.
> Then, let us embrace and truly love our
>   gay neighbors as ourselves.

-Written for the Brethren/ Mennonite Supporting Congregations Network Gathering,
1998.

Ruth Linscheid celebrated her 70th birthday in 2001. She grew up near Goessel, Kansas, where she and her husband J. Willard (d. 1992) taught in the local schools for many years. The couple's three sons and their mates are: David (Cynthia), John (Ken), and Steven (Anne). They have two grandsons: Aaron and Joel. Ruth enjoys reading, china painting, and quilting, and occasionally she does some writing.

Ruth Linscheid is the mother of John Linscheid. John Linscheid and Ken White tell their story on page 32.

After I came out, I mourned the loss of my social power, but I came to recognize that true power belongs to God. Surrendering the power that had for so long protected me, I was forced to rely on God's power.

The witness of other gay brothers and sisters confirms that in coming out and "losing everything" we find our greatest power. We feel free, undominated, fully human (even though some now regard us as less than human).

~ John Linscheid,

Christians & Homosexuality: Dancing Toward the Light
Special issue of *The Other Side*

~ *thirty-two* ~

A Great Marriage Ended

Clarissa Brooks*

In my family, twenty-one was marrying age. By my twenty-fifth birthday, I was scared that I was doomed to spinsterhood. I decided I had better get professional help to find out why I was so unsuccessful relating to men.

The day of my first therapy session was also the evening Bob and I had our first date. We had both graduated from Wheaton College in 1978, although we didn't meet there. After college, he became friends with my brother-in-law. I was both interested in him and wary. For the most part, I kept him at a distance. When he began to ask me for dates, I declined, but I finally agreed to go out with him in December of 1981.

I remember talking to him on our first date about my therapy session that had happened earlier that day. I felt good talking to Bob; he was a good listener. We shared many values and interests, and he was good looking.

Dating him was a victory for me. All through high school and college, I had always broken off relationships as soon as we began any passionate kissing. I was certain this was because of the difficult relationship I had with my father growing up. He was a hard man to know and talk to, reserved, domineering, and sometimes violent. Bob, on the other hand, was warm, gentle, kind, caring, and had a gift for friendship. I enjoyed spending time with him.

We dated, broke up, and dated again. We began to talk about getting married. We both wanted to be very sure this marriage

---

* All names in this story have been changed

would work before we made a commitment. I was deeply committed to doing whatever it took to make a marriage work – to hang in, talk things through, pray, get help. The quality in Bob that was most important to me was that he, like me, had the capacity to make the changes needed to have a successful long-term relationship.

When we were married, it seemed to me that my therapy goals had been reached. I felt comfortable enough with a man to marry him. But suddenly, within a month of our wedding, I ran into an abyss of memories of tangled experiences that had happened to me while I was growing up. Amid the normal difficulties we faced with being newly married, I slid into a deep depression. Bob was in his second year of medical school. At times I was too depressed to do anything but work and come home to hide under a blanket on the sofa. Within a year, he began a grueling call schedule that had him exhausted all the time.

During that time, I found, as I had for so long, that my relationships with women commanded my attention more than my relationship with Bob. Because of this, within a year of my wedding, I wondered if I was gay. But my therapist and I decided I had a lot of other issues I needed to address before I would be ready to look at that one.

The core of what gripped me was that I thought I had to look, think, feel, and be the image my mother had of me. I had to make myself into what would keep her comfortable, to take care of her, to be her "good little girl." On top of that, I grew up in a very conservative Christian environment. There was only one option – to be a perfect Christian, get married and have children. Growing up, I strove to be the image of what I was supposed to be. What I had then was an image rather than anything that felt like real human substance.

I spent nearly a decade battling for wholeness. There were times when the impulse to kill myself was nearly overwhelming. Bob was in medical school and residency. Our relationship was only occasionally in the foreground. Nevertheless, we got through it. I healed internally and began to see more of my own person emerge. I started feeling more whole and balanced, with a clearer sense of who I was and what was important to me. When we had the energy, Bob and I worked on developing healthy ways to communicate. Our relationship improved. We learned to fight fairly and to care more deeply.

In the summer of 1992, I spent six weeks in a tipi in the mountains in Montana on a spiritual retreat. During that time, I began to feel that there was some kind of connection missing between Bob and me. I identified it as a spiritual connection. I had the sense that Bob did not understand who I was on some deep levels. I felt our marriage was in jeopardy. At the same time, I realized that while I had been developing my spiritual life, every ounce of his energy had been spent becoming a doctor. I realized I needed to give him a chance to develop parts of himself that he had neglected during the brutal rigors of medical school and residency. I put my concerns on hold.

In December of 1992, I became pregnant. With Shelly's birth we were thrown into the new challenges of parenthood, and we began to thrive. We discovered deep places of love. Together, we faced difficulties with more and more grace. We developed a spiritual synergy that helped us each cope with the difficulties we faced with greater maturity and wisdom. Our love deepened. We found we worked well around the daily events of life. We talked about everything. Many of the difficulties that had troubled me earlier in our relationship seemed to fade.

One of the outlets for my creative energy was serving on our church council. In 1996, our state's denominational leaders were trying to *disfellowship* our congregation because we accepted members without regard to sexual orientation.

The battle with the denomination was bruising. I had to prepare spiritually before meetings. After the meetings, I had to consciously work to let go of anger when vicious things had been said about us by denominational leaders. But after the meeting in which delegates voted to begin the procedures to remove us from membership, I simply could not let go of my anger. After six weeks I had to ask myself, *Why? Why was I taking this so personally?* My answer came instantly. I realized I identified with the gay and lesbian community. I realized I was bisexual.

The first person I talked to about what I was feeling was Bob. He tilted his head, looked at me sideways and said, "This is news to you?" Yes, it was! It was not news to Bob. It was not news to my father. It was not news to my sister. But it was news to me! Before that moment, I had not had a context into which to put my powerful feelings toward women. The idea that homosexuality was about who you fall in love with had never occurred to me.

I felt certain that accepting this information about myself would have no bearing on my marriage. I would not leave Bob if I became attracted to someone, whether that person was a man or woman. My family was profoundly important to me. I knew how damaging divorce was for children, and I could not even imagine entertaining the possibility that Bob and I would do that. Our relationship was too good.

Coming out as bisexual took courage, but I found support among all of my friends and family. I was surprised and delighted by their response.

There were other almost immediate consequences to my new awareness. I felt my creativity and spiritual life deepen. Where in the past my relationship to Christianity had been distant, I began to sense Jesus beckoning to me. I began to slowly look again at my faith. I found it ironic that rather than my sexuality pushing me further from God, it drew me closer.

After the birth of our second child David in 1996, we began two fast paced, high stress years that included building a house and dealing with a baby and toddler on top of a host of other challenges. We worked consciously to use the circumstances to grow individually and as a couple. Bob and I did well with the challenges that faced us as a family. But at quieter times, I still felt something was missing between us. I did not have the energy to question myself more deeply. I was relieved when months would go by without me having any sexual thoughts about women.

Our love was warm and deep. I just figured we were too busy and tired. I worked hard to get over my continuing resistance to sexual intimacy. I talked about my dissatisfaction. Night after night I lay in bed looking at Bob's sleeping face and prayed, "Please, God, make me love him the way I want to."

At the end of those two years, my creativity and spiritual resources were spent. I decided taking piano lessons would be a good way to reenergize myself, and I found a teacher in our town. By my third lesson, I was passionately in love with Gail! Suddenly, feelings awoke in me that I had never experienced before. I had never known how the brush of a hand could electrify my entire body.

For months, I struggled to not have an affair. I talked to Bob about what was going on. I tried to figure out why I didn't have the same response to him that I had to her. I was sure that I would never leave Bob for her. I would not do that. I also would not have an affair, though that took every bit of self-discipline I had. Realizing I could not be "just friends" with Gail, we ended the relationship. I felt heartbroken.

The difficulty in our marriage intensified. In almost every respect I was very happy. I had a husband I loved. We had two healthy, happy children. We lived in a house we had built in a beautiful setting. Our life was rich with good friends and caring family. *So why did I periodically have an intense urge to pack up my mini-van and disappear into the West? Why did I feel like some part of me was suffocating under ice?*

As I shared with Bob my continued frustration about the sexual aspect of our relationship, we both began to recognize that our relationship was in crisis. I realized some of our conversations hinted at the possibility of divorce. I was stunned by the thought. I felt I was looking into an abyss that terrified me. I could not bear the thought that we might break up a family in which there was such an abundance of love and happiness.

Being sexual was an important aspect of our relationship. It helped us feel close in many ways. But the more I looked at my feelings about being sexual with Bob, the more I realized that I have always felt uncomfortable with even the mildest forms of intimate relationships with the few men I had dated in my life. I had always ended relationships after the first few kisses. All the years of therapy – the years of prayer – all the things books and magazines tell you to do – none of them worked!

Finally, one night I dreamed that I was a prostitute. I realized I was only being sexual with Bob because I wanted to keep the marriage happy. I had to stop – for at least a while – to try to sort out my feelings and try to see what this was about.

Bob and I went into therapy again. We worked hard, and I hoped it would help. But the longer I went without being sexual with Bob, the more relieved I felt.

Still, I was not willing to admit that I was lesbian. I felt to do so would mean ending a relationship that had been deeply important to me for twenty years. I could not reconcile the two sides of myself: the side that knew that I could not stay in a sexual relationship with a man and the side that would not hurt the man I loved and our children. I felt like draft horses were pulling me in two different directions.

When I finally said to myself, "I am lesbian," I became suicidal. I knew those thoughts were coming from a conservative Christian upbringing that implied homosexuality was the ultimate evil and needed to be destroyed. I knew I would not follow those impulses. They were from old self-hatred I now rejected. However, I knew if I had come out to myself when I had first asked the question sixteen years earlier, I would not have had the internal resources to resist the impulse to kill myself.

When I was able to let go of the hatred toward myself, I felt a huge surge of relief and release of energy. I realized the effort to hide the knowledge of my sexuality from myself had drained energy from many areas of my life. Almost immediately, I felt more energy and attention for my children.

My relief from depression was short-lived. On a Saturday morning I told Bob that I knew I was lesbian. Within twenty minutes, we had decided to divorce. I was stunned. I did not expect to come to that conclusion. I expected we would talk about it and try to find a way around it. We both cried all weekend.

We spent the next seven months swinging back and forth between deciding to divorce and trying to work something out. Because Bob had been so comfortable when I had told him I was bisexual, I was shocked by his anger. I was naïve. I thought Bob and I would have the maturity to work this out in a friendly way. However, the anger and sudden difficulty communicating was not about maturity. I realized his anger was out of profound pain. He believed being gay was what I wanted. As I watched his pain and knew how difficult this would be for our children, I had the constant feeling of a maul hammering into my chest.

I was shocked by my friends, especially my church friends. I had expected care from my supportive congregation. I had expected sympathy, at least, and hoped for celebration that I had finally owned who I really was. I had not counted on the grief people felt as they saw a very good marriage end. I felt terribly vulnerable as a gay person and as a woman dependent on a man for financial support.

I had expected a measure of generosity – not just financial, but also emotional and spiritual – from Bob, my family, and our friends. Instead, longtime friends told me they would never be able to trust my wisdom or integrity again. Friends who had studied the issue of homosexuality in great detail, very well-educated, bright, sensitive, sophisticated people told me I had made a *decision* to be homosexual. One friend told me I wasn't acknowledging the pain I was causing.

My parents decided I was mentally ill. My father told me that he would have preferred to learn I had a terminal illness rather than that I was gay. I had friends say I was the moral equivalent of a violent drunk. It was as though I was suddenly in some sub-human category. Many of the same friends who had been supportive when I came out as bisexual said I had made a *choice* to be gay – as though it was possible for anyone to choose their sexuality.

In order to come out, I risked every single relationship I had – family, friends, and neighbors. I risked my social standing as a doctor's wife in an upper middle-class community. I risked my financial security. I lost my home, my best friend, and the right to sleep in the same house every night with our children.

However, I knew that to continue to force myself to be in a relationship with a man meant shutting down my creativity, my spirituality, my emotional energy, my capacity to care about others, and my very sense of feeling alive and human. I felt angry that I had to make the terrible decision between shutting down who I was as a woman and keeping my family. I felt even angrier that many who loved me could not see it was not a choice about my sexuality, but rather a choice about staying alive, and that it was earth-shattering.

When I finally realized I could not continue to try and fix something that had no hope of working, I moved out of our house. I felt my courage was completely spent. I had lost so much, only to be alone.

Then I met Joy! She came into my life at a time when I needed to regain my courage. Through her love and care, I found the strength to begin to heal relationships that had been damaged. I realized that the deep connection I felt to her was what was missing from my life for so long. There was nothing Bob and I could have done to make things work for us sexually. He simply was the wrong gender.

I had hoped Joy and I would be together for the rest of our lives. However, we soon found we were geographically incompatible. She needed to move back West to be close to friends and because the midwestern winters were too much for her.

Some months after Joy and I broke up, Gail and I ran into each other again. We resumed our friendship and began to explore something deeper. We are letting things unfold slowly while enjoying the gift of being together.

As Bob and I have begun our post-divorce life, many of the skills we worked so hard to develop are helping us. We both seem to have let go of much of our anger. Our children, Shelly and David, went through several months of depression. We made sure they got the kind of attention they needed from us, from friends, and from family, as well as professionals. My heart still feels crushed when I think of the long-term consequences our divorce will have on them. Hopefully, the commitment Bob and I made to each other to continue to work well together as parents will mitigate the most negative consequences. I also believe that I am a better mother now that I am not constantly weighed down with depression.

I may never fully shake my sense of vulnerability. But I am grateful that the dire predictions of many have not come true. Most of the relationships that were hurt in my process of coming out are largely healed. And much to my surprise, rather than being estranged from God because of my supposed *choice*, I have a profound sense of being carried in the arms of Divine Love. I am created in the image of the Divine. In claiming who I am fully, I am more fully able to be the loving, creative, healing person God created me to be.

~ *thirty-three* ~

A Tribute to My Lesbian Daughter

Lois Kenagy

In healthy families, the relationship between parents and their adult children is one that provides great joy and satisfaction. Although sometimes complicated, the relationship between a mother and daughter can be a very special one. Certainly that has been my experience with our oldest child, our lesbian daughter, now in her early forties.

The joy of her parents at the time of Susan's birth was so evident that my mother-in-law inquired of Clif, "What did you do before she was born?" To which he replied, "We wished for her." She was planned for and expected with joyful anticipation. Both of us were over thirty years of age, and we were very ready to devote time and effort to this child's nurture. And what a remarkable child she was! We think she continues to be a remarkable person, one of whom we are very proud.

Early on, she gave evidence of her own unique personality – she not only had a mind of her own, but seemed to have a strong sense of who she was. An aunt made two lovely dresses for her second birthday. Not about to wear something new, she would not let me put them on her until they had hung in the closet for many months. She loved toy cars and trucks and toys for constructing things such as Legos, blocks, and Tinker-Toys. Dolls were of no interest. One time we found her lying on her back under the family Volkswagen, wrench in hand.

When Susan was three and a half, our third child was born. As I tried to cope with the work involved with caring for three preschoolers, I fear I may have put too much responsibility on her at that young age. Without question, she helped a great deal then and all through the years of her childhood.

Susan was eight years old when our fourth child was born. I shall long remember the interchange between Susan and her younger brother when the new baby came home from the hospital. Peter (nineteen months younger than Susan) objected when Susan wanted to hold the new baby, "But you don't like babies." To which Susan replied, "But this is *our* baby!" And indeed the special relationship between her and that little brother continued until his death at age nineteen. The bonding was strong and her grief was immeasurable. She felt he understood her and had a heart like her own.

In the '70s, public school required that girls wear dresses. That made life difficult for both Susan and me. The constraints of our own financial situation and her strong opinions about what she would find comfortable to wear made finding ready-made dresses difficult. Therefore, I sewed her dresses, although finding fabrics she would approve was not easy. No floral prints were acceptable, so we went with paisleys and geometric prints. When she entered seventh grade, the rules changed and she could wear jeans to school. This made life easier for her and for her mother.

I made a long cotton print dress that she wore to church and to school programs. We smiled on seeing her enter the church foyer with farm boots and the long dress. When she arrived at school for the junior high band program, her band director greeted her with surprise and open arms. He had never before seen her in a dress! She protected herself from his welcoming embrace by placing her trombone firmly in front of her.

A good friend who had difficulty understanding Susan urged me to work harder to help her to be *more feminine*. I replied that my responsibility as a parent is to help each of my children be true to who they are and not to force them to become someone they are not. My goal was that she should be a happy child, happy with who she is, not that she conform to others' expectations of how she should act. I'm not sure where I had developed such a wise philosophy of child rearing. I only know that I am grateful that I had such an approach during Susan's childhood.

Susan regularly accompanied her parents to church. She participated in Sunday evening classes for her age group and in Mennonite Youth Fellowship. She hated the girls' club which did projects most girls enjoyed. Since she didn't object to other church functions, we permitted her to withdraw from girls' club. During junior high, she made the decision to be baptized and to become a member of Albany (Oregon) Mennonite Church, a decision that her father and I welcomed.

Susan was fortunate to be born into a farm family. Her father welcomed her participation in all the farm activities. She was a good tractor driver, farm mechanic, agricultural planner, and a very practical person with a good understanding of what we now call "appropriate technology." If ever I were stranded on a desert island, I would want Susan for my companion.

During her high school years, we hired a custom operator to harvest our green beans. With her carefully saved dollars Susan purchased a used bean picker, and we then hired her to do the custom harvesting. I recall her departure for college. We were in the car on the way to the airport when she turned around to wave one last fond good-bye to her very own bean picker.

During college years, between terms and on vacations, Susan worked on the farm. It was her love – her joy. After college she planned to be more directly involved with the farm operation and, together with her brother, purchased a small farm parcel owned by their grandmother. However, after a few years, she realized that although her brother was ready to make a life-long commitment to be tied down to the farm, she wasn't. She wanted to retain more flexibility with her time. She also wanted to reserve for herself the option of being a mother and of being involved in community service and advocacy for peace and justice issues that would require time away from farm work. Consequently, she decided to study engineering at Oregon State University while she continued working on the farm.

Susan had not dated during high school years, and only briefly in college. While living in Corvallis and working on the farm, she told me one day that she needed to get out of town because she was becoming too involved with the lesbian community. She suggested that I might find it helpful to talk to the Quaker parents of two young lesbians she knew. She also gave me permission to talk to friends in my women's prayer group. I declined to do either. I was fearful that if others knew anything about this, they would lock her into that identification. If she was lesbian, I knew life could be very difficult. As I think about it now, I realize I was also not ready to deal with this possibility. While I assured her I would be supportive when she had "made her decision" regardless of what that was, to my regret I did not offer to walk with her during her journey of self-discovery.

In retrospect, I am amazed at my own fears. I was hesitant to receive the newsletter from BMC – the Brethren/Mennonite Council on Gay and Lesbian Concerns – in the mail. While both Clif and I were interested in the subject of homosexuality because of knowing others whose lives were involved, at denominational gatherings he felt free to attend workshops on the subject. On the other hand, I would not attend, fearing someone might conclude we had a gay child. Oh, dear, I was fearful that if it was known I had a gay child, it would somehow be a reflection on me.

Susan spent a semester at a seminary, and when she returned home the subject of sexual orientation did not come up. She dated a few men, but apparently found those relationships unsatisfactory. She continued her membership at Albany Mennonite Church, but when the leader of a Sunday school study on human sexuality refused to spend time on the chapter regarding homosexuality, she discontinued attending and found her spiritual home at a congregation of the United Church of Christ. She has narrated the story of her own struggle to be Christian and lesbian in *From Wounded Hearts.*[1]

Our nineteen-year-old son Eric died in a bicycle-car accident while Susan was still in her engineering studies. It was a moment of truth for all of us – today we have life – tomorrow is uncertain. Her relationship with a current boyfriend was terminated immediately. That was in August. In October a good friend of her sister and her sister-in-law visited Oregon from New York. The attraction happened. During the next months and years, there were frequent cross-country trips and long phone conversations. No longer was there uncertainty about her orientation. Biene became her beloved partner, and they planned to live together when Susan completed her engineering degree.

At that point it all came together for me. Even as I believed the little girl should not be forced into a traditional mold, but should be allowed to develop in her own direction, I now understood that her self-acceptance as a lesbian was an expression of that personal integrity. She was being true to who she is.

The same week that she defended her master's degree thesis, she received an offer from Steinway Piano Company in New York City for a job as an engineer. She moved to Long Island where Biene works in a family landscaping business. That was in 1988, and Susan continues at Steinway as a senior engineer. Very soon after she was there, they assigned her the task of engineering and designing a new line of pianos, later named Boston. What a satisfaction it has been for Clif and me to follow the development of this work and eventually to own a five-foot, ten-inch Boston piano! More recently, she has designed another line for Steinway called the Essex.

In 1991, after being together several years, Susan and Biene entered into a formal covenanted agreement. They had a beauti-

---

[1] *From Wounded Hearts* by Roberta Showalter Kreider was published by Chi Rho Press, Gaithersburg, Maryland, in 1998.

ful service in a UCC church with both families in attendance. Susan's dad read Scripture, and I led several congregational hymns. Two of my brothers and one sister, plus several nieces and nephews, attended. It was a grand celebration.

Susan had always wanted to have children. Even though dolls were not a part of her childhood, her experience with younger siblings must have provided understanding of what joy children bring to their parents. It wasn't easy, but eventually they found a donor – a man whom they know and respect – and she became pregnant by alternative conception. Hannah is now eight years old. A second daughter, Anja, is almost five. The joy of knowing and loving a wonderful daughter is comparable only to knowing and loving wonderful granddaughters.

Fortunately Steinway has been cooperative with Susan's parenting responsibilities. She is able to work three days a week on a flexible schedule. Susan, Biene, and their daughters live close to the landscape and nursery business owned by Biene's family. So even though they are distant from the Oregon farm, they do have access to growing plants.

This loving family is deeply involved in a small Methodist church in their neighborhood. Hannah loves to learn Bible verses and sing hymns. At her request I gave her a special edition of our denomination's *Hymnal: A Worship Book* that she treasures. Her parents are nurturing their children with Anabaptist Christian values in the midst of an affluent community where materialism is a constant influence.

All three of our adult children and our six grandchildren bring great joy. I have special admiration for Susan because she refused to compromise her own identity and did the hard work of self-understanding on a journey that has led to becoming a healthy, mature adult and a wonderful nurturing parent. I am so very proud to be her mother.

Lois Kenagy has been a partner with her husband Clif in the operation of the family farm. Now retired, they both continue their advocacy for sexual minority persons. They are the parents of four children: Susan (about whom Lois writes in this chapter); Peter, who now manages the farm; and Marguerite, in a management position in Oregon's state government. Their youngest son Eric died in 1986 at age nineteen. They have six grandchildren.

In the past, Lois' volunteer work included service on several denominational and district conference boards and committees. She has also been active in peace work, including mediation and victim-offender reconciliation work, and has just completed eight years as a member of the Oregon Dispute Resolution Commission where her efforts were directed at providing and strengthening community mediation programs.

> We don't have to obey any person, any thing, or any power that tells us to go against the ways of Jesus – ways of love, healing, radical equality, and liberation.
>
> ~ Kathleen Temple

~ *thirty-four* ~

Celebration

Janet Hartzell

Come on, Lord, celebrate with us,
as we worship and adore You
and give thanks to Your Holy name.
So, come on, Lord, celebrate with us!

We thank You for this beautiful land we live on –
Land You have so generously given to us.
What's that, Lord?
It was the Native People You gave it to?
Surely You must have intended it to be for us.
After all, they were just savages, Lord,
and You know we had no choice but to kill them for it.
We are committed and faithful followers of You,
and we did our very best to convert them.
But for some reason they couldn't hear our message.
They had their own way of worshipping, they said;
something about a Great Spirit and having respect and honor
for the land, and water, and air and all living things ....pagans,
aren't they, Lord?

What's that, Lord?
Everyone is precious in Your eyes?
We should love and respect all people?
Oh, we do, Lord, we do!
Didn't we finally give them land
so they could have reservations to build their homes on?
Oh, I know most of it was undesirable, but it was good enough
for them.
After all we needed so much more land than they did ....or did
we, Lord?

So, come on, Lord, celebrate with us!

Did I hear You say something?
"Love one another as I love you."

Oh, we do, we do!

And, Lord, we praise You for setting those Negroes free.
For Abe Lincoln, Rosa Parks, and Martin Luther King.
Hallelujah!   Praise Your Name!   They're free at last!
We confess to You most earnestly it was wrong to make them slaves.
But now, Lord, just look at the mess they've made of their lives,
and that's the thanks we get!
Why, they haven't learned a thing from us.
They don't come close to living up to our standards.
Just look at the slums they live in.

What's that, Lord?
Everyone is precious in Your eyes?
We should love and respect all people?
Oh, we do, Lord, we do!
We just don't want them living in our neighborhoods,
and neither would You!
Just tell them to "get a job"!
That would solve all their problems …….. or would it, Lord?

So, come on, Lord, celebrate with us!

Did I hear You say something?
"Love one another as I love you."

Oh, we do, we do!

And, Lord, we just give thanks to You for always
being on our side when we went to war.
"In God We Trust" is our motto, and we sure do.
And when we killed, maimed, raped, and destroyed,
we did it in Your name, for we knew You were with us.
I guess Vietnam was a mistake though.
Wasn't it 58,000 of our men and women that died?

That sure was a good lesson for us, Lord, and we're grateful!
We learned so much from that experience.
The wars we fought since then have been short-lived,
and only a few of our own men and women were killed, and we won!
We praise You, Lord!

What's that, Lord?
Others were killed, and You loved them too?
Everyone is precious in Your eyes?
We should love and respect all people?
Oh, we do, Lord, we do!
We just don't understand those people in
Israel and Palestine, Northern Ireland, and the like.
It's so dreadful and senseless to keep hating like they do,
isn't it, Lord?
They sure don't know You like we do …….. or do they, Lord?

So, come on, Lord, celebrate with us!

Did I hear You say something?
"Love one another as I love you."

Oh, we do, we do!

And we thank You for sending us those migrant workers
to harvest the fields of bountiful goodness for us.
If it weren't for those poor, little people,
why we would just have to do it ourselves!
And just look at our righteousness; we've given them jobs!
Who are they, and where do they come from anyway, Lord?
"Why they're …….."
Oh, it doesn't matter, we don't care, they're not like us.
Just keep them harvesting those fields of plenty
so we can eat and keep our bellies full.
What's that, Lord?
Everyone is precious in Your eyes?
We should love and respect all people?
Oh, we do, Lord, we do!

We pay them – granted it's not much,
but we do give them some food and shelter.
Probably better than what they are used to,
and that sure is good enough for them …….. or is it, Lord?

So, come on, Lord, celebrate with us!

Did I hear You say something?
"Love one another as I love you."

Oh, we do, we do!

And we thank You, most Holy One
That we were born Adam and Eve.
I know this is the way You intended it to be …….. isn't it?
It's just disgusting, Lord,
Man with man, woman with woman.

What's that Lord?
Everyone is precious in Your eyes?
We should love and respect all people?
For you created all of us....and loved us....and knew us
even before we were formed in the womb?
Oh, we do, Lord, we do!
But certainly You don't mean them, Lord!
You know how hard we've tried to change them.
We've counseled them, beat them, tried to demoralize them,
and kill their spirits.
Others have even killed their bodies,
and hung them on split-rail fences.
Why, even some of their own families have disowned them.
Now we know that's wrong, Lord, because we believe in You!
And yet, Lord, even You cast a great affliction upon them,
and still they choose to live that way......... or do they, Lord?

Well, I know you're proud of us, Your body of believers.
We work hard doing Your will by keeping them out
of our churches and places of worship.

They can't preach in our pulpits!
And we sure don't want them coming through our doors
if we know they are …….. *one of them.*
We love them, Lord, please don't misunderstand,
but we hate their sin.
And You surely don't want those queers in Your house
unless they change …….. or do You, Lord?

So, come on, Lord, celebrate with us!

Did I hear You say something?
"Love one another as I love you."

Oh, we do, Lord, we most certainly do!

What's that? …………………….You don't feel like celebrating with us?
Why? ……………. We just don't understand.

Are they tears I see flowing out of Your eyes,
falling down Your face
spilling onto the ground?

Is that a trail of tears I see behind me and ahead of me?

But why are You weeping?

Janet Hartzell lives in Souderton, Pennsylvania, with her husband Barry. She has two sons and four grandchildren and is a member of Zion Mennonite Church. She has been a hospice volunteer for many years, where she works primarily with AIDS patients. In 1990, Janet organized *A Walk Together,* a support group that meets on a weekly basis to help those living with or affected by HIV/AIDS. In 1991, she initiated Thanksgiving and Christmas dinners, serving hundreds of meals at Zion Mennonite Church for people from the community. These events are for those in need of food or fellowship. Four years ago these dinners were expanded to become *The Table of Plenty* where Janet coordinates the serving of free lunches on Monday, Wednesday, and Friday. The great passions of her life, in addition to her service to the community, are her husband, children, grandchildren, her pug Happy, writing poetry, and reading.

> Whenever you see persecution, there is more than a probability that the truth is on the persecuted side.
>
> ~ Hugh Latimer

~ *thirty-five* ~

A Father's Message to the Church

Clif Kenagy

My Closet

As the father of a lesbian daughter, my experience has been typical of many parents. When a child exits the closet, the parent enters a closet. Our closet time is usually spent seeking truth. We have the promise that "the truth will make us free."[1] So, we pray, we read widely, we process new information, and occasionally share with a *safe* friend. The church is *not* a helpful resource.

A half-decade in the closet convinced me that the church today is caught in a dilemma comparable to that experienced by the church of the nineteenth century. It is becoming increasingly difficult for the present-day church to ignore the suffering of those oppressed by church dogma. Earlier, it was the suffering of God's African-American children under slavery. Today, it is God's gay children and their families suffering under a stigma imposed by church dogma for a condition over which they have no choice.

The closet experience can mature a parent to where he can no longer be silent. Just as it is expected for a child to scream if a two-hundred-pound man persists in standing on the child's foot, I also came to realize that the church was "standing on my foot," and I needed to scream. John Fortunato, an Episcopalian author, has written that "...the appropriate response to injustice

---

[1] John 8:32. Unless otherwise noted, all Scripture references are from the King James Version.

is outrage and protest, not polite dialogue...."[2] I believe that a stance less than confrontation is a sin of omission. While dialogue is being both promoted and resisted, little is accomplished at any level.

Reality

The parent is caught in a double bind. It seems impossible to bring relief to our children who are stigmatized by a church that has ears, but does not hear. The second bind is that we are complicit in the oppression by virtue of being members of and loving the offending church. *Lord, have mercy!*

Giving up and leaving the church is not a responsible option for parents. The church needs us. I am not without hope. Change is happening, although it is at glacial speed. Hope is possible, because the change – though slow – is in a forward direction. I don't expect relief in my lifetime. It will come later, but only if we work at it today.

Jesus Didn't Say...(?)

It is often stated that Jesus didn't say anything about homosexuality. We don't actually know that. It is more accurate to say: *"There is NO RECORD of him saying anything about homosexuality."* Scripture indicates he said many things that were not written down.[3] If he did say something, would it be more likely to have fallen through the cracks if his comments were positive, or if they were negative? Ponder that.

We do know that Jesus said: "But whoso shall offend one of these little ones which believe in me, it were better for him that a millstone were hanged around his neck..."[4] We also know that our gay and lesbian children are offended by a church-imposed stigma for something over which they have no choice.

---

[2] Quoted by Elsie Steelberg in *To Continue the Dialogue*, C. Norman Krause, ed. (Telford, PA: Pandora Press, 2001), p. 296.

[3] John 20:30

[4] Matthew 18:6

Where Is the Love?

Gays and lesbians are modern day equivalents to the victim in the story of the good Samaritan[5] who, when going from Jerusalem to Jericho, fell among thieves, was robbed, beaten, and left to die. A traveling priest and Levite did not come to his aid, but passed by on the other side. It was left up to one of those despised Samaritans to exemplify God's love to him.

Gays and lesbians are beaten down with an abusive stigma, robbed of their dignity, excluded from the table, and left to die. Religious leaders still pass by on the other side. And, just as the priest and Levite would have had a hard time convincing the victim in that story that they loved him, so also do religious leaders of today have a hard time convincing gays and lesbians that they are loved by the church.

Calling the Church to Repentance

1. The church needs to acknowledge the stigma and unfathomable pain its position imposes upon gays, lesbians, and their families because of a condition over which they have no choice.

2. The church needs to acknowledge the "collateral damage" experienced by straight persons who innocently marry a closeted gay or lesbian person.

3. The church needs to acknowledge that if an understanding of Scripture hurts people because of a condition over which they have no choice, that understanding of Scripture must be revisited.

4. The church needs to convene a "Jerusalem Conference."[6]

We love our gay and lesbian children.

Won't you love them too?

---

[5] Luke 10:29-37
[6] Acts 15:1-35

Clif Kenagy and his wife Lois are the parents of two daughters and two sons (one deceased). Clif served in Civilian Public Service during World War II and with Mennonite Central Committee in Poland and Germany after the war. He attended Hesston College (Kansas), Goshen College (Indiana), and Oregon State University. Clif and Lois are now retired after forty-five years of farming in Oregon.

> For freedom Christ has set us free.
>
> Stand firm, therefore, and do not submit again to a yolk of slavery.
>
> Galations 5:1

Resources

~ Books ~

Aarons, Leroy. *Prayers for Bobby: A Mother's Coming to Terms with the Suicide of Her Gay Son.* San Francisco: Harper, 1995.

Bess, Howard H. *Pastor, I Am Gay.* Palmer, AK: Palmer Publishing Co., 1995.

Boenke, Mary, editor. *Trans Forming Families: Real Stories About Transgendered Loved Ones.* Imperial Beach, CA: Walter Trook Publishing, 1999.

Borhek, Mary V. *Coming Out to Parents.* Cleveland: The Pilgrim Press, 1983. Revised and updated, 1993.

_____. *My Son Eric.* Cleveland: The Pilgrim Press, 1979.

Boswell, John. *Christianity, Social Tolerance, and Homosexuality: Gay People in Western Europe from the Beginning of the Christian Era to the Fourteenth Century.* Chicago: The University of Chicago Press, 1980.

Buxton, Amity Pierce. *The Other Side of the Closet: The Coming Out Crisis for Straight Spouses.* Santa Monica, CA: IBS Press, Inc., 1991.

Cantwell, Mary Ann. *Homosexuality: The Secret a Child Dare Not Tell.* San Rafael, CA: Rafael Press, 1996.

Cole, Beverly. *Cleaning Closets: A Mother's Story.* St. Louis: Chalice Press, 1995.

Comstock, Gary David. *Gay Theology Without Apology.* Cleveland: The Pilgrim Press, 1994.

Eichberg, Rob. *Coming OUT: An Act of Love.* New York: Penguin Books USA Inc., 1990.

Galluccio, Jon and Michael with David Groff. *An American Family.* New York: St. Martin's Press, 2001.

Glaser, Chris. *Come Home! Reclaiming Spirituality and Community as Gay Men and Lesbians,* 2nd ed. Gaithersburg, MD: Chi Rho Press, 1998.

_____. *Uncommon Calling: A Gay Christian's Struggle to Serve the Church.* Louisville: Westminster John Knox Press, 1988.

Grimsrud, Ted. *God's Healing Strategy.* Telford, PA: Pandora Press U.S., 2000.

Handel, Linda. *Now That You're Out of the Closet, What About the Rest of the House?* Naperville, IL: Sourcebooks, Inc., 1998, 2000.

Helminiak, Daniel A. *What the Bible Really Says About Homosexuality.* San Francisco: Alamo Square Press, 1994.

Kreider, Roberta Showalter, editor. *From Wounded Hearts: Faith Stories of Lesbian, Gay, Bisexual, and Transgendered People and Those Who Love Them.* Gaithersburg, MD: Chi Rho Press, 1998.

Marcus, Eric. *Is It a Choice? Answers to 300 of the Most Frequently Asked Questions About Gays and Lesbians.* San Francisco: Harper/SanFrancisco, 1993.

McNaught, Brian. *Now That I'm Out, What Do I Do? Thoughts on Living Deliberately.* New York: St. Martin's Press, 1997.

_____. *On Being Gay: Thoughts on Family, Faith and Love.* New York: St. Martin's Press, Inc., 1989.

McNeill, John J. *The Church and the Homosexual.* 3rd ed., Boston: Beacon Press, 1988.

Morrison, Melanie. *The Grace of Coming Home: Spirituality, Sexuality, and the Struggle for Justice.* Cleveland: The Pilgrim Press, 1995.

Pearson, Carol Lynn. *Good-Bye, I Love You: A True Story of a Wife, Her Homosexual Husband, and a Love That Transcended Tragedy.* New York: Random House, 1980.

Pennington, Sylvia. *Ex-Gays? There Are None! What It Means To Be a New Creature in Christ.* Hawthorne, CA: Lambda Christian Fellowship, 1989.

Perry, Troy. *Don't Be Afraid Anymore: The Story of Reverend Troy Perry and the Metropolitan Community Churches.* New York: St. Martin's Press, 1990.

_____. *The Lord Is My Shepherd and He Knows I'm Gay.* 1972. West Hollywood, CA: Universal Fellowship of Metropolitan Community Churches, 1994.

Piazza, Michael S. *Holy Homosexuals: The Truth About Being Gay or Lesbian and Christian.* 2nd ed. Dallas: The Sources of Hope Publishing House, 1995.

Scanzoni, Letha and Virginia Ramey Mollenkott. *Is the Homosexual My Neighbor? Another Christian View.* San Francisco: Harper & Row, 1978, 1994.

Scholinski, Daphne. *The Last Time I Wore A Dress: A Memoir.* New York: Riverhead Books, 1997.

Scroggs, Robin. *The New Testament and Homosexuality.* Philadelphia: Fortress Press, 1983.

Spahr, Jane Adams, et al, editors. *Called OUT! The Voices and Gifts of Lesbian, Gay, Bisexual, and Transgendered Presbyterians.* Gaithersburg, MD: Chi Rho Press, 1995.

Switzer, David K. *Coming Out As Parents.* Louisville: Westminster John Knox Press, 1996.

Truluck, Rembert S. *Steps to Recovery from Bible Abuse.* Gaithersburg, MD: Chi Rho Press, 2000.

Waun, Maurine C. *More Than Welcome: Learning to Embrace Gay, Lesbian, Bisexual, and Transgendered Persons in the Church.* St. Louis: Chalice Press, 1999.

White, Mel. *Stranger at the Gate: To be Christian and Gay in America.* New York: Simon & Schuster, 1994.

Wiltshire, Susan Ford. *Seasons of Grief and Grace: A Sister's Story of AIDS.* Nashville: Vanderbilt University Press, 1994.

Wink, Walter, editor. *Homosexuality and Christian Faith: Questions of Conscience for the Churches.* Minneapolis: Fortress Press, 1999.

Booklets

Barnett, Walter. *Homosexuality and the Bible: An Interpretation.* Wallingford, PA: Pendle Hill Publications, Pamphlet #226, 1979. Order toll free: (800) 742-3150

Blair, Ralph. *Homosexuality: Faith, Facts, and Fairy Tales.* New York: Evangelicals Concerned, 1991. Contains two messages given to a United Methodist Church.

Cook, Ann Thompson. *And God Loves Each One: A Resource for Dialogue About the Church and Homosexuality.* Washington, DC: Task Force on Reconciliation, Dumbarton United Methodist Church, 1988, 1990.

Friesen, Walter S. *A Personal Witness About Biblical Faith and Homosexuality*, 2000. 2009 Clover Lane, Newton, KS 67114. Phone: (316) 283-5250   E-mail: wcfriesen@juno.com

Human Rights Campaign Foundation. *Finally Free: Personal Stories: How Love and Self-Acceptance Saved Us from "Ex-Gay" Ministries*, 2000.

Kreider, Roberta Showalter. *Personal Sharing with my Church Family* and *Fifteen Reasons Why I Have Changed my Mind,* 1996. Order from Ray L. Moyer, 6 Eagan Street, Pottsville, PA 17801-1002. E-mail: rlm@infi.net

Liechty, Ruth Conrad, series editor. *Welcome to Dialogue Series: A Search for Inclusiveness* (booklets), 2001. Series includes:
1. *Sharing Personal Convictions*
2. *Historical Perspectives*
3. *Discerning Church Membership, Part I*
4. *On Biblical Interpretation*
5. *Biological and Psychological Views*
6. *Discerning Church Membership, Part II*
Order from Ruth Conrad Liechty, 1568 Redbud Court, Goshen, IN 46526.

PFLAG, *Opening the Straight Spouse's Closet: A guide for understanding issues facing families with gay, lesbian, bisexual, or transgendered spouses* (no date).

The Other Side. Christians & Homosexuality: Dancing Toward the Light (special issue). Philadelphia, 1994.

The Renaissance Transgender Association, Inc., compiler. *Background Papers*, Wayne, PA, 1997.

Transgender Special Outreach Network of PFLAG. *Our Trans Children*, 1998.

Wink, Walter. *Homosexuality and the Bible.* A booklet of an earlier version of this article that appeared in the *Christian Century* magazine, Christian Century Foundation, 1979. Revised version, 1996 by Walter Wink. Order from Fellowship Bookstore, Box 271, Nyack, NY 10960.   Phone: (914) 358-4601.

~ *Periodicals* ~

Open Hands: Resources for Ministries Affirming the Diversity of Human Sexuality. Chris Glaser, editor. *Open Hands* is the quarterly magazine of the Welcoming church movement, a Christian consortium of denominational church programs in Canada and the United States whose ministries encourage and assist individuals and faith communities in welcoming and affirming lesbian, gay, bisexual, and transgender people and their families and friends. *Open Hands*, 3801 N. Keeler Avenue, Chicago, IL 60641. Phone: (773) 736-5526.   E-mail: openhands@RMNetwork.org Web: www.RMNetwork.org/openhands/index.html

The Other Side. Doug Davidson, Dee Dee Risher, co-editors (published bi-monthly). The *Other Side* magazine advances a healing Christian vision that is biblical and compassionate, appreciative of the creative arts, and committed to the intimate intertwining of personal spirituality and social transformation. The magazine has been an active advocate for the church's full inclusion of LGBT people since 1978. *The Other Side,* 300 W. Apsley, Philadelphia, PA 19144. Phone: (800) 700-9280.   E-mail: editors@theotherside.org Web: www.theotherside.org

~ *Videos* ~

Body of Dissent: Lesbian and Gay Mennonites and Brethren Continue the Journey. (39 min.) Toronto: Bridge Video Productions, 1994. Personal stories of lesbian and gay people from Mennonite and Brethren backgrounds.
BMC, PO Box 6300, Minneapolis, MN 5534-0300.
Phone: (612) 722-6906   E-mail: BMCouncil@aol.com

Family Stories: Journeys of Spirit in Mixed Orientation Families. (35 min.) Wayne, PA: John Davis Producer, 2001. Roberta Showalter Kreider and Mary Lou Wallner tell short stories of their journey to truth. Introduction by Rev. Peter J. Gomes, author of *The Good Book.* Order from John Davis, 417 Teresita Boulevard, San Francisco, CA 94127   E-mail: JOHNBO11@aol.com

Growing up Gay. (80 min.) Denver, Co: KBDI-TV, 1992. Brian McNaught tells what it is like to grow up as a gay individual.
To order: Phone: (800) 876-7676

How Can I Be Sure God Loves Me Too? (23 min.) *The Rhetoric of Intolerance* (29 min.) *The Trials of Jimmy Creech* (28 min.) *There's a Wideness in God's Mercy: Dr. Lewis Smedes on Romans One.* (30 min.) Soulforce, PO Box 4467, Laguna Beach, CA 92652. E-mail: melwhite@soulforce.org
Phone: (949) 455-0999   Toll free: (877) 705-6393
Web: www.soulforce.org

Marsha Stevens Live in Concert. (95 min.) Costa Mesa, CA: BALM Publishing, 1993. Marsha Stevens, who wrote and composed the song, "For Those Tears I Died," when she was sixteen years old, presents fourteen songs that were written by her and composed with the aid of others from the Universal Fellowship of Metropolitan Community Churches. She also shares anecdotes and her personal story of being a lesbian woman of faith. Available from BALM Publishing, PO Box 1981, Costa Mesa, CA 92628.

Ma Vie En Rose (My Life in Pink). (89 min.) English subtitles. Columbia/Tristar Studios, 1997. Alain Berliner's movie is the story of an innocent little boy who wants to be a girl. It is a mix of innocent fantasy and childhood cruelty and a family that struggles to come to terms with Ludo. A reviewer's comment: "A well-thought-out and beautifully told story of transgenderism." Available from www.Amazon.com

Two Sides of a Christian View of Homosexuality. (50 min.) Tony and Peggy Campolo speaking in North Park College Chapel, February 29, 1996. ($10.00) Available from North Park University, 3225 West Foster, Chicago, IL 60625. Contact: Bill Hartley. Phone: (773) 244-5579   (Audio tape: $7.00.)

~ Organizations ~

American Educational Gender Information Service (AEGIS)
PO Box 33724, Decatur, GA 30333   Phone: (404) 939-0244
A source of general information about transgender issues.

Brethren/Mennonite Council for Lesbian and Gay Concererns
Amy Short, Executive Director
PO Box 6300, Minneapolis, MN 55406-0300
Phone: (612) 722-6906   E-mail: BMCouncil@aol.com
Web: www.webcom.com/bmc/

Children of Lesbians and Gays Everywhere (COLAGE)
3543 18th St., #17, San Francisco, CA 94110
Phone: (425) 861-5437   E-mail: colage@colage.org

Connecting Families
Ruth Conrad Liechty, Contact Person
1568 Redbud Court, Goshen, IN 46526
E-mail: rliechty@juno.com

Evangelicals Concerned, Inc.
Dr. Ralph Blair, Director
311 East 72nd Street, New York, NY 10021
E-mail: ecincnyc@aol.com

Family Pride Coalition
PO Box 50360, Washington, DC 20091
Phone: (619) 296-0199   Web: pride@familypride.org

Gay, Lesbian, Straight Education Network
121 West 27th Street, Suite 804, New York, NY 10001
Phone: (212) 727-0135   Web: www.GLSEN.org
GLSEN is the largest national organization that brings together
concerned citizens from all walks of life in order to end the destructive effects of anti-gay bias in K-12 schools across the country.

Humans Rights Campaign Foundation
919 18th Street, NW, Suite 800
Washington, DC 20006   Phone: (202) 628-4160
E-mail: hrc@hrc.org   Web: www.hrc.org

International Federation for Gender Education (IFGE)
PO Box 367, Wayland, MA 01778   Phone: (617) 889-2212
Catalogue available of books and pamphlets about transgender issues.
Most of the books cited can be obtained through IFGE.

Lambda Legal Defense Education Fund
666 Broadway, 12th Floor, New York, NY 10012
Phone: (212) 995-8585   Web: www.lambdalegal.org
A national organization committed to achieving full recognition of
the civil rights of LGBT and people with HIV or AIDS through
impact litigation, education, and public policy work.

Parents, Families, and Friends of Lesbians and Gays (PFLAG)
(Now includes Bisexuals and Transgenders)
1726 M Street, NW, Suite 400, Washington, DC 20036
Phone: (202) 467-8180   E-mail: info@pflag.org
Web: www.pflag.org

Phoenix Communications
Dotti Berry, President   Phone: (859) 489-4791
E-mail: dotti@EmpoweringDiversity.com   dotti@GLBTcoach.com
Web: www.EmpoweringDiversity.com   www.GLBTcoach.com
www.EmpoweringDiversity.com/JabezPrayerapostles
Dotti is a diversity and sexuality educator, working on her doctorate
in Human Sexuality at Widener University, Chester, PA. She serves
as a "coach" for the GLBT community.

The Renaissance Transgender Association, Inc.
987 Old Eagle School Road, Suite 719, Wayne, PA 19087.
Phone: (610) 975-9119   Web: www.ren.org

Soulforce
PO Box 4467, Laguna Beach, CA 92652
Phone: (949) 455-0999   Toll free: (877) 705-6393
E-mail: RevMel@aol.com   Web: melwhite@soulforce.org
A network of friends learning nonviolence from Gandhi and King
seeking justice for God's lesbian, gay, bisexual, and transgender
children.

Straight Spouse Network
8215 Terrace Dr., El Cerrito, CA 94530-3058
Phone: (510) 525-0200   E-mail: dir@ssnetwk.org

TranScience Research Institute
PO Box 28089, Richmond, VA 23228
Phone: (804) 421-2428   E-mail: Transcience@earthlink.net
Web: www.transcience.org

Universal Fellowship of Metropolitan Community Churches
8704 Santa Monica Blvd., 2nd Floor, West Hollywood, CA 90069
Phone: (310) 360-8640   E-mail: UFMCCHQ@aol.com
Web: www.ufmcc.org

What Jesus wants is not admirers,
but disciples.

~ Karl Heim

About the Editor

Roberta Showalter Kreider was born during a huge snowstorm on April 3, 1926, in a farmhouse near the small town of Inman in McPherson County, Kansas. Her three older brothers remember that they were sent upstairs to play, and when they came down they had a baby sister. Two young cousins took a team and wagon across the fields to meet the doctor and bring him the remainder of the way. Roberta arrived before the doctor did.

On November 1, 1929, her youngest sibling was born – another boy! She did not get the sister she had wanted, but her parents helped to ease the disappointment by letting her name her brother. She called him Baby Ray, and he became her pride and joy. They grew up together as playmates and friends. In 1984, Ray died of AIDS.

Roberta and her brothers received their elementary education in a two-room country school near Yoder, Kansas. Her father was president of the small town bank and her mother was a homemaker. In 1943, Roberta graduated from a Mennonite high school in Hesston, Kansas.

Her preacher brother, who later became a psychologist, often asked her to teach summer Bible school in several states, including Kansas, Oklahoma, Texas, Mississippi, and Alabama, beginning after she was a freshman in high school.

There was a shortage of teachers during World War II. After one semester of college, Roberta was granted an emergency certificate to teach. She and a friend boarded with a local family and taught in a two-room country school near Meade, Kansas. The first year she taught grades one through four, and the second year she moved to grades five through eight so another friend could teach the lower grades. As the upper grade teacher, she also served as principal. Janitorial services were shared by both teachers.

In April of 1946, Roberta married Harold Glenn Kreider, a farmer's son from Palmyra, Missouri. He was ordained to the Christian ministry in the Mennonite Church in 1950. Harold finished college and seminary when their children were in elementary and secondary schools. The couple served in pastorates at Palmyra and Hannibal in Missouri and Osceola and Goshen in Indiana. Harold served two terms as an interim pastor in a team ministry at Perkasie Mennonite Church in Perkasie, Pennsylvania.

In 1983, they moved to rural Sellersville, Pennsylvania, where they remodeled an old stone house with their daughter and son-in-law. The Kreiders live in the first floor apartment and enjoy being near their children and grandchildren in the two-floor apartment above them. Another daughter lives in Kansas City, Missouri; her husband is deceased. The Kreiders' youngest daughter and her husband live in Eugene, Oregon, with their two sons.

Roberta has always enjoyed books. When Harold was in seminary, she worked part-time in the seminary library. After they moved to Pennsylvania, she worked part-time in the Resource Center of Franconia Mennonite Conference for seven years.

In their retirement years, Roberta and Harold are involved in seeking justice for their lesbian, gay, bisexual, and transgender friends, and they enjoy the many friends that God has brought into their lives.

There is no victory in "defeating" an enemy. There is only victory when relationships are restored.

~ Dotti Berry

How to Order

Ask for *Together in Love* at your local bookstore or order from on-line retailers.

To order directly from the author:

Order from: Roberta Showalter Kreider
P.O. Box 101
Sellersville, PA 18960

Single copies: U.S. $24.00 (postpaid)
Canada $40.00 (postpaid)

Sales tax: Pennsylvania residents, add 6% to all orders
($1.44 per book)

Bulk rate: Six or more copies to one address:
U.S. $20.00 each (postpaid)
Canada $36.00 each (postpaid)

For discount to bookstores:
Contact Roberta Kreider   (215) 257-7322
kreiders@netcarrier.com.

Roberta@EmpoweringDiversity.com.

Please print.

Name _____

Address _____

_____

City _____ State _____ Zip _____

Telephone _____

E-mail address _____

No. of books ordered _____ at $_____ = $_____

Send Check or Money Order to:
Roberta Showalter Kreider
P.O. Box 101, Sellersville, PA 18960

"You shall love the Lord
your God with all your heart,
and with all your soul,
and with all your mind."

This is the greatest and
first commandment, and
a second is like it:

"You shall love your neighbor
as yourself."

Jesus
(Matthew 22:37-39)

~ ~ ~

If you continue in my word,
you are truly my disciples;
and you will know the truth,
and the truth will make you free.

Jesus
(John 8:31b-32)